Transcription of the "Poor Book" of the tithings of Westbury-on-Trym, Stoke Bishop and Shirehampton from A.D. 1656-1698; with introduction and notes

England Westbury-on-Trym

With the Author's compliments

TRANSCRIPTION OF THE "POOR BOOK."

Transcription
of the
"Poor Book"
of the
Tithings of Westbury-on-Trym, Stoke Bishop & Shirehampton
from
A.D. 1656—1698

WITH

Introduction and Notes

BY

H. J. WILKINS, D.D.
Vicar of Westbury-on-Trym
and
Reader of Redland Chapel, Bristol

BRISTOL
J. W. ARROWSMITH, 11 QUAY STREET
LONDON
SIMPKIN, MARSHALL, HAMILTON, KENT & CO. LIMITED

1910

Antiquarian Essays

By the same Author.

THE DISAGREEMENT BETWEEN THE DEAN AND CHAPTER OF WESTBURY AND THE VICAR OF HENBURY, WITH TERMS OF SETTLEMENT, IN A.D. 1463. By The Right Reverend JOHN CARPENTER, D.D., Lord Bishop of Worcester and Westbury. ALSO NOTES ON THE EARLIEST EFFORTS TO FOUND A BISHOPRIC FOR BRISTOL.

THE LETTERS PATENT OF KING HENRY VIII, GRANTING WESTBURY-ON-TRYM COLLEGIATE CHURCH AND COLLEGE, TOGETHER WITH ALL THEIR ENDOWMENTS, TO SIR RALPH SADLEIR.

THE LETTERS PATENT OF KING EDWARD VI, GRANTING HENBURY MANOR AND CHURCH, STOKE BISHOP, SNEYD PARK, PEN PARK, OLVESTON, ETC., TO SIR RALPH SADLEIR.

COPY OF THE DEED OF THE SALE OF THE NEXT PRESENTATION BUT ONE TO HENBURY VICARAGE, IN A.D. 1678.

SOME CHAPTERS IN THE ECCLESIASTICAL HISTORY OF WESTBURY-ON-TRYM—

1. Desecration of Bishop Carpenter's Tomb.
2. Decay of the College Buildings.
3. Dispersion of Church Lands.
4. Alieination of Tithes.
5. Sale of Living.

TO WHICH IS APPENDED

A LIST OF ABBOTS, DEANS AND VICARS SINCE A.D. 715.

Can be obtained separately or in one volume, bound in Cloth, price 10/- net.

BRISTOL
J. W. Arrowsmith, 11 Quay Street
LONDON
Simpkin, Marshall, Hamilton, Kent & Co. Limited

INTRODUCTION.

IN connection with the history of Bristol, the value of this "Poor Book" (hitherto unpublished), relating to the Tithings of Westbury-upon-Trym, Stoke Bishop and Shirehampton, can scarcely be overestimated; for it is the only book which can give the information it contains, in reference to a district which is now the largest "residential" part of Bristol, and which also embraces the recently-opened magnificent dock at Avonmouth, part of the Tithing of Shirehampton.

This book deals with disturbed or unsettled periods of English history, for it runs from A.D. 1656 to 1698, a period embracing part of the Protectorate (1653–9), the restored Commonwealth (1659), the reign of Charles II (1660–85), the reign of James II (1685–88), and of William and Mary to 1689.

Westbury had suffered very heavily from the Civil Wars, for the College buildings (which Bishop Carpenter, with the aid of Dean Canynges, had so splendidly erected in A.D. 1447) were almost destroyed. We are told that on Sunday, July 23rd, 1643, Prince Rupert, who was on his way to Bristol, fixed his quarters at Westbury College. Before leaving he set fire to the buildings, in order to prevent their occupation by the Parliamentary forces. All that now remains of the original buildings is a massive square tower (the twin of the one built by Bishop Carpenter at Hartlebury Castle and destroyed by the eighteenth-century bishops) and two small towers, together with a small portion of the west front and of the boundary walls of the Trym.[1]

The parish church (which in a monastic or collegiate form had existed since about A.D. 715) also suffered great damage,[2] yet for the most part life during this period went steadily on in the three tithings: the parish business was quietly and regularly performed, and the tending and relief of the poor carefully and, in a measure, sympathetically given. Still there are a few items showing that the times were times of difficulty and unsettlement.

These three tithings, *i.e.* the ancient parish of Westbury-on-Trym,[3] now form an integral part of Bristol, having been included in 1904.

[1] *Cf.* p. 19 in *Some Chapters in the Ecclesiastical History of Westbury*, by the present writer.

[2] *Ibid.*, p. 10.

[3] It is necessary to remember that Westbury parish extended, roughly speaking, from the top of the present Park Street to Henbury Hill; and from Avonmouth (Shirehampton) to Horfield.

So it will be of interest, before we examine the assessments in this book in reference to the tithings, to glance at the population of Bristol in the seventeenth century. A letter by Mr. J. Landfear Lucas, of Hinehead, in the *Standard* of November 1st, 1909, puts the matter very clearly in the form of a comparison of Norwich with Bristol:—

"In connection with the visit of His Majesty to Norwich, surprise has been widely expressed that no English king had visited that city, until last Monday, since Charles II in 1671; and this is the more to be wondered at seeing that Norwich occupied then, and for long after, so prominent a position in this country.

"On a discussion taking place lately between some members of a London livery company as to the relative importance of Bristol and Norwich in the seventeenth century, I consulted the town clerks on this point, and their replies may be of interest.

"Mr. Edmund J. Taylor, Town Clerk of Bristol, writes:—

"'I cannot ascertain from our records what was exactly the population of Bristol in the reign of Charles II, but Lord Macaulay, in his *History of England*, states that Bristol and Norwich were equal in population, with 29,000 each.'

"Mr. Arnold H. Miller, Town Clerk of Norwich, writes:—

"'The result of the inquiries I have made of the honorary archivist of the city is that there is no record belonging to the city giving the population of Norwich in the reign of Charles II. The honorary archivist computes it at about 25,000 at the beginning of the reign (1660), and about 27,000 at the close of it.'

"Macaulay tells us that Bristol had, in 1685, 5,300 houses, and estimates the population at about 29,000. Norwich, he says, in 1693 had between 28,000 and 29,000. He describes them, after the capital, as the first English seaport and the first English manufacturing town, and of Norwich he remarks that no place in the kingdom, except the capital and the universities, had more attractions. It had, moreover, a court in miniature, the old palace of the Dukes of Norfolk being said to be the largest town house in the kingdom, out of London."

In the first assessment in this book—it is for the year 1656—we find the following number of persons were rated for the relief of the poor:—

For the Tithing of Westbury	32	persons.
,, ,, Stoke Bishop	36	,,
,, ,, Shirehampton	41	,,
Total	109	,,

The Rate was three-halfpence in the pound, and produced from Westbury,

£5 0s. 4½d.; from Stoke Bishop, £5 8s. 6d.; and from Shirehampton £5 12s. 4½d. So the total for the three tythings was £16 1s. 3d.

In the last assessment (A.D. 1697) given in the book we find:—

For the Tithing of Westbury	39	persons.
,, ,, Stoke Bishop	38	,,
,, ,, Shirehampton	42	,,
Total	119	,,

The Rate was eightpence in the pound, and produced from Westbury, £27 10s. 4d.; from Stoke Bishop, £30 14s. 8d.; and from Shirehampton, £23 15s. 0d. The total for the three tythings being £82.

So from 1656 to 1697 there was an increase of ten persons assessed for the relief of the poor, and also a slight increase in the total value of the assessment.

Taking the total number of persons rated in 1697 in the three tithings, viz. 119, and allowing five persons for each household (perhaps a little above the average number, judging from Atkyns, quoted below) we find the whole population to have consisted of 595 persons.

Atkyns[1] in 1712 states: "There are one hundred and forty houses in this parish, and about six hundred and fifty inhabitants, whereof thirty are freeholders.

"Yearly { Births 23
{ Burials .. .. 22"

The enormous change which has taken place in these three tithings will be seen from the following figures:—

The population of Bristol at the commencement of 1909 was estimated at 372,785, to which number the area, which composed these three tithings at the period with which our book deals, contributed (roughly) the following:—

Westbury	30,487
Stoke Bishop	1,629
Shirehampton	6,000
Total	38,116

Therefore the number of the houses and population of these tithings now exceeds the total number of the houses and population of the whole of Bristol in the reign of Charles II.

The names of the persons, mentioned in the assessments, are full of local interest, and it is interesting to find that many of those names still continue

[1] Cf. *History of Gloucestershire*, p. 423.

prominent in Bristol. Stoke Bishop then, as now, was a favourite place of residence for Bristol merchants and of knights and baronets. *Cf.* page 183.

In considering the expenditure of the Poor Rate, it will be seen that each tithing appointed at the parish vestry its own overseer, and was responsible for its own poor.

Blackstone[1] gives the following instructive account of the origin of tithings :—

> "The civil division of the territory of England is into counties, of those counties into hundreds, of those hundreds into tithings or towns ; which division, as it now stands, seems to owe its original to King Alfred, who, to prevent the rapines and disorders which formerly prevailed in the realm, instituted tithings, so called from the Saxon because *ten* freeholders with their families composed one. These all dwelt together, and were sureties or free pledges to the king for the good behaviour of each other, and if any offence was committed in their district they were bound to have the offenders forthcoming ; and therefore, anciently, no man was suffered to abide in England above forty days unless he were enrolled in some tithing or decennary. One of the principal inhabitants of the tithing is annually appointed to preside over the rest, being called the tithing-man, the head-borough (words which speak their own etymology), and in some counties the borsholder, or borough's-ealder, being supposed the discreetest man in the borough, town or tithing.
>
> "Tithings, towns or vills[2] are of the same signification in law, and are said to have had, each of them, originally a church, and celebration of divine service, sacraments and burials, though that seems to be rather an ecclesiastical than a civil distinction."

The value and purchasing power of money at the time of these accounts are difficult to estimate.

From Professor Thorold Rogers's *History of Agriculture and Prices* we find :—

"A.D. 1643–1702 :

AVERAGE WEEKLY WAGE.	s.	d.		YEARLY WAGE—50 WEEKS. £	s.	d.
Carpenter	10	2¾	..	25	11	5½
Mason	9	10¾	..	24	14	9½
Pair of Sawyers	19	0¼	..	43	1	0½
Tiler or Slater	9	8¾	..	24	6	2½
Tiler's Help	5	3½	..	13	4	7
Artisan's Labourer	6	7¾	..	16	3	3½
Agricultural Labourer : first class	6	4¾	..	15	19	9½

[1] *Cf.* his *Commentaries*, 1809, i, 113.

[2] In the 13 and 14 Car. II, c. 12, which provides that when a parish is so large that it cannot have the benefit of overseers and provision for the poor, appointed by the 43 Eliz., c. 2, two overseers may be appointed for every township or village in such parish.

"*The average price* of wheat, 41s. 11¼d. a quarter; malt, 22s. 2¼d.; oatmeal, 52s. 11d.; beef, 3s. 5½d. the stone of 14 lb., or nearly 3d. a pound; mutton and pork, ditto; butter, a little over 6d. a pound. [It is probable that the peasants had a cow, as the Irish cottiers now have, and so would not need to purchase butter.]

"Now if we allow a family two quarters of wheat, two of malt and one of oatmeal yearly, the cost at the above prices comes to £9 1s. 2d. The rent of his cottage and garden will not be less than 6s. a quarter, or 24s. a year, and the fuel of his household at least 26s. yearly. This brings up the necessary charges to £11 11s. 2d. Four pounds of meat weekly raises the sum to £14 3s. 2d. The annual cost of tools is set by Arthur Younge at 15s., and of clothing £6 9s. At such a rate of expenditure the wages of the unskilled workman are insufficient to meet the cost of living."

So the lot of the poor, and particularly of those in receipt of parochial relief, must have been one of some hardship at the best, while for wayfarers it must have meant great privations. A short consideration of the history and state of the Poor Law will help towards the better understanding and appreciation of this book.

Without entering into the earlier laws relating to the poor, or into the controversial question as to what was the effect upon the condition of the poor of the dissolution of the monasteries, the first enactment it is necessary to notice is that of A.D. 1601 (43 Eliz., c. 2), re-enacting almost word for word the Statute of 1597 (39 Eliz., c. 3), which directed the parish officers to find materials for "setting the poor on work," and also to provide money towards the relief of the old, lame, blind, and others not able to work; it also directed children, able to do so, to support their parents. This Act formed a landmark in legislation for the support of the poor, and started a new epoch. It defined rateable property, and extended and defined the family obligation to support its members, and also directed the formal apprenticing, instead of placing out, of children. This Act also contains provisions for the rendering of accounts by the overseers. So now henceforward the care of the poor became rather a matter for the State than for the Church.

The Act of 1601 was not altogether satisfactory, and so another Act (7 James I, c. 4) followed, having special reference to houses of correction and illegitimate children: it also dealt with officers and accounts.

In 1630 there was a Royal Commission, and in 1656, owing to the increase of vagabonds, another law was passed.

In 1662 it was ordered (13 and 14 Charles II, c. 12), owing to many persons endeavouring to leave their own parishes and to settle "where there is best stock, the largest commons or waste to build cottages, and the most woods for them to burn and destroy, and, when they have consumed it, then to another parish, and at last become rogues and vagabonds, to the great discouragements of parishes to provide stocks where it is liable to be devoured by strangers," justices of the peace, upon complaint of the parish officers, within forty days after any such person's coming to settle as before mentioned in any tenement under the yearly value of £10, should be empowered by warrant to remove such person to the parish where he was last legally settled, either as a native, householder, sojourner, apprentice or servant, for not less than forty days, unless he gave sufficient security for the discharge of the parish.

Thus arose the law of settlement. But this same Statute allowed persons " to go into any county, parish or place to work in time of harvest, or at any time to work at any other work," if they had a certificate from the minister of their parish, or one of the parish officers.

This Act led to great restraint upon the free removing of the working classes to places where employment might be obtained, and also to subterfuges. Some, by concealing themselves in a parish for forty days, had in times past gained a settlement, but 1 James II, c. 17, had sought to remedy this by requiring notice of intended settlement to be given. But the poor person, giving such notice and being unable to " give security," was generally refused permission to settle.

This mischievous result was sought to be avoided by a certificate of acknowledgment of settlement, and then and not before, on becoming chargeable to another parish, the certificated person could be sent back to the parish whence it was brought (8 and 9 Will. III, c. 30).

This Statute also enacted " to the end that money raised only for the relief of such as are as well impotent as poor, may not be misapplied and consumed by the idle, sturdy and disorderly beggars ; that persons receiving parochial relief, and their wives and children, should (under the punishment for refusal of imprisonment and whipping, or of having reliefs abridged or withdrawn) wear a badge on the shoulder of the right sleeve—that is to say, a large ' P '—together with the first letter of the name of the parish or place, cut in red or blue cloth ; and a penalty was imposed on churchwardens and overseers relieving poor persons not wearing such a badge." [1]

Such was the state of the Poor Law during the period, with which our book is concerned.

Having regard to the above-mentioned enactments, reflecting the spirit of the times, it will be readily admitted that the overseers of Westbury, Stoke Bishop and Shirehampton Tithings carried out their duties to their poor, with as much kindness and consideration as was possible (which might even now be copied with advantage) : and at the same time displayed the necessary firmness to prevent the parish being burdened with the poor of other parishes and parts.

The monthly payments, made to the poor, will compare very favourably with those made in the present day, and more so when it is found, on referring to the "Audit Money Book" (1664–1703), which contains an account of the disbursements of the parochial charities, that the recipients of Poor Law relief were almost always recipients of these charities.

[1] *See* " Poor Laws " in *Ency. Brit.*

It may be urged that these "charity gifts" do not show kindly consideration on the part of those, who administered the charities, but that the "relief of the rates" was the main object. To this end points the fact that the Charity Commissioners on December 3rd, 1880, ordered that "the funds of the charities shall in no case be applied directly or indirectly in relief of the Poor Rate of the said Parish, or so that any individual shall become entitled to a periodical or recurrent benefit therefrom." But there is the other side, even though it be not the wiser, which can be strongly urged for the conduct of our predecessors, who lived in "different times," and were in a better position to enter into the intentions of the donors of those charities.

The various entries in our book bear testimony to the kindly manner, in which the wants and needs of the local poor were met. Regular relief is given, and special difficulties are considered: food, firing, lighting, clothing, shoes, hats, etc., are given, and incidentally the prices of materials and labour (*cf.* p. 164) can be noted. No detail is too small to be attended to, *cf.* page 298, "Itt paide to Thomas Everatt for *taping* James Whitchurches shoes 00 00 10d."; and page 312, "Itt for grafting a pair of Stockins for Henry Jayne 00 00 06d."; and, "Itt for lengthing Sarah Onions coat 00 00 04." Filial duty is encouraged, *cf.* page 36, "Geaven to Jane Jeffiries for tending her mother 00 02 00," and "Geaven to Jane Jefferies towards the buring of her mother 00 06 00"; and page 247, "Payd to William White to relieve his mother in her sickness 00 05 00." Kindness comes out in such an entry as that on page 213, "Given to Widow Vaughon being weake and feeble this year 00 18 06." Care for the children is very marked, as many entries will prove, *cf.* page 215, "Paid Ellen Squire for the *Tabling* of Henry Fishpoole at a quarter of a yeare at 1s. 3d. p week 00 17 06"; and page 300, "Itt paide for a truss for the child 00 00 06." Education is valued and made possible, *cf.* page 21, "Paid to John Gee for to *parrell* his son when he went to the free school £01 05 10." "Boarding out" of the parish children is no much-vaunted modern discovery; it appears to have been the rule, *cf.* page 213, "Sarah pullins boy 5 mo at 4s. p mo to Thomas Grant 01 00 00."

Great care seems to have been taken in the apprenticing of children, both boys and girls, *cf.* page 267, "Gave with *Anne* Williams to bind her apprentice 05 00 00." And if a parent could not provide the whole premium he was helped, *cf.* page 212, "Paid to William Jones *towards* the binding out of his son apprentice."

The overseers were careful guardians of the parish, and could use stern means; but at the same time they showed wisdom beyond the present times, and so knew how to prevent infanticide and suicide, while at the same time defending the sanctions of morality, as will appear from a careful study of the disbursements in reference to illegitimate children.

Some items of relief appear strange, but speak volumes for the kindness shown and the power of entering into that which is often the greatest anxiety to the poor, viz. the payment of rent, *cf.* page 271, "Itm pd Mr. Lane Goody

Palmers house rent 02 00 00." The old lady must have been very grateful, for the value of "home," be it only very poor, is not always considered in dealing with poor folk seeking relief—the "house" can never be "home." In another case relief was given to the old lady, who enjoyed her home till death, and then her things were sold by the overseers for part repayment, *cf.* page 187, "Moe for goods of Edith Williams when shee dyed 02 13 00." Other unusual items appear, *e.g.* page 15, "Paid towards the mending of Jane lanes house 00 02 06"; also page 219, "Paid for 3 horse loade of Cole for William Smith 00 03 03."

To help people to start in business money was borrowed at interest from the Charities, and the interest paid, *cf.* page 227, "To mo pd ye Clark for ye use of £10: £00 12 00"; and page 178, "Paid for the use of ten pounds Gooddy Gyllett 00 12 00." Misfortune also met with sympathy, *cf.* page 56, "Itt payd to Mr. Davis and Mr. Wasborow for fetching Robert Everat out of Newgate 00 01 09." He was probably an unfortunate debtor, who had been cast into that evil-smelling and disreputable prison near Bristol Castle precincts, and of which Latimer in his *Annals* gives so heart-rending an account.

Sickness and the claims of motherhood were readily recognised, and unusual items are found, *cf.* page 271, "Itt pd ffrances Wasborow for *ale* for Margarett Haskins in her tyme of sickness 00 1 07"; also page 159. The regular medical practitioner is employed, *cf.* page 227, "To pay ye doctor 01 05 06"; and page 255, "Payd to Chirugion for cureing of Richard Jones Legg 00 10 00." The midwife is also to be found, *cf.* page 158; and kindly disposed women are employed as nurses, *cf.* page 266, "It gave to Abigail Parker for tending of Tom Playford in ye small pox 00 05 00." But isolation and disinfectants are unknown or unused, and so it is small wonder that a subsequent entry runs, "It Gave to Abigail Parker in the time of her child's sickness in ye smallpox 00 06 06," the additional 1s. 6d. probably indicating sympathy, in that she has conveyed the smallpox to her own child. Skill, other than that of the recognised doctor, is employed, *cf.* page 197, "Pd Elnor Cooke for ye cureing Sarah Pullins Legg 00 06 00"; and page 310, "Paid Elizabeth Giles for curring Tants child 00 04 06." The bone-setter is also employed, *cf.* page 134, "Spent that day that Edward boure bones was set 00 05 06"; and, "Paid the bone setter 00 10 00." But the following suggestive entry comes next, "Paid for a chest and shroud for Edward Boure 00 12 00"; and, "Paid to the Currinor 00 13 04." And yet another catastrophe, *cf.* page 144, "Paid to the bone setter for him (John Pullin) 00 05 00"; then on the same page, "Paid towards the buring of John pullin 00 02 06."

Great care seems to have been taken with burials, and it could not be written of the deceased poor of these tithings :—

"Rattle his bones over the stones!
He's only a pauper, whom nobody owns!"

Thomas Noel in "The Pauper's Ride."

For *cf.* page 285 :—

" It Gave to Joane Jones in sickness	00	12	06
It Paid for drink and Biskett for those yt carried her to ye grave	00	06	00
It Paid ye Clerk and Sextone	00	03	08
It Paid for a Shroud for her	00	02	06
It Paid to them yt Laid her out	00	01	00
It Paid for a Coffin for her..	00	07	00
It Paid ye minister	00	02	06
It Paid for Coales	00	02	00
It Paid to two women yt made oath	00	01	00
It Paid to woman to looke to her in her sickness..	00	02	00 "

Here and elsewhere it will be noticed that drinking and eating were necessary incidents in a funeral, even though it was a "parish funeral"; but it was probably a "corrupt following" of what was customary, even down to recent times, in higher walks of life.

But when we leave the picture of the life of the resident poor of these tithings (which, for the most part, appears to have been not an unhappy one, although the "branding of poverty grates upon the feelings"—*cf.* page 298, "Itt paide for the Cloth and makeing the letters for the poore people 00 02 06"—even though the law so directed, *cf.* page x), and come to that of the "outside" poor, we are in a different atmosphere. There we find hard treatment, with only just bare consideration in the majority of cases, although here and there a touch of human kindness comes out.

Strangers can on no account be allowed to acquire a settlement in the tithings, *cf.* page 30, "Itt for riding to the Justice for a warrant for Thomas Stephens being an intruder 00 02 0"; page 111, "Spent when we went to Kingsland wth a warrant of disturbance to goe out of the parish 00 00 06"; and page 164, "for exspenses sev times going about to warne people for taking in strangers 00 02 06." The very last entries in this book refer to an effort to prevent settlements: "Aug. 27, 'Go by Christmas or to give security'"; "Walter Rudge and his wife late of Clifton to bring a Certificate by ye 8th September"; and "ffrances Osborne and his wife of Blagdon in Sommersettshire now living at ye Gallows Hill ye persons at ye house say they are going away at Michaelmas."

Small sums of money are given to strangers, who arrive with the necessary passes or certificates, and occasionally human nature asserts itself, even though the allowance is small, *cf.* page 43, "Itt geaven to a poore gent woman wth a pass and 4 children 00 01 00"; page 170, "A good minister and his wife in August 00 01 00." Motherhood must be recognised, but no "settlement" can be permitted, *cf.* page 56.

Some entries speak of the troubles of the times, *cf.* page 105, "Geaven to 2 seamen that were taken by the Dutch"; page 203, "It gave several disbanded souldiers that came with a pass party" ; and page 249, " It gave 3 seamen wch was taken in January 00 03 00."

In life the tithings would have nothing to do with strangers ; it was equally so in death, *cf.* page 205, " Payd the Coroner that sate upon ye man killed by ye fall of ye house at Gallows Hill and wh was then spent upon him and ye jury that sate upon him and given that this pish might not be at ye charge of his buriall 01 01 02."

The dealing with cripples appears very severe, and life must have been very hard for wayfaring children, as there are many entries relating to cripples, *cf.* page 53, " Payd for carrying away 3 cripples and exspenses 00 01 06" ; also page 64, " Payd for carring away a cart load of cripples and releef 00 02 06." But it must be remembered that they were only being dealt with according to the Statute of Ed. VI.

Legal proceedings were resorted to, rather than allow any claim of "settlement" to be made on the parish (*cf.* pp. 150 and 310), and immoral characters are removed to prison (*cf.* p. 212).

Sunday is to be observed as a day of rest, and there is to be no disturbance of the peaceful village Sabbath, *cf.* page 117, " Receaved of a drover driving uppon the Sabboth day 1 0 0" ; and so 3 Car. I, c. 1, which inflicted a penalty of 20s. on any carrier or drover, pursuing his calling on the Lord's Day, was enforced.

The accounts are kept in a perfectly simple manner : additions, subtractions and alterations are made after the accounts have been made up. If a person thinks his assessment is too high, he quietly refrains from paying the whole, and there appears an entry in the accounts on the part of the collector, " I crave allowance for." All ranks adopt this method, *cf.* page 286, " It I crave allowance for wh Sr Thomas Cann stoped which was 04 17 06" ; and page 172, " I crave allowance for Sr ffraunces Fane 00 06 08." If rent is due to a landlord from a poor tenant, the landlord does not hesitate to deduct the amount out of his own rate, *cf.* page 260, " I crave allowance i could not receve Mr: Richard Lane stopt for rent palmer house 2 0 00" ; also page 302, " I crave allowance of Alderman Lane for the rent of Pitt 02 00 00." A poor person does not need to trouble about his rate, and is "allowed" year after year, *cf.* page 260, " Gills nuosse 0 0 3½." If the rate has not produced sufficient for the year's needs, the collectors or overseers meet the difficulty by advancing the money.

The various handwritings, with their indications of the characters of the writers, are most interesting, but, of course, this is lost in the transcription. Some of the handwriting is splendid, but many evidently sign the book with very great difficulty, while both churchwardens in A.D. 1679 were unable to sign their names, and therefore made their marks. The spelling often depends upon the writer's fancy, or the sound of the word ; so both handwriting and spelling place the transcriber in some difficult positions, from which he is only able to extricate himself by careful comparisons.

The Parish Meetings were held at the Inn, and this, without a doubt, helped towards decency and order ; certainly in the treatment of public-houses our forefathers were wiser than their descendants.

There is no difficulty about the provision of refreshments for those engaged in public work, even though they be Justices of the Peace ; and these good people would have failed to understand the outcry, sometimes raised, against refreshments for guardians and councillors at the public expense when engaged on public work, *cf.* page 227, " To Mo paid when ye Justices met for wine and beere 00 13 00."

The office of overseer was served by the owners or tenants of the various properties, and ladies were expected to take their share or find a substitute, *cf.* page 272, where Lady Yeaman is nominated.

Lime-burning then, as now, was carried on in the parish, *cf.* page 47, " Geaven to the poore woman at the lime Kills at sev times 00 10 00." Pipe-making was also carried on (but now no longer), *cf.* page 198, " Payd Thomas Grant of Westbury pipe maker wt due to him in taking Martha Andrewes apprentice 01 00 00." This is in A.D. 1686, but it is interesting to note that in July, 1644, smoking had become so general that the House of Commons imposed an excise duty on " tobacco pipes of all sorts to be paid by the first buyer for every grosse fourpence."

It would be interesting to know, how the members of the Berkeley Hunt, which dates from 1613, would have looked upon overseers whose accounts in 1666 stated, " Itt payd for a fox head 00 01 00." [1]

Legal business was transacted not at Bristol, but at Old Sodbury, *cf.* page 6, " For going to Sadbury to confirme our rates, 00 02 00 " ; and, " For going to Sadbury another time for a warrant, 00 02 00."

There is one entry, which points to the breaking in upon the accustomed quiet of the parish, and it is easy to picture the excitement of that day, *cf.* page 53, " Spent uppon them that kept Christopher Smith in hold a night and day being taken with a hue and cry, 00 03 06." Blackstone in his *Commentaries* gives the following interesting account of " hue and cry " :—

> " There is yet another species of arrest, wherein both officers and private men are concerned, and that is upon an *hue* and *cry* raised upon a felony committed. An hue (from *huer*, to shout and cry), *hutesium et clamor*, is the old common law process of pursuing, with horn and with voice, all felons, and such as have dangerously wounded another. It is also mentioned by Statute Westms., 13 Edw. I, c. 9, and 4 Edw. I *de Officio Coronatoris*. But

[1] Against this early date, which has been claimed for the Berkeley Hunt, must be placed the statement in the *Badminton Library—Hunting*, p. 28 (1886):—"Some few years ago there was in the *Field* an engraving of a hunting horn in the possession of the then master of the Cheshire hounds, on which was the following inscription: 'Thomas Boothby, Esq., Tooley Park, Leicester. With this horn he hunted the first pack of fox-hounds then in England 55 years: born 1677, died 1752.'" Beyond this I cannot carry this subject.

the principal Statute relative to this matter is that of Winchester, 13 Edw. I, c. 1 and 4, which directs that from thenceforth every country shall be so well kept that, immediately upon robberies and felonies committed, fresh suit shall be made from town to town, and from county to county, and that hue and cry shall be raised upon the felons, and they that keep the town shall follow with hue and cry, with all the town and the towns near; and so hue and cry shall be made from town to town until they be taken and delivered to the sheriff. And, that such hue and cry may more effectually be made, the hundred is bound by the same Statute, cap. 3, to answer for all robberies therein committed, unless they take the felon; which is the foundation of an action against the hundred in case of any loss by robbery. By Statute 27 Eliz., c. 13, no hue and cry is sufficient unless made with both horsemen and footmen. . . . Hue and cry may be raised either by precept of a justice of the peace, or by a peace officer, or by any private man that knows of a felony. The party raising it must acquaint the constable of the vill with all the circumstances which he knows of the felony, and the person of the felon; and thereupon the constable is to search his own town, and raise all the neighbouring vills, and make pursuit with horse and foot; and in the prosecution of such hue and cry the constable and his attendants have the same powers, protection and idemnification as if acting under the warrant of a justice of the peace. But if a man wantonly or maliciously raises an hue and cry, without cause, he shall be severely punished as a disturber of the public peace."

The reservation, added by the Justices of the Peace to their sanction of the accounts, provokes a smile: *cf.* page 313, "3 April 1700 allowed of this account *if true* Richard Haynes, Nath Wade, Tho Walter."

There is a pleasing monotony about the accounts, and also the names both of the recipients and of those transacting the parochial business, so that the following lines could truly be applied to these tithings:—

"Far from the madding crowd's ignoble strife
Their sober wishes never learned to stray,
Along the cool sequester'd vale of life
They kept the noiseless tenor of their way."

Gray's "Elegy in a Country Churchyard."

Yet their vision was not bounded by a narrow parochialism, but an interest was taken in the "larger world," for we find on page 30, "Itt spent uppon the ringers the Coronation day 01 10 00." There was much truth in Charles II's remark: "It is my own fault," laughed the new king with characteristic irony, "that I had not come back sooner, for I find nobody who does not tell me he has always longed for my return."[1] At any rate, Westbury had lost heavily in the late troublous times in the destruction of its college buildings, involving

[1] Green's *History of the English People*, p. 582.

the departure of the hospitable Ralph Sadleir,[1] and in the damage to its church.

This wider interest also appears on page 56, dated A.D. 1666, "Itt payd for making Rates for Royall Ayd 00 02 00"; and, "Spent when the tithing did meet about the Royall Ayd 00 07 06."

The tithings again shared in the national rejoicings in connection with the landing of William III, *cf.* page 227, "To Wade for ye Ringers and other expenses Wn ye King landed 00 11 03."

There are two buildings, mentioned in this book, of special local interest:—

1. *The College*, for which the reader is referred to *Some Chapters in the Ecclesiastical History of Westbury-on-Trym*, where he will find the history of this building somewhat fully dealt with.

2. *The Almshouse cf.* page 76, "Payd afterwards for mending the Almshouse 00 16 06."

The history of this almshouse is full of interest. The original buildings, which were on the north side of the church, were most probably the work of of Bishop Giffard. *The Victoria History—Gloucestershire*, edited by William Page, F.S.A., gives the following interesting statement: "It has usually been assumed that afterwards (*i.e.* after Bishop Simon, 1123–51, had restored the Church of Westbury with its dependent chapels to the prior and convent of Worcester) Westbury was merely a parish church until 1288, when Bishop Giffard founded a College of Canons against the will of the prior and convent of Worcester (Tanner, *Notitia Monastica* (ed. 1744), p. 142, and *Clifton Antiquarian Club Proceedings*, iv, 33). However, Giffard's registers prove conclusively that from the earliest times of his episcopate (1268) a dean and canons were in possession (*Worc. Epis. Reg.*, Giffard (Worc. Hist. Soc.), 20, 49, 54, 71, 123, etc.), and indeed that his predecessor, Walter de Cantilupe, collated his clerks to the prebends of Westbury (*ibid.*, 4)." At any rate, whatever was the previous history, these buildings (which afterwards became the almshouses) were in Bishop Giffard's time the residences of the collegiate body, and continued to be so till the time of Bishop Carpenter (1444).

The Victoria History continues: "In 1447 Bishop Carpenter began to rebuild the college on a much larger scale, and revised its statutes and ordinances with the object of increasing its sphere of usefulness (*Worc. Epis. Reg.*, Carpenter, i, fol. 183*d*). He built almshouses for six poor men (*Worc. Epis. Reg.*, Carpenter, i, fol. 231 in 1466) and six widows (*Clifton Antiquarian Club Proceedings*, iv, 36; *Valor Eccles.* (Rec. Con.), ii, 434), vesting the right of nomination in the dean and chapter."

In Pryce's *Canynges' Family*, etc., is the following statement: "In addition to the share William Canynges had in the re-erection of the Benedictine College at Westbury, he built an almshouse also in its vicinity for the reception of poor men and women, leaving lands for its support, as well as to pay £44 yearly to the Sheriffs of Bristol for vehicles to pass through the gates of the town toll

[1] See *Letters Patent of Edward VI*, published for the present writer by Arrowsmith.

free when conveying provisions to his charity, and probably the College at Westbury."

Dr. Harvey, in his *Westbury Church*, writes: "But it does not appear whether the twelve aged men and poor widows were sheltered under the collegiate roof."

It would seem that Bishop Carpenter, in building his new buildings, (with the aid of Dean Canynge, who was a wealthy man,) for the college did not fetter himself with Bishop Giffard's buildings, but utilised an adjacent site hard by these buildings, but separated from them by a small lane. (*See* Plan A.D. 1792, in *Eccles. Hist. of Westbury*.) It appears most probable that the old buildings were made into almshouses for the six poor widows, while the six aged men lived under the collegiate roof.

These almshouses are mentioned in the parish *Terrier*, dated May 3rd, 1806, viz.: the churchyard is "bounded on the north by certain Tenements belonging to the parish of Westbury-on-Trym."

In 1840 the eminent architect, the late John Norton, wrote, after he had visited the place: "The Grounds belonging to the Monastery (*i.e.* the College of Bishop Carpenter) were extensive, including the Church and Almshouse, and endowed by Bishop Carpenter for six poor men and six poor women and a row of Buildings, said to be erected on the site of the old cloisters now sometime since converted into eight houses occupied by the poor of the Parish rent free. They were separately entered from a narrow alley in length about 130 feet, and are situated under the north wall of the churchyard." Without entering into John Norton's history, which is inaccurate, his testimony to the existing almshouse is important. He gives the accompanying sketch of the entrance, which is the more valuable, for after patient inquiry and also personal search in the Bristol Central Library and at the Bodleian Library and elsewhere, I have been unable to find any view of Westbury earlier than about 1852. A view, evidently dating before the partial restoration of the church in 1852, has been presented to the Church Museum by Miss Taylor, sometime district nurse. It remains to be seen if any exist in the library of the Earl of Leicester at Holkham, where is the "celebrated and perhaps matchless collection of maps and views in nearly one hundred volumes" of John Innys, who was churchwarden of Westbury in 1764.

The almshouses were no longer in existence in 1853, when Pryce (continuing the statement given above) wrote: "The site of the almshouse may still be

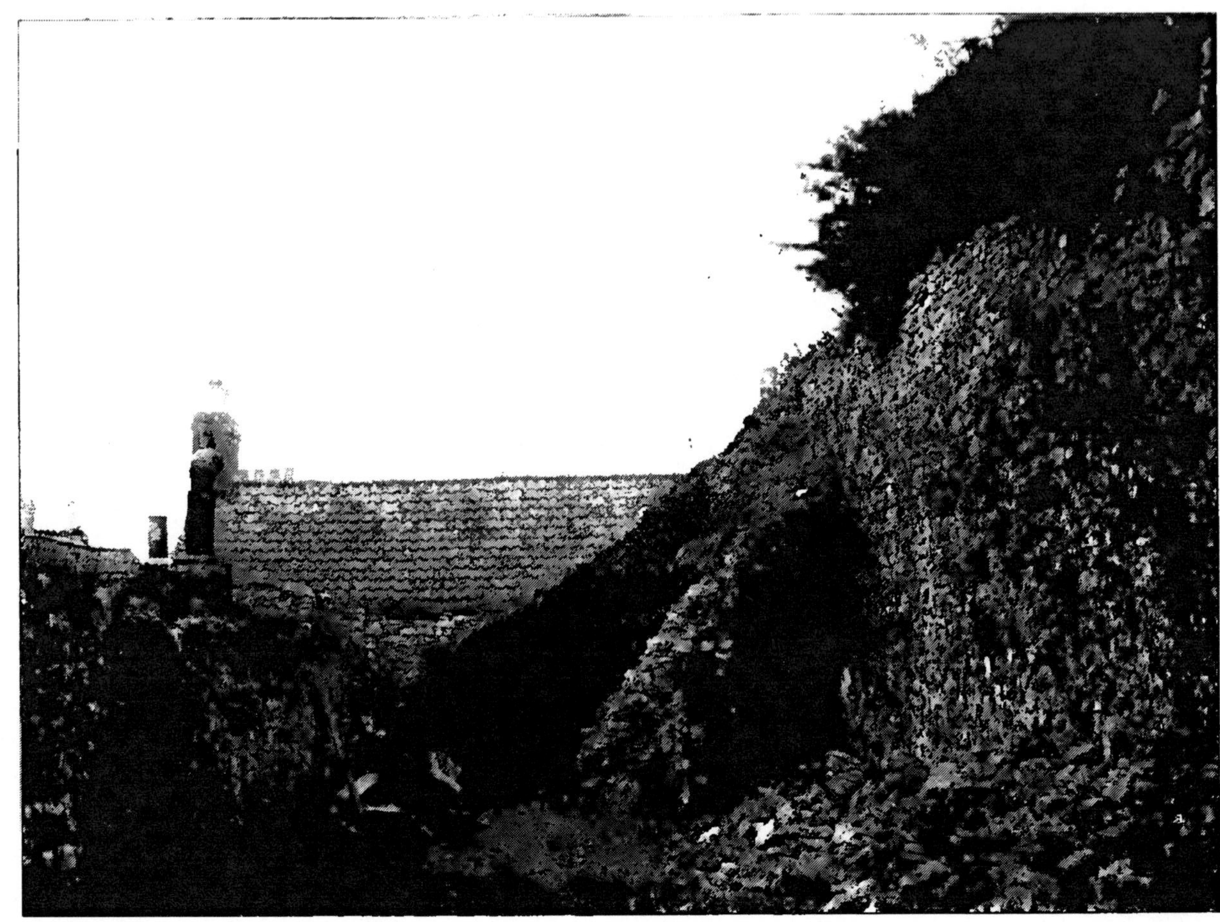

Feb. 1905. *From a photo taken by Mr. Frank Richardson (who was one of the Churchwardens of Westbury at that time), and kindly given to the writer.*

recognised by sundry doorways, etc., built up with more modern portions of dwelling-houses, but they are of too insignificant a character to remark."

The destruction of these almshouses about 1852 was quite in keeping with the spirit of that time at Westbury. The old parish clerk, now deceased, told the present writer in 1900 that the reason they were destroyed was because "the people wouldn't behave themselves: they were shut in at night" (the almshouses were situated inside the west gates of the churchyard, which were locked at sunset), "and used to let cans down over the wall and get folks to fetch them beer, and so they pulled the houses down." For such a paltry reason, to which other old inhabitants testify, was destroyed what would have been a most interesting specimen of a mediæval monastery.

All that now remains is the massive north wall, dating from not later than 1288, and the mouldings of a window at the east end of the entrance to the almshouses. Mr. J. B. C. Burroughs (to whom Westbury owes a great debt of gratitude, since he was the first to move in the matter of the preservation of the remains of the college, and so, with others, saved them from the fate of the almshouses) writes October 26th, 1909: "This building was used as a Parish Poor House, and was dismantled and the materials sold about sixty years ago. I had these remains inspected by Sir John Maclean and Mr. T. S. Pope in 1892, who pronounced the details" (these would not include the north wall) "to be of late fifteenth or early sixteenth century, and window with circular head and quaint moulding of same date."

On part of the site of the almshouse was built a small Vestry Hall in 1853 from the materials of the bone or charnel house, which was then pulled down from the south-west end of the south aisle of the church, and which involved a further loss to the church, for John Norton wrote in 1840: "In the Bone house is a Piscina bearing the same date," *i.e.* Early English, "and an altar tomb of a later character," both of which have disappeared. The other part of the site has been long used as a rubbish tip. When in 1905 a partial clearance was made a portion of a dividing wall was discovered, giving an idea as to the extent of each compartment.

For the notes to the names in the book I am largely indebted to Latimer's *Seventeenth-Century Annals of Bristol* and to some Westbury documents.

It would not be right to conclude this introduction without expressing our deep sense of gratitude to our esteemed parishioner, Mr. Peter Forrest (Churchwarden of Westbury, 1902–5). When District (or Parish) Councils came into existence in 1894, the civil duties of the Vestry were transferred to that body, who, laying claim to civil documents, swooped down upon Westbury Church and carried off—so careless was the examination of documents or the guardianship of them—*inter alia*, would it be believed! *A Book of Common Prayer* (Charles I); the first volume—extremely rare, as it is an undoubted church copy—of Erasmus's *Paraphrase of the New Testament*, first published in 1523; a large bundle of churchwardens' accounts and two "Poor Books"—the one now under consideration and the other for 1700–29. When Westbury was incorporated with Bristol in 1904, thanks to Mr. Forrest's suggestion, the above documents were returned to Westbury Church, and so we conclude with our best thanks to Mr. Forrest and those concerned in the restoration of those interesting documents.

H. J. WILKINS.

1909.

"POOR BOOK."

Page 1.

1656 | 1698. A ratement or an asseasment made for the relief of the poore of the p'rish of Westbury-uppon-trim by Thomas Hort and John Berry churchwardens Anthony Hort John Young and John Smith overseers of the poore of the sayd p'rish for this yeare 1656 according to the valuacon of every mans land or living at the rate of three half pence a pound as followeth vigt :—

		£	s.	d.
Imp	Mris. Barker[1]	096	12	00
	Mr. Walter	095	11	10
	Mr. Wasborow	090	11	03
	William Stephens	090	11	03
	Widdow Wasborow	030	03	03
	Mr. Lane	042	05	03
	Mr. Ffloyd	030	03	09
	Robert Wasborow	023	02	10
	Thomas Adlam	025	03	01
	Mris. Arendall	029	03	07
	Widdow White	024	03	00
	Thomas Grant	020	02	06
	Widdow Hort } Mr. Hort }	039	04	10
	Mris. Lardy	024	03	00
	Mr. Meredy	025	03	01
	John Atkins	025	03	1
	Edward Rumney	018	02	3
	Mr. Cox	014	01	9
	Mr. King	011	01	4
	Mr. Walter	006	00	6
	Mr. Grig	006	00	9
	Samuell Lanford	010	01	03
	Robert Effington	005	00	07
	Thomas Hort	008	01	00
	Mr. Sommerset	006	00	09
	Edward Sampson	012	01	01
	Samuell Cutler	004	00	01
	Widdow Adlam	003	00	09
	Widdow Weare	001	00	01
	Widdow Creed	002	00	03
	William Hicks	001	00	01
	£ 5 s. 0 d. 4½	05	00	4

[1] Mris. Barker was the widow of Alderman John Barker, M.P. (son of a former mayor of Bristol), who espoused the cause of the Bristol merchants in 1634, as they were suffering unjust exactions at the hands of the king's mercenary officials.

Page 2. THE TITHING OF STOKEBISSHOP.

		£	s.	d.
Imp	Mr. Wallis	056	07	00
	Mr. Shermon	038	04	09
	Docter Martin	077	09	07
	Mr. Jackson	080	10	00
	Mr. More	076	09	06
	Mr. Sommerset	038	04	09
	Mris. Charleton	054	06	09
	William Dimmock	051	06	04½
	Jeorum Cuffe	024	03	00
	Robert White	036	04	06
	Mr. Rutland [1]	033	04	01½
	Mr. Godman	26	03	03
	Mr. Norris	022	02	09
	Mr. English	026	03	03
	Mris, Tillotdam	020	02	06
	William Hurtnoll	014	01	09
	Mr. Can	014	01	09
	Mris. Child	012	01	06
	Mr. Haswerd	010	01	03
	Edward Lewes	011	01	04½
	Mris. Boulten	008	01	00
	Thomas Hort	026	03	03
	Mr. Can	006	00	09
	Mr. Bawldin	007	00	10½
	Richard Wellington	008	01	00
	Mr. Lane	006	00	09
	Thomas Adlam	004	00	06
	Thomas Maunsell	008	01	00
	William Hurne	010	01	03
	Mris. Hungerford	040	05	00
	Mris. Jones	002	00	03
	Robert Wasborow	002	00	03
	Wathen Adlam	002	00	03
	Mr. Lewes	004	00	06
	William Baddam	001	00	01
	Mr. Sommersett	018	02	03
		£005	08	06

[1] Mr. Rutland was Minister of Westbury (See *Eccles. Hist. of Westbury*). He left ' 5 pounds to ye Poor in Cote for ever."

 THE TITHING OF SHEREHAMPTON.

	£	s.	d.
Mris. Rogers	80	10	00
Mr. Grummell	40	05	00
Mris. Bush	55	06	10 *ob*
Widdow Hort and John berry	28	03	06
Mr. Gibbs	50	06	03
Widdow Rome	12	01	06
Richard Parker	05	00	07 *ob*
John Matthews	03	00	04 *ob*
John Green	36	04	06
John Smith	14	01	09
Christopher Smith	41	05	01 *ob*
Widdow Clement	07	00	10 *ob*
John Stokes	28	03	06
Mr. Chilton	24	03	00
John Wasborow	17	02	01 *ob*
Widdow Dee	09	01	01 *ob*
Walter Parker	16	02	00
Christopher Peacock	19	02	04 *ob*
Richard Lot	14	01	09
Widdow Heskins	50	06	03
Elizabeth Hellin	36	04	06
for Avenhouse	20	02	06
John Gunning	33	04	01 *ob*
Widdow Wasborow	05	00	07 *ob*
Mr. Mats	16	02	00
Richard Street	28	03	06
William Greenfeild	50	06	03
Mr. Lock	16	02	00
James Harris	16	02	00
Mr. Diton	10	01	01 *ob*
William Cottrell	09	01	01 *ob*
William Parker	24	03	00
Morris Smith	15	01	10 *ob*
John Smith	25	03	01 *ob*
Petre Dee	09	01	01 *ob*
John Berry	05	00	07 *ob*
Thomas Herring	11	01	04 *ob*
John Gunning	04	00	06
Thomas Willis	05	00	07 *ob*
John Matthews	14	01	09
	£05	12	4½

Page 4.

The Accompt of Anthony Hort one of the collectors of the poore of the prish of Westbury-uppon-trim made the tenth day of Aprell 1657.

		£	s.	d.
Imp	this accomptant chargeth himself wth a rate of 3*ob* a pound	05	00	4 *ob*
	more receaved of the ould collectors	04	08	00
	The disbursements as followeth the total is	09	08	04½
Imp	John Wade 10 moneths att 4s. p month	02	00	00
	Richard deane 9 moneths	01	02	06
	Jane Lane 5 mo att 1s. 6d. and 4 M att 2. p m ..	00	15	06
	Joane Button 9 moneths at 3s. a moneth	01	07	00
	Christopher bugher at 4 moneths 1 6 and 4 mo att 2	00	15	06
	Elizabeth foord 9 moneths 8 mo att 1s. 6d. and 1 mo att 26	00	14	00
	geaven unto John Wade and his in their sickness..	00	07	00
	geaven unto Goddy Coats	00	02	00
	payd for a new book..	00	04	06
	payd unto William Arnall for nursing a child ..	02	00	06
	payd to John Hunt for nursing the same child ..	00	05	00
	spent uppon accompt day the last year	00	08	00
	spent at the Downe to meet Mr. Bush	00	04	00
	the totall of my disbust	£10	05	06

Soe it appeareth that there is dew unto me uppon this accompt 17s. 2d*ob*.

Page 5.

The Accompt of John Young one of the collectors of the poore of the prish of Westbury-uppon-trim made the tenth day of Aprell 1657.

		£	s.	d.
Imp	this accomptant charget hhimself wth a rate of 3*ob* a pound	05	08	06
	The disburstments as followeth			
Imp	payd John wade 3 moneths at 4s. a moneth ..	00	12	00
	payd to Christopher bushey 4 moneths at 2s. a moneth	00	08	00
	geaven to John Reynolds	00	04	00
	payd to Richard deane 4 moneths at 2s. 6d. a moneth	00	10	00
	payd to Joane Button 4 moneths at 3s. a moneth ..	00	12	00
	payd to Jane Lane 4 moneths at 2s a moneth.. ..	00	08	00
	payd to Widdow foord 4 moneths	00	09	06
	payd for the rates and ingrossing the book	00	02	06
	payd to John Hunt for nursing the child	00	15	00
	the total is	£04	01	00

	£	s.	d.
Soe it appeareth that there is dew unto the prish uppon this accompt	1	7	6
Now I craveth allowance for money that I cannot gather—			
William Hobson	0	0	9
Richard Edwards	0	1	0
Mris. Jones	0	0	3
Matthew peerre	0	0	1 *ob*

	£	s.	d.
now there is dew to the prish ..	1	5	4 *ob.*

	£	s.	d.
payd to Anthony Hort of this money that is dew to the prish	00	15	2½
more payd to John Smith	00	10	02

soe it appeareth it is all payd.

Page 6.

The Accompt of John Smith one of the collectors of the poore of the prish of Westbury-uppon-trim made the tenth of Aprell 1657.

	£	s.	d.	
Imp this accomptant chargeth himself wth the rate of three half pence a pound wch commeth to	05	12	04	*ob*
more hee chargeth himself with money that hee receaved of the ould collectors wch is ..	00	17	00	
the totall is	£06	09	04	*ob*

The disburstments as followeth :—

	£	s.	d.
Itt payd to Thomas faux 7 moneths at 2 shillings a moneth	00	14	00
more payd to him	00	10	00
payd the widdow boure 12 moneths at 3s. 6d. a moneth	02	02	00
payd the Widdow wood 12 moneths at 2s. a moneth ..	01	04	00
payd Edward Lansdown 12 moneths at 2s a moneth ..	01	04	00
payd the widdow drinckwater 12 moneths at 1s. 6d. a moneth	00	18	00
geaven to Elizabeth Berry in her sickness	00	04	00
more geaven her in her sickness	00	05	00
for going to Sadbury to confirme our rates	00	02	00
for going to Sadbury another time for a warrant ..	00	02	00
the totall of my disburstments ..	£07	05	00

Now hee craveth allowance for money that hee cannot gather of Richard parker 7d*ob*.

soe it appeareth there is dew unto him from the prish 06s. 3d.

John: Codrington
Sa: Codrington

	£	s.	d.
more dew unto him 7s. being forgotten			
soe there is dew unto him in the whole	00	13	03
Paide John Smith	00	05	10
	£00	07	05

This accompts seen and allowed by wee whose name are under written
Wee doe nominate and appoint to serve the office of collectors for the yeare ensuinge
George Lane
John White
Richard Street

Edmund Rutland Minist ibid.
Robert Wasborow
Thomas Adlam
Thomas Hort
John Edney
John Besey.

Page 7.

ratement made by the inhabitants of the prish of Westbury-uppon-trim for and towards the reliefe of the poore of the said prish for this yeare 1657 at the rate of 2 pence the pound as followeth :—

		£	s.	d.
Imp	Mris. Barker	96	16	00
	Mr. Walter	95	15	10
	Mr. Wasborow	90	15	00
	William Stephens	90	15	00
	Widdow Wasborow	30	05	00
	Mr. Lane	42	07	00
	Mr. floyd	30	05	00
	Robert Wasborow	23	03	10
	Thomas Adlam	25	04	02
	Mris. Arendall	29	04	10
	John Sampson	24	04	00
	Thomas Grant	20	03	04
	Widdow Hort	20	03	04
	Mr. Hort	19	03	02
	Mr. Davis	24	04	00
	Mr. Meredy	25	04	02
	Widdow Atkins	25	04	02
	Widdow Rumny	18	03	00
	Mr. Cox	14	02	04
	Mr. King	11	01	10
	Mris. Walter	06	01	00
	Mr. Grigg	06	01	00
	Samuell Sanford	10	01	08
	Robert Essington	05	00	10
	Thomas Hort	08	01	04
	Mr. Sommerset	06	01	00
	Samuel Tucker	04	00	08
	Widdow Adlam	03	00	06
	Edward Sampson	12	02	00
	Widdow Weare	01	00	02
	Widdow Creed	02	00	04
	William Hicks	01	00	02

Page 8. THE TITHING OF STOKEBISSHOP.

		£	s.	d.
Imp	Mr. Wallis..	56	09	04
	Mr. Shermon	38	06	04
	Docter Marten	77	12	10
	Mr. Jackson	80	13	04
	Mr. Somersett	38	06	04
	Mris. Charleton	54	09	00
	William Dimock	51	08	06
	Jeorom Cuff	24	04	00
	Robert White	36	06	00
	Mr. Rutland	33	05	06
	Thomas Godman	26	04	04
	Mr. Norris..	22	03	08
	Mr. English	26	04	04
	Mr. Standfast	20	03	04
	William Hurtnoll	14	02	04
	Mr. Hobson	16	01	04
	Mris. Child	12	02	00
	Mr. Haswerd	10	01	08
	Edward Lewes	11	01	10
	Mris. Boulton	08	01	04
	Thomas Hort	26	04	04
	Mr. Can	14	02	04
	Mr. Bawldin	07	01	02
	Richard Willington	08	01	04
	Mr. Lane	06	01	00
	Thomas Adlam	04	00	08
	Thomas Maunsell	08	01	04
	William Hurne	10	01	08
	Mris. Hungerford..	40	06	08
	Mris. Jones	02	00	04
	Robert Wasborow	02	00	04
	Mathew Adlam	02	00	04
	Mr. Somerset	18	03	00
	Mr. Lewes	04	00	08
	William Baddam	01	00	02

Page 9. THE TITHING OF SHEREHAMPTON.

		£	s.	d.
Imp	Mris. Rogers	80	13	04
	Captaine Grummell	40	06	08
	Mris. Bush	55	09	02
	Widdow Hort and John Berry	28	04	08
	William Harris	50	08	04
	Widdow Rome	18	03	00
	Richard parker	05	00	10
	John matthews	17	02	10
	John Green	36	06	00
	John Smith	10	01	08
	Christopher Smith	41	06	10
	Widdow Clement	07	01	02
	John Stokes	28	04	08
	Mr. Chilton	24	04	00
	Widdow wasborow	17	02	10
	Widdow Dee	09	01	06
	Walter parker	16	02	08
	Christopher peacock	19	03	02
	Richard Lot	14	02	04
	Widdow Heskins	50	08	04
	Elizabeth Hellin	36	06	00
	for Avenhouse	20	03	04
	John Gunning	38	06	04
	Widdow wasborow	00	00	00
	Mr. Mats	16	02	08
	Richard Street	28	04	08
	William Greenfeild	50	08	04
	Mr. Lock	16	02	08
	Mr. Rutland	16	02	08
	Mr. Diton	10	01	08
	William Cotterell	09	01	06
	William parker	24	04	00
	Morris Smith	15	02	06
	John Smith	25	04	02
	Petre Dee	09	01	06
	John Berry	05	00	10
	Thomas Herring	11	01	10
	John Gunnng	04	00	08

Page 10.

The accompt of Mr. Georg Lane one of the collectors of the poore or the prish of Westbury-uppon-trim made the xxiiith day of Aprell 1653.

		£	s.	d.
Imp	this accomptant chargeth himself wth the rate of 2d a pound wch commeth unto	06	14	06
	The disburstments as followeth			
Imp	paid to John hunt for keeping a child 53 weeks ..	05	06	00
	more paid to Christopher busshell 12 moneths ..	01	16	00
	more paid to John Lane 12 moneths	01	04	00
	more spent when wee went to Sadbury	00	05	00
	more paid to Robert Wasborow	00	00	06
	more paid to the Cleark for making the rate and ingrossing	00	00	10
	more geaven to ould wade at 2 sevall times	00	02	00
	the total of my disbur ..	£08	14	04
	Soe it appeareth that there is dew unto mee.. ..	01	19	10

The accompt of John White one of the collectors of the poore of the prish of Westbury-uppon-trim made the xxiiith day of Aprell 1658.

		£	s.	d.
Imp	this accomptant chargeth himself wth the rate of two pence a pound wch commeth unto	07	05	00
	The disburstments as followeth			
Imp	paid to John Wade 12 months	02	08	00
	paid to Joane button 12 moneths	01	16	00
	paid to Richard deane 12 moneths	01	10	00
	paid to widdow foord 12 moneths	01	10	00
	geaven to John wade in his sicknes	00	06	00
	geaven to Gooddy osborne in her sicknes	00	05	00
	geaven to Gooddy Coats in her sickness	00	03	00
	the totall of my disbursm	£07	18	00
	Soe it appeareth there is dew unto me..	00	13	00

Page 11.

The accompt of Richard Street one of the collectors of the poore of the prish of Westbury-uppon-trim made the xxiiith day of Aprell 1658.

		£	s.	d.
Imp	this accomptant chargeth himself wth the rate of two pence a pound wch commeth	07	10	00
	The disburstments as followeth			
Imp	the Widdow boure paid 13 moneths	02	15	06
	more paid the Widdow wood 13 moneths	01	12	06
	more payd Edward Lansdown 13 moneths ..	01	06	00
	more paid the Widdow drinckwater 12 moneths ..	00	18	00
	more paid Thomas faux towards keeping a child ..	01	04	00
	more geaven unto Hester Gale in her sickness ..	00	09	02
	more for keeping a child 14 weeks	01	01	00
	more paid to John Smith	00	02	04
	more paid for making the rate and ingrosing ..	00	01	00
		£08	19	06
	Now I Crave allowance for Richard parker 10d			
	Soe it appeareth that there is dew unto me dew ..	01	09	06

This accopmts allowed by wee whose names are underwritten

John Codrington	Edmund Rutland Minst	
Sa: Codrington	Anthony Hortt and	Church
	John Gunning	Wardens
	Thomas Adlam	
	John Molyenes	

Wee doe nominate and appoint collectors of the poore for the yeare ensuing John Wade Davee Haswerd John Matthews.

Page 12.

A rate made by the Churchwardens and other of the inhabitants of the parrish of Westbury-uppon-trim for and towards the releife of the poore of the said parrish for this yeare 1658 at the rate of three pence the pound as followeth :—

		£	s.	d.
Imp	Mris. Barker	96	24	00
	Mr. Walter	88	22	00
	Mr. Wasborow	90	22	06
	William Stephens	90	22	06
	Widdow Wasborow	15	03	09
	Mr. Lane	42	10	06
	Mr. Walter	07	01	09
	Mr. floyd	30	07	06
	Robert Wasborow	23	05	09
	Thomas Adlam	25	06	03
	Mris. Arendall	25	06	03
	Mris. Sarah Lardy	04	01	00
	John Sampson	24	06	00
	Thomas Grant	20	05	00
	Widdow Hort	22	05	06
	Mr. Hort	17	04	03
	Mr. Davis	24	06	00
	Mr. Meredy	25	06	03
	Widdow Atkins	25	06	03
	Widdow Rumney	18	04	06
	Mr. powell	14	03	06
	Mr. King	11	02	09
	Mris. Walter	06	01	06
	Mr. Grigg	06	01	06
	Samuel Sanford	10	02	06
	Richard Street	05	01	03
	Thomas Hort	08	02	00
	Mr. Sommerset	06	01	06
	John Sampson	12	03	00
	Samuel Tucker	04	01	00
	Widdow Adlam	03	00	09
	Widdow weare	01	00	03
	Widdow Creed	02	00	06
	William Hicks	01	00	03

	£	s.	d.	
William atwood	10	02	06	£10 03 06
Mr. Rutland	05	01	03	

Page 13. THE TITHING OF STOKEBISSHOP.

		£	s.	d.
Imp	Mr. Wallis..	56	14	00
	Mrs. Shermon	36	09	06
	Docter Martin	77	19	03
	Mr. Jackson	80	20	00
	Mr. More ..	76	19	00
	Mr. Sommerset	38	09	00
	Mris. Charleton	54	13	06
	William Dimmock	51	12	09
	Mr. Cuff ..	24	06	00
	Robert White	36	09	00
	Mr. Rutland	33	08	03
	Mr. Godman	26	06	06
	Mr. Norris..	22	05	06
	Mr. Gled ..	26	06	06
	Mr. Sommerset	18	04	06
	Nicholas parker	20	05	00
	William Hurtnoll..	14	03	06
	Mr. Can ..	14	03	06
	Mris. Child	12	03	00
	Mr. Haswerd	10	02	06
	Edward Lewes	11	02	09
	Mris. Boulton	08	02	00
	Thomas Hort	26	06	06
	Mr. Can ..	06	01	06
	Mr. Bawldin	07	01	09
	Richard Willington	08	02	00
	Mr. Lane ..	06	01	06
	Thomas Adlam	04	01	00
	Thomas Maunsell	08	02	00
	William Hurne	10	02	06
	Mris. Hungerford..	40	10	00
	Mris. Jones	02	00	06
	Robret Wasborow	02	00	06
	Mathew Adlam	02	00	06
	Mr. Lewes	04	01	00
	William Baddam	01	00	03
	Mris. Arendall	05	01	03
		10	17	06

Page 14. THE TITHING OF SHEREHAMPTON.

		£	s.	d.
Imp	Mris. Rogers	80	20	00
	Captaine Grummell	40	10	00
	Mris. Bush	40	10	00
	Mris. Bush	15	03	09
	Widdow Hort	19	04	09
	Mr. Gibbs	50	12	06
	Widd Rome	18	04	06
	Richard parker	05	01	03
	John Mathews	17	04	03
	John Green	36	09	00
	John Smith	10	02	06
	Widdow Smith	14	10	03
	Widdow Clement	07	01	09
	John Stokes	28	07	00
	Mr. Chilton	24	06	00
	Widdow Wasborow	17	04	03
	Widdow Dee	09	02	03
	Walter parker	16	04	00
	Christopher peacock	19	04	09
	Richard Lot	14	03	06
	Widdow Heskins	50	12	06
	Elizabeth Hellin	36	09	00
	for Avenhoues	20	05	00
	John Gunning	38	09	06
	Mr. Mates	16	04	00
	Richard Street	28	07	00
	Mr. Lock	16	04	00
	William Greenfeild	50	12	06
	Mr. Rutland	16	04	00
	Mr. Diton	10	02	06
	Christo: peacock and John Green	09	02	03
	William Parker	24	06	00
	Morris Smith	15	03	09
	John Smith	25	06	03
	Petre Dee	09	02	03
	John Berry	14	03	06
	Thomas Herring	11	02	09
	John Gunning	04	01	00

Page 15.

he accompt of John Wade one of the Collectors of the poore of the parish of Westbury-uppon-trim made the xith day of Aprell 1659.

		£	s.	d.
Imp	This accomptant chargeth himself wth the rate of 3d. a pound more hee chargeth himself with £7 14s. receaved of Davee Haswerd which commeth unto	17	17	06
	The disburstments as followeth			
Imp	paid to John Wade one moneth	00	04	00
	more paid to John Wade for 13 moneths at 5s. a month	03	05	00
	more paid to Christopher Bussher for 14 moneths at 3s. a moneth	02	02	00
	more paid to Jane lane for 14 moneths at 2s. a moneth	01	08	00
	more paid to Joane Button 14 moneths at 3s. a month	02	02	00
	more paid to Richard deane 14 moneths at 2s. 6d. a moneth	01	15	00
	more paid to the Widdow foord for 3 moneths ..	00	09	00
	more paid to her for a 11 moneths at 4s. a moneth ..	02	04	00
	more paid to John Hunt for keeping the child six weeks	00	12	00
	more paid for buring of the child and for a shroud and for making the woeman drinck	00	04	00
	geaven to Robert Smith in the whole yeare at sev times	00	08	06
	geaven to Jane Phillips towards the keeping of her child	00	08	00
	geaven to John Wade	00	02	06
	paid towards the mending of Jane lanes house ..	00	02	06
	geaven to Agnes Smith	00	01	00
	geaven to Elizabeth Cooke	00	01	06
	geaven to 6 poore people that was brought by a pas..	00	00	08
	geaven unto a poore woeman and 3 children that was brought by a pass	00	00	06
	paid for a horse and for bred and drink for to carry a creeple to henbury	00	00	08
	paid for buring a poore woeman	00	01	02
	paid to Mr. lane the money that hee laid out last yeare	01	19	10
	paid for making a grave for Thomas Cas	00	00	06
	for making the rates and in grossing the book.. ..	00	02	06
	for a warrant	00	00	06
	Soe there is dew unto the prish 0s. 3d.	17	15	4

Iow I Crave allowance
or money I cannot gather

William hicks	3
Widdow weare ..	3
Widdow Creed	6

Page 16.

The accompt of Davee haswerd one of the Collectors of the poore of the prish of Westbury-uppon-trim made the xith day of Aprell 1659.

		£	s.	d.
Imp	this accomptant chargeth himself wth the rate of three pence a pound wch commeth to	10	17	06
	The disburstments as followeth			
Imp	paid to Thomas hollins	07	14	00
	more paid for mending Jane lane house	00	02	06
	more paid towards buring the poore child	00	02	00
	more paid William Coats	00	03	00
	more geaven to Robert Smith	00	05	00
	more geaven to John Reynolds	00	02	00
	more geaven to Jane Phillips at sevral times towards the keeping of her child	00	10	00
	geaven to the poore woeman at Olam Slade	00	01	03
	geaven to gooddy Dogget	00	01	03
	geaven to 6 poore people with a pas	00	00	06
		09	01	06

	£	s.	d.
Now I Crave allowance for 3d. wch I could not gather			
Now there is dew to the prish	01	16	03
Now of this £1 16s. 03d. there is paid to John White 13s. ood.			
Soe there is dew from me to the pish	01	03	03
now this £1 3s. 3d. is payd to the now churchwardens			

Wee doe nominate and appoint to serve the office of Collectors for the poore for the yeare ensuing

Thomas Cuff
Anthony Elsworthy
Roger Gray

Page 17.

he accompt of John Matthews one of the collectors of the poore of the prish of Westbury-uppon-trim made the xith day of Aprell 1659.

		£	s.	d.
Imp	this accomptant chargeth himself with the rate of three pence in pound wch commeth to	11	04	00
	The disburstments as followeth			
Imp	paid to yeady Boure 13 moneths at 3s. 6d. a moneth ..	02	05	06
	paid to widdow woods 13 moneths at 2s. 6d. a moneth	01	12	06
	paid Eward Lansdown 13 moneths at 2s. od. a moneth	01	06	00
	paid to widdow drinckwater 13 mo. 1s. 6d. a moneth ..	00	19	06
	paid to Thomas faux	01	04	00
	paid for keeping a child 13 moneths at 6s. a moneth ..	03	18	00
	geaven to Thomas Base in the time of his sicknes ..	01	05	00
	paid to Richard Street	00	12	00
		13	2	6

[ow I Crave allowance for money
hat I cannot gather of Richard parker 1s. 3d.
oe it appeareth there is dew unto mee 01 19 09
ow this £1 19s. 9d. is paid to John
Iathews by John Smith

This accompts allowed by wee whose
names are underwritten

ohn Codrington
a: Codrington

Edmund Rutland Minist
William Dymocke
Anthony Hortt
Robert White
Thomas Adlam
John Norris

Page 18.

A rate made by the inhabitants of the prish of Westbury-uppon-trim for and towards the releife of the poore for this year 1659 at the rate of three pence the pound as followeth :—

		£	s.	d.
Imp	Mris. Barker	96	24	00
	Mr. Walten	88	22	00
	Mr. Wasborow	90	22	06
	William Stephens	90	22	06
	Mr. Walter	07	01	09
	Widdow Wasborrow	15	03	09
	Mr. Rutland	05	01	03
	Mr. Wood	10	02	06
	Mr. Lane	42	10	06
	Mr. ffloyd	30	07	06
	Robert Wasborow	17	04	03
	John England	06	01	06
	Thomas Adlam	25	06	03
	Mris. Avendall	26	06	06
	Mr. Wasborow	03	00	09
	John Sansom	24	06	00
	Thomas Grant	20	05	00
	Widdow Hort	20	05	00
	Mr. Davis	43	10	09
	Mr. Meredy	25	06	03
	Widdow Atkins	25	06	03
	Widdow Rumney	18	04	06
	Mr. Powell	14	03	06
	Mr. King	11	02	09
	Mirs. Walter	06	01	06
	Mr. Hort	06	01	06
	Samuel Sanford	10	02	06
	Richard Street	05	01	03
	Thomas Hort	08	02	00
	Mr. Sommerset	06	01	06
	Samuel Tucker	04	01	00
	Widdow Adlam	03	00	07
	John Sampson	12	03	00
	Widdow Weare	01	00	03
	Widdow Creed	02	00	06

Page 19. THE TITHING OF STOKE BISHOP.

		£	s.	d.
Imp	Mr. Wallis..	35	08	09
	Mr. Shermon	38	09	06
	Docter Martin	77	19	03
	Mr. Jackson	80	20	00
	Mr. More	76	19	00
	Mr. Somerset	38	09	06
	Mris. Charleton	54	13	06
	Mr. Dimmock	51	12	09
	Mr. Cuffe	24	06	00
	Robert White	36	09	00
	Mr. Rutland	24	07	03
	Mr. Godman	36	09	00
	Mr. Norris..	22	05	06
	Mr. Gleed	30	07	06
	Nicholas Parker	20	05	00
	William Hurtnoll..	14	03	06
	Mr. Hobson	06	01	06
	Mr. Shore	12	03	00
	Mris. Haswerd	10	02	06
	Widdow paine	21	05	03
	Edward Lewes	11	02	09
	Mris. Boulten	08	02	00
	Thomas Hort	26	06	06
	Mris. Arendall	05	01	03
	Mr. Can	24	06	06
	Mr. Bawldin	06	02	00
	Richard Willington	08	02	00
	Mr. Can	06	01	00
	Thomas Adlam	03	09	00
	Thomas Maunsell	08	02	00
	William Hurne	10	02	06
	Mris. Hungerford..	40	10	00
	Mris. Jones	02	00	06
	John England	02	00	06
	Mathew Adlam	02	00	06
	Mr. Sommerset	18	04	06
	Mr. Lewes	04	01	00
	Mr. Licence	03	00	09

Page 20. THE TITHING OF SHEREHAMPTON.

		£	s.	d.
Imp	Mris. Rogers	80	20	00
	Captaine Grummell	40	10	00
	Mr. Bush	55	13	09
	Widdow Hort	19	04	09
	William Harris	50	12	06
	Widdow Rome	18	04	06
	John Mathews	17	04	03
	John Green	42	10	06
	John Smith	10	02	06
	Widdow Smith	41	10	03
	Widdow Clement	07	01	09
	John Stokes	28	07	00
	Mr. Chilton	24	06	00
	Widdow wasborow	17	04	03
	Widdow Dee	09	02	03
	Walter parker	16	04	00
	Christo peacock	21	05	03
	Richard Lot	14	03	06
	Widdow heskins	50	12	06
	Elizabeth hellen	36	09	00
	for Avenhouse	20	05	00
	John Gunning	38	09	06
	Mr. Mats	16	04	00
	Richard Spratlee	28	07	00
	Mr. Lock	16	04	00
	William Greenfeild	50	12	06
	Mr. Rutland	16	04	00
	Roger Gray	10	02	06
	William parker	26	06	06
	Morris Smith	15	03	09
	John Smith	25	06	03
	Petre Dee	09	02	03
	John berry	14	03	06
	Thomas herring	11	02	09
	John Gunning	04	01	00

Page 21.

'he accompt of Thomas Cuff one of the collectors of the poore of the prish of Westbury-uppon-trim made the 5th day of May 1660.

	£	s.	d.
mp this accomptant chargeth himself wth the rate of 3d. a pound wch commeth unto	10	03	03
more he chargeth himself wth money receaved of his partner	09	09	09
	£19	13	00

The disburstments as followeth

	£	s.	d.
tt paid to John Gee for to parrell Thomas Cas his son when hee went to the free schools	01	05	10
tt paid to the widdow hollister for tending wid: button . ..	00	10	00
tt paid to the lame man	00	16	00
tt paid unto him since we were ordered by the Sessions at 2s. a week	01	12	00
tt for 8 jorneis to the Justice	01	04	00
tt for my riding to the Sesions	00	16	00
tt for 2 warrants for Robert Coats	00	01	00
tt geaven to William Coats his wife	00	02	00
tt spent when wee went to move Coats out of his fathers house	00	02	00
tt spent at the Inn about the lame man	00	02	00
tt for ingrossing the book	00	02	06
tt for signing of 2 rates	00	01	00
tt paid an Attorney fee concerning Coats	00	03	04
tt paid the wid foord 13 moneths at 4d. a moneth	02	12	00
tt paid Jane Lane 13 moneths at 2s. a moneth	01	06	00
tt paid to Richard deane 13 moneths at 2s. 6d. a moneth ..	01	12	06
tt paid to Christop bussher 5 moneths at 3s. 6d. a moneth ..	00	17	06
[tt paid to christo: bussher 2 moneths at 3s. od. a moneth ..	00	16	00
[tt paid to Christo bussher 6 moneths at 4s. a moneth	01	04	00
[tt paid to widd button 2 moneths at 3s. a moneth	00	06	00
[tt paid her 2 moneths more at 3s. 6d. a moneth	00	07	00
[tt paid her 9 moneths more at 4s. od. a moneth	01	16	00
[tt paid Jo: wade 7 moneths at 5s. od. a moneth	01	15	00
[tt paid him 2 moneths at 6s. od. a moneth	00	12	00
[tt paid to Joane wade 4 moneths	00	12	00
[tt paid to Ro: Smith 13 moneths at 2s. a moneth	01	06	00
Disburst	21	19	08

	£	s.	d.
Soe it appeareth that there is dew unto me from the parish	02	06	08
now I have receaved of that £2 6s. 8d. of Anthony Elsworthy	01	00	00
Soe there is dew unto me ..	01	06	08

Page 22.

The accompt of Anthony Elsworthy one of the collectors of the poore of the prish of Westbury-uppon-trim made the 5th day of May 1660.

	£	s.	d.
This accomptant chargeth himself wth the rate of 3d. a pound wch commeth to	11	04	03
The disburstments as followeth			
I paid to my partner Thomas Cuff	09	09	09
Itt geaven to the poore woeman of the slad	00	10	06
Itt geaven to her at another time	00	02	00
Itt spent at the Inn	00	02	00
Soe it appeareth that there is dew unto the prish from me 20s. disburst	£10	04	03

The accompt of Roger Gray one of the collectors of the poore of the prish of Westbury-uppon-trim made the 5th of May 1660.

	£	s.	d.
first this accomptant chargeth himself wth the rate of 3d. a pound wch commeth unto	11	01	03
The disburstments as followeth			
Imp paid to Thomas faucks	01	05	00
paid to John Mathews for keeping a child	03	10	00
paid for keeping Mary Chant and putting her prentice ..	01	17	06
paid for sending John Gunnings man to bath	01	04	00
for riding to the Justice sevrall times	00	12	00
for the lame mans diett and lodging 9 weeks and od daies	01	16	00
paid for the lame mans Cloths to his master	00	12	06
paid for sending him to the place of his birth	00	05	06
paid for him another time	00	01	00
paid for haling him to his masters house and for drinck wch they had	00	01	08
paid for his diett and lodging that time	00	01	00
geaven to John wade	00	02	02
geaven to poore people that had a breef	00	00	06
for signing 2 rates	00	01	00
paid Edward lansdown for 9 moneths	00	18	00
paid Edward lansdown for 5 moneths	01	00	00
paid to widdow wood 14 moneths	01	08	00
paid to wid: drinckwater 14 months..	00	14	00
paid to Richard Street	00	05	00
allowed to Richard parker being not able to pay.. ..	00	00	03
his disburstmens	16	09	1
Soe it appeareth that there is dew unto mee..	05	07	10

Seene and allowed by us whose names are here under written	Abell Meredith John Smith Church Wardens	Edmund Rutland Minist William Dimmocke Robert Wasborrow

Soe there is dew to Richard Street	00	12	00

Page 23.

/ee doe nominate and appoint William Walter Richard Walter and Roger Gray the Overseers for ye yeare ensuing.

ɔhn Codrington

a: Codrington

Page 24—blank.

[1] Mr. Jackson, mentioned on page 25, was Mayor of Bristol in 1651, Master of the erchant Venturers 1654–5, M.P. for Bristol 1657. "The Common Council," states atimer, "seems to have been reminded by the election that the 'wages' of the Members Parliament of 1654 were still unpaid, and Messrs. Aldworth and Jackson were voted ;o each for 150 days' service. Subsequently Aldworth received £138 (including some rears), and Alderman Jackson £53 for attending the Parliament in 1656–7." For further story of the Jackson family, see *Eccles. Hist. of Westbury.*

Page 25.

A pound rate agreed on by the inhabitants and freeholders of the tithing of Stokebisshop the 16th day of May 1660 to wch are subscribed their hands as followeth

		£
Imp	Mr. Wallis	35
	Mr. Sheremon	38
	Docter Martin	80
	Mr. Jackson[1]	80
	Mr. More	66
	Mr. Sommerset	38
	Mris. Charleton	54
	Mr. Dimmock	52
	Mr. Cuff	24
	Robert White	36
	Mr. Rutland	24
	Mr. Godman	36
	Mr. Norris	22
	Mr. Gleed	32
	Nicholas parker	20
	William hurtnoll	14
	Mr. hobson	06
	Mr. Shore	12
	Mris. haswerd	10
	Widdow paine	21
	Edward Lewes	11
	Mris. Boulton	08
	Thomas hort	26
	Mris. Arendall	05
	Mr. Can	30
	Mr. Bawldin	08
	Richard Willington	08
	Thomas Adlam	03
	Thomas Maunsell	08
	Widdow Hurne	10
	Mris. Hungerford	40
	Mris. Jones	02
	John England	02
	Matthew Adlam	02
	Mr. Sommerset	18
	Mr. Lewes	04
	Mr. Licence	03

Gabriel Yeman — Edmund Rutland
Jeremy Martin — William Dimocke
ffrancis Gleed — Tho Moore — Robert White

[1] See page 24.

Page 26

A rate made by the inhabitants of the prish of Westbury-uppon-trim for and towards the reliefe of the poore for the yeare 1660 at the rate of fower pence the pound as followeth:

		£	s.	d.
Imp	Mris. Barker	96	32	00
	William Walten	88	29	04
	Henry Wasborow	90	30	00
	William Stephens	90	30	00
	Richard Walter [1]	07	02	04
	Widdow Wasborrow	15	05	00
	Mris. Rutland	05	01	08
	William Wood	10	03	04
	Georg Lane	42	14	00
	John ffloyd	30	10	00
	Robert Wasborow	17	05	08
	John England	06	02	00
	Thomas Adlam	25	08	04
	Elizabeth Arendall	26	08	08
	Thomas Wasborow	03	01	00
	John Saunson	24	08	00
	Thomas Grant	20	06	08
	Widdow Hort	17	05	08
	Richard Davis	46	15	04
	Abel Meredy [2]	25	08	04
	Widdow Atkins	25	08	04
	Widdow Rumney	18	06	00
	Charles Powell	14	04	08
	Arthur King	11	03	08
	Mris. Walter	06	02	00
	Anthony Hort	06	02	00
	Samuel Sanford	10	03	04
	Richard Street	05	01	08
	Thomas Hort	08	02	08
	Mr. Sommerset [3]	06	02	00
	Samuell Tucker	04	01	04
	Widdow Adlam	03	01	00
	Jo: Sampson	12	04	00
	Widdow Weare	01	00	04
	Widdow Creed	02	00	08
		13	11	00

[1] Pd this to Sam Sandford Augt 4th 1661 and tho hopkins.

[2] Itt: pd this to Sam Sandford and tho hopkins.

[3] Itt: pd this to Sam Sandford and thos: hopkins.

Page 27.

THE TITHING OF STOKEBISSHOP.

		£	s.	d.
Imp	Mr. Wallis	35	11	08
	Mr. Sheremon	38	12	08
	Docter Martin	77	25	08
	Mr. Jackson	80	26	08
	Mr. More	76	25	04
	Mr. Sommerset	38	12	08
	Mris. Charleton	54	18	00
	William Dimmock	51	17	00
	Jeorum Cuff	24	08	00
	Robert White	36	12	00
	Mr. Rutland	24	08	00
	Mr. Godman	36	12	00
	Mr. Norris	22	07	04
	Mr. Gleed	30	10	00
	Nicholas Parker	20	06	08
	William Hurtnoll	14	04	08
	Mr. hobson	06	02	00
	Mr. Shore	12	04	00
	Mris. haswerd	10	03	04
	Widdow Paine	21	07	00
	Edward Lewes	11	03	08
	Mris. Boulton	08	02	08
	Thomas Hort	26	08	08
	Mris. Arendall	05	01	08
	Mr. Can	30	10	00
	Mr. Bawldin	08	02	08
	Richard Willington	08	02	80
	Thomas Adlam	03	01	00
	William Hurtnoll	08	02	00
	Widdow Hurne	10	03	04
	Mris. Hungerford	40	13	04
	Mris. Jones	02	00	08
	John England	02	00	08
	Mathew Adlam	02	00	08
	Mr. Sommerset	18	06	00
	Mr. Lewes	04	01	04
	Mr. Licence	03	01	00
		14	16	08

Page 28. THE TITHING OF SHEREHAMPTON.

		£	s.	d.
mp	Mris. Rogers	80	26	08
	Captaine Grummel	40	13	04
	Mris. Bush	55	18	04
	Widdow Hort	19	06	04
	William Harris	50	16	08
	Widdow Rome	12	04	00
	Thomas Willis	05	01	08
	John Mathews	17	05	08
	John Green	42	14	00
	John Smith	14	04	08
	Widdow Smith	41	13	08
	Mr. Smethum	07	02	04
	John Stokes	28	09	04
	Mr. Chilton	24	08	00
	Widdow Wasborow	17	05	08
	Widdow Dee	09	03	00
	Widdow Parker	20	06	08
	Christo Peacock	21	07	00
	Richard Lot	14	04	08
	Widdow Heskins	50	16	08
	Elizabeth Hellen	36	12	00
	for Avenhouse	16	05	04
	John Gunning	38	12	08
	Mr. Mats	16	05	04
	Richard Spratlee	28	09	04
	Mr. Lord	16	05	04
	William Greenfield	50	16	08
	Mr. Rutland	16	05	08
	Roger Gray	10	03	04
	William Parker	26	08	08
	Morris Smith	15	05	00
	John Smith	25	08	04
	Peter Dee	09	03	00
	John Berry	14	04	08
	Thomas Herring	11	03	08
	John Gunning	04	01	04
		14	16	04

Page 29.

The Accompt of William Walter one of the collectors of the poore of the prish of Westbury-uppon-trim made the 26 day of Aprell 1661.

	£	s.	d.
Imp This accomptant Chargeth himself wth the Rate of fower pence a pound wch commeth unto	13	11	00

The Disburstments as followeth

Itt payd to the Widdow foord 13 moneths at fower shillings a moneth	02	12	00
Itt payd to Joane Wade 12 moneths at three shillings a moneth	01	16	00
Itt payd to her one month at fower shillings	00	04	00
Itt payd the Widdow button 12 moneths at fower shillings a moneth	02	08	00
Itt payd a months pay wch was left to pay in Thomas Cuffe time	00	11	00
Itt geaven to Elizabeth Cook at sevll times	00	05	00
Itt geaven to John Reynolds	00	02	00
Itt geaven to William Coats his wife	00	03	00
Itt spent at Sadbury about the poore busines	00	02	00
Itt payd for making of the Rate	00	00	06
geaven to ould William Coats..	00	04	00
some—	£08	07	06
Soe it appeareth that there is dew to the pish	05	03	06

Now I crave allowance for money
that I cannot gather

	s.	d.
Samuell Tucker ..	1	4
Elnor Creed	0	8
Widdow Weare ..	0	4

Hue Rumney 8d.

William Curtiss
Curate

Soe there is dew to the pish .. £ 5 s. 0 d. 6

Jo Whittington

Now this £ 5 s. 0 d. 6 is payd
to the new collectors.

Jem Arundell

Page 30.

'he Accompt of Richard Walter one of the Collectors of the poore of the prish of Westbury-uppon-trim made the 26 day of Aprell 1661.

	£	s.	d.
mp This accomptant Chargeth himself wth the rate of fower pence a pound wch came to	14	16	08
The disburstments as followeth			
tt spent riding to Sadbury to the Justice	00	01	06
tt paid to Robert Smith 13 moneths at two shillings six pence a moneth	01	12	06
tt paid Richard Deane 13 moneths at two shillings six pence a moneth	01	12	06
tt paid Jane Lane 13 moneths at two shillings six pence a moneth	01	12	06
tt paid to Christopher busher 8 moneths at fower shillings a moneth	01	12	00
tt paid to Christopher busshell 5 moneths at 5s. a moneth ..	01	05	00
tt paid one moneths pay to all this people being left unpaid by Thomas Cuff	00	11	06
tt geaven to a poore woeman that doth live at the lime kills at sev'll times	00	04	00
tt geaven to William Coats his wife at sevall times	00	07	00
tt for riding 2 sev' times to the Justice and for a warrant ..	00	04	00
tt geaven to John Reynolds	00	02	00
tt for riding to the Justice for a warrant for Thomas Stephens being an intrueder..	00	02	00
tt spent uppon the ringers the Coronation day	01	10	00
tt for ingrossing the book	00	02	06
tt for making the Rate	00	00	06
t geaven to Jane Wade	00	02	06
FS	11	02	00
oe it appeareth that there is dew nto the prish	03	14	08

£ s. d.

'ow this 3 14 08 is payd to sayd

l. 16s. 00d. to Roger Gray }
l. 06s. 06d. to Thomas Cuff } Th: Rose being 12s. 02d. to the new Collectors.

Page 31.

The Accompt of Roger Gray one of the Collectors of the prish of Westbury-uppon-trim made the 26th of Aprell 1661.

	£	s.	d.
Imp This accomptant Chargeth himself wth the rate of fcwer pence a pound wch commeth to	14	16	04
The disburstments as followeth			
Itt dew unto me uppon my last accompts	05	07	10
Itt paid to Edward James Downe 13 mounthes at 4 shillings a mounth	02	12	00
It paid to Thomas Baker 13 Mounthes at 2 shillinges a mounth..	01	06	00
It paid to the widow woode 13 mounthes at 2s. 6d. a mounthe	01	12	06
It paid ffor keping John woodes child 14 mounthes at 5s. a mounth	03	10	00
It paid to widow Drinke watter 13 mounthes at 1s. 6d. a mounth		19	06
It paid to sevrall poore peopell and straingers	00	03	04
If ffor Riding to the Justic ffor warants	00	15	00
It to william Deane	00	00	03
It for Making the Rate	00	00	06
It payd to Jo: Smith for money dew unto him	00	05	08

	£	s.	d.			
	16	12	03			
	14	16	04			
FS ..	1	15	11	16	12	03

Soe it appeareth there is dew unto him one pound ten shillins and seaven pence

Tho Stephens
Gab Lowe
John Codrington
Tho Chester

William Curtiss
Curate
Jo Whittington
Tom Arundell
Robert White

This accompt seen and allowed by wee whose are heare unto subscribed

Wee doe nominate and appoint Samuell Sanford Thomas Green and Morrice Georg the oversseres of the poore for the yeare ensuing

Page 32.

	£	s.	d.
Morrice Georg being one of the Collectors of the poore receaved the third day of May 1661 of Richard Walter being left in his hands as the remainder of his accompt..	00	12	06

age 33.

ıte made by the inhabitants of the prish of Westbury-uppon-trim for and towards the releef of the poore for the yeare 1661 at the rate of 2d. *ob* a pound as followeth :—

	£	s.	d.
Mris. Barker	96	20	00
William Walter	81	16	10 *ob*
Henry Wasborow	90	18	09
William Stephens	90	18	09
Richard Walter	14	02	11
Widdow Wasborow	15	03	01 *ob*
Mris Rutland	05	01	00 *ob*
William Wood	10	02	01
Georg Lane..	42	08	09
John ffloyd	30	06	03
Robert Wasborow	17	03	06 *ob*
John England	06	01	03
Thomas Adlam	25	05	02 *ob*
Mris. Arendall	26	05	05
Thomas Wasborow	03	00	07 *ob*
John Saunson	24	05	00
Thomas grant	16	03	00
Thomas Adlam	04	00	10
Widdow hort	17	03	06 *ob*
Richard Davis	46	09	07
Abell Meredy	25	05	02 *ob*
Widdow Atkins	25	05	02 *ob*
Widdow Rumney	18	03	09
Charles Powell	14	02	03 *ob*
Arthur King	11	02	03 *ob*
Richard Walter	04	00	10
Anthony hort	08	01	08
Samuell Sanford	10	02	01
Richard Street	05	01	00 *ob*
Thomas hort	08	01	08
John Sommerset	06	01	03
Samuell Tucker	04	00	10
Widdow Adlam	03	07	00 *ob*
John Sampson	12	02	06
Widdow Creed	02	00	05
Widdow Weare	01	00	02 *ob*
	08	00	04 *ob*

Page 34. THE TITHING OF STOKEBISSHOP.

	Name	£	s.	d.	
Imp	Mr. Humphrey Hoot	70	14	07	*ob*
	Mr. Wallis	35	07	03	*ob*
	Mr. Sheremon	38	07	11	
	Docter Martin	80	16	08	
	Mr. Jackson	80	16	08	
	Mr. Sommerset	38	07	11	
	Mris. Charleton	38	07	11	
	William Dimmock	52	10	10	
	Jeorum Cuff	24	05	00	
	Robert White	36	07	06	
	Mris. Rutland	24	05	00	
	Mr. Godman	36	07	06	
	Mr. Norris	22	04	07	
	Mr. Gleed	32	06	08	
	Nicholas Tucker	20	04	02	
	William Hurtnoll	22	04	07	
	Mr. Hobson	06	01	03	
	Mr. Shore	12	02	06	
	Mris. Haswerd	10	02	01	
	Mr. Husbands	21	04	04	*ob*
	Edward Lewes	11	02	03	*ob*
	Mris. Boulton	08	01	08	
	Mr. Can	30	06	03	
	Thomas Hort	26	05	05	
	Mris. Arendall	05	01	00	*ob*
	Mr. Bawldin	08	01	08	
	Richard Willington	08	01	08	
	Thomas Adlam	03	00	07	*ob*
	Widdow Hurne	10	02	01	
	Thomas Parker	40	08	04	
	Mris. Jones	02	00	05	
	John England	02	00	05	
	Mathew Adlam	02	00	05	
	Mr. Sommerset	18	03	09	
	Mr. Licence	03	00	07	
	Mr. Lewes	04	00	01	
		09	05	10	

?age 35. THE TITHING OF SHEREHAMPTON.

		£	s.	d.	
p	Mris. Rogers	80	16	08	
	Captaine Grumell	40	08	04	
	Mris. Bush	55	11	05	*ob*
	Widdow hort	19	03	11	*ob*
	William harris	50	10	05	
	Widdow Rome	12	02	06	
	Thomas Willis	05	01	00	*b*
	John Mathews	17	03	06	*b*
	John Green..	42	08	09	
	John Smith..	14	02	11	
	Widdow Smith	31	06	05	*b*
	Mr. Smethum	07	01	05	*b*
	John Stokes	28	05	10	
	Mr. Chilton..	24	05	00	
	Widdow Wasborow	17	03	06	
	Widdow Dee	09	01	10	*ob*
	Widdow parker	20	04	02	
	Christopher peacock	21	04	04	*b*
	Richard Lot	14	02	11	
	Widdow Heskins	50	10	05	
	Elizabeth Hellen	36	07	06	
	Avenhouse	16	03	04	
	John Gunning	38	07	11	
	Mr. Mats	16	03	04	
	Richard Spratlee	28	05	10	
	Mr. Lock	16	03	04	
	William Greenfeild	50	10	05	
	Mris. Rutland	16	03	04	
	Roger Gray	10	02	01	
	William parker	26	05	05	
	Morrice Smith	15	03	01	*b*
	John Smith..	25	05	02	*b*
	Petre Dee	09	01	10	*b*
	John Berry..	14	02	11	
	Thomas Herring	11	02	03	
	John Gunning	04	00	10	
	Richard Smith	10	02	01	

Page 36.

The accompt of Samuell Sanford one of the Collectors of the poore of the prish of Westbury-uppon-trim made the 11th day of Aprell 1662.

	£	s.	d.
This accomptant Chargeth himself wth the value of 2d. *ob* a pound wch commeth to	08	09	04 *ob*
More hee chargeth himself wth money receaved of the ould collectors the last yeare	02	09	06
	£10	18	10
The disburstments as followeth			
Imp payd to the Widdow foord 12 moneths at 4 shillings a moneth	02	08	00
paid to Jane Lane 13 moneths at 2s. 6d. a moneth ..	01	12	06
paid to Robert Smith 13 moneths at 2s. 6d. a moneth	01	12	06
paid to Richard Deane 13 moneths at 2s. 6d. a moneth	01	12	06
	07	05	6
geaven to John hunt at sev times	00	08	00
geaven to William Coats..	00	01	00
geaven to Elizabeth Cook at sev times..	00	03	00
paid for a shroud for a poore man that died at Coat ..	00	03	02
geaven to the Widdow hollister	00	04	00
geaven to Jane Jefferies towards the buring of her mother	00	06	00
geaven to Robert Smith	00	00	06
geaven to Robert Smith another time	00	00	06
geaven to Jane Lane	00	00	06
geaven to Richard Deane	00	00	06
geaven to Jane Jeffiries for tending her Mother ..	00	02	00
disbursted	08	14	02
Soe there is dew to the pish	02	02	03

Now I crave allowance for money that I cannot gather

Samuell Tucker .. 10d.

Widdow Creed .. 05d.

Widdow weare .. 02d.

Page 37.

he accompt of Thomas Green one of the Collectors of the poore of the prish of Westbury-uppon-trim made the 11th day of Aprell 1662.

	£	s.	d.
his accomptant chargeth himself with the rate of 2d. *ob* a pound wch commeth to	09	05	10
ore he chargeth himself wth money receaved of the ould collectors the last yeare	02	11	00
	11	16	10

The disburstments as followeth

	£	s.	d.
np payd to Christopher Bussher 8 months at 5s. a moneth ..	02	00	00
payd to Joane Wade 13 moneths at 4s. a moneth	02	12	00
payd to William Coats 13 moneths at 2s. 6d. a moneth ..	01	12	06
payd to John Hunt 5 moneths at 2s. a moneth	00	10	00
	06	14	6
geaven to William Coats at 3 sev times	00	03	00
payd for a payer of shoes for him	00	03	06
payd to his Lanlady for his rent	00	01	06
geaven to Jane Wade at sev times	00	06	00
geaven to Welch Jeane at sev times..	00	10	00
geaven to John Reynolds'	00	02	06
payd for buring a poore man and a shroud	00	05	06
payd for carring away a cripple and for bread and drinck	00	01 ?	09
geaven to a poore woeman and 2 children with a pas ..	00	00	06
payd for buring Christo: bussher	00	01	02
payd for buring of a poore man that died at Coat	00	01	06
geaven to John hunt	00	01	06
geaven to a lame man that came from the bath	00	00	06
geaven to Susan Smith	00	01	00
geaven to Agnes Smith	00	01	00
payd for carring of a cripple to Stoke and for drinck ..	00	00	08
geaven to a poore woeman and one child with a pas ..	00	00	04
geaven to bes Cook	00	01	00
for making the rates and ingrosing the book	00	04	00
disbursted	09	00	05
Soe ther is dew to the pish ..	02	16	05

Page 38.

The accompt of Morrice Georg one of the Collectors of the prish of Westbury-uppon-trim made 11th day of Aprell 1662.

	£	s.	d.
This accomptant chargeth himself wth the rate of 2d. *ob* a pound wch commeth to	09	06	05 *ob*
More he chargeth himself wth money receaved of the ould Collectors the last yeare	00	12	06
	08	18	11
The distburstments as followeth			
Imp geaven to Alis Davis for her sicknes	00	01	00
geaven to a poore man	00	00	04
geaven to Alis Davis	00	02	00
geaven to a poore woeman and 2 children	00	02	08
geaven to Ane Reece	00	01	00
geaven to John Calee	00	02	00
payd house rent for Alis Davis	00	02	06
geaven to Mary Playford	00	01	00
geaven to Ane Reece	00	01	00
geaven to Ane Jones	00	03	00
geaven to Joane wood in her sickness	00	02	06
geaven to Ane Jones	00	02	00
geaven to Edward Lansdowne	00	01	00
geaven to Thomas vaux..	00	01	00
geaven to Alis Davis	00	01	00
geaven to John Calee	00	02	00
geaven to Alis Davis	00	01	00
geaven to Ane Jones	00	01	00
Grace Jones	00	02	00
Payd to Edward Lansdowne at 4s. a moneth.. ..	02	12	00
payd Thomas vaux for 13 moneths 3s. a moneth ..	01	19	00
payd to widdow Drinckwater for 13 moneths.. ..	00	19	06
payd Joane wood for 6 moneths at 2s. 6d. a moneth ..	00	15	00
payd Joane wood for 7 moneths at 4s. a moneth ..	01	08	00
	09	03	06
Soe there is dew unto the prish ..	00	15	05

Ro: Poyntz [1]
John Codrington
Tho Chester
John Smyth [2]

Nath: Raven
Clerke

William Dimmocke
Anthony hortt
Rob Wasborrow

Richard Davis, William harris } Churchwardens

Thomas Grannth

[1] Sir Robert Poyntz, J.P., of Iron Acton, was fined by Cromwell's agents £723. He owned property in Bristol, and "Poyntz Pool," upon which St. Jude's Church was subsequently built, was his property.

[2] John Smyth, see *Eccles. Hist. of Westbury.*

Page 39.

Wee doe nominate and appoint John King Joseph Cleark and John Helleing to bee overseers for the poore for the yeare ensuing.

The money that was left in the three Collectors hands was payd to Mr. Davis towards the money that was dew unto him uppon his accompt.

Page 40.

A rate made by the inhabitants of the prish of Westbury-uppon-trim for and towards the releef of the poore for this yeare 1662 at the rate of 2d. *ob* a pound as followeth.

	£	s.	d.	
Imp Mr. Lock or his teanaunt	90	18	09	
Mr. Lock or his tenaunt	06	01	03	
William Walter	81	16	10	*ob*
Henry Wasborow	90	18	09	
William Stephens	90	18	09	
Richard Davis	47	09	10	
Richard Walter	14	02	11	
Sisly Wasborow	15	03	01	*ob*
Mris. Rutland	05	01	00	*ob*
William Atwood	10	02	01	
Georg Lane	42	08	09	
Edward Morgan	30	06	03	
Robert Wasborow	17	03	06	*ob*
John England	06	01	03	
Tho: Adlam	29	06	00	*ob*
Mris. Arendall	25	05	02	*ob*
Tho: Wasborow	03	00	07	*ob*
John Saunson	24	05	00	
Thomas Grant	16	03	04	
Mary Hort	17	03	06	*ob*
Abell Meredy	25	05	02	*ob*
Widdow Atkins	25	05	02	*ob*
Widdow Rumney	18	03	09	
Charles Powell	14	02	11	
Mr. Tompson	11	02	03	*ob*
Richard Walter	04	00	10	
Anthony hort	08	01	08	
Samuell Sanford	10	02	01	
Richard Street	05	01	00	*ob*
Tho: hort	08	01	08	
John Sommerset	06	01	03	
Samuell Tucker	04	00	10	
Alnos Adlam	03	00	07	*ob*
Jo: Sampson	12	02	06	
Widdow Creed	02	00	05	
Widdow Weare	01	00	02	*ob*
	08	08	09	

Page 41. THE TITHING OF STOKE BISSHOP.

	£	s.	d.	
Imp Sr. Robert Can [1]	30	06	03	
Sr. Humphry Hook [2]	70	14	07	
Mr. Wallis	35	07	03	*ob*
Mr. Shermon	38	07	11	
Docter Martin	80	16	08	
John Merefeild	80	16	08	
Mr. Sommerset	38	07	11	
Mr. Sommerset	54	11	03	
William Dimmock	52	10	10	
Jeorum Cuff	24	05	00	
Robert White	36	07	06	
Mris. Rutland	22	04	07	
John Sampson	02	00	05	
Tho: Godman	36	07	06	
John Norris	22	04	07	
Mr. Gleed	32	06	08	
Nicholas Parker	20	04	02	
William Hurtnoll	22	04	07	
Mr. hobson	06	01	03	
Mr. Shore	12	02	06	
Mris. haswerd	10	02	01	
Mr. husbands	21	04	04	*ob*
Edward Lewes	11	02	03	*ob*
Widdow Boulton	08	01	08	
Tho hort	26	05	05	
Mris. Avendall	05	01	00	*ob*
Mr. Bawldin	08	01	08	
Richard Willington	08	01	08	
Tho: Adlam	03	00	07	*ob*
Hue Rumney	10	02	01	
Tho Parker	40	08	04	
Mris. Jones	02	00	05	
John England	02	00	05	
Mathew Adlam	02	00	05	
Mr. Sommerset	18	03	09	
Mr. Licence	03	00	07	*ob*
Mr. Lewes	04	00	10	

[1] See *Eccles. Hist. of Westbury*, p. 60. He was Master of the Merchant Venturers 1658, and Mayor of Bristol 1662.

[2] Sir Humphry Hook was Keeper of Kingswood and Fillwood Forests, a vehement Royalist, and was knighted by Charles II. Became M.P. for Bristol after a disputed election, the Earl of Ossory holding the seat till raised to the peerage, when Sir Humphry Hook's claim prevailed. He supported Sir Robert Can in the struggle for the precedency of Knights in the Bristol Council (See *Eccles. Hist. of Westbury*, p. 60). In 1663, for the King's Subsidy, his goods were assessed by "partial" commissioners at £13, while Sir Robert Can, above-mentioned, who was a wealthy merchant, was assessed at £10 and paid £2 13s. 4d.! He died in October, 1677.

Page 42. THE TITHING OF SHEREHAMPTON.

		£
Imp	Mris. Rogers	80
	Captain Crummell	40
	Mris. Bush	55
	Widdow hort	19
	William harris	50
	Widdow Rome	12
	Thomas Willis	05
	John Mathewes	17
	John Smith	14
	John Green	42
	Widdow Smith	31
	James Smethum	07
	John Stokes	28
	Mr. Chilton	24
	Widdow Wasborow	17
	Widdow Dee	09
	Widdow Parker	20
	Christo: Peacock	21
	Richard Lot	14
	Widdow Heskins	50
	John hellen	36
	Avenhouse	16
	John Gunning	36
	John Smith	02
	Mr. Mats	16
	Richard Spratlee	28
	Mr. Lock	16
	William Greenfeild	50
	Mris. Rutland	16
	Roger Gray	10
	William Parker	26
	Morrice Smith	15
	John Smith	25
	Petre Dee	09
	John Berry	14
	Tho: Herring	11
	John Gunning	04
	Richard Smith	10

Page 43.

The accompt of Richard King one of the Collectors of the poore of the prish of Westbury-uppon-trim made the 4th day of May 1663.

	£	s.	d.
This accomptant Chargeth himself wth the rate of 2d. *ob* a pound wch commeth to	08	08	09
Imp payd to Mr: Joseph Cleark	06	16	06
Itt payd to Samuell Sanford for a warrant that hee brought from the Justice to bring in the new Collectors.. ..	00	01	00
my disburstments	06	17	03

Now I crave allowance for money that I cannot gather

Widdow Tucker	.	10d.
Widdow Creed	..	05d.
Widdow Weare	..	02d.

	£	s.	d.
Soe it appeareth there is dew to the prish	01	10	01

The accompt of Mr. Joseph Cleark one of the Collectors of the poore of the prish of Westbury-uppon-trim made the 4th day of May 1663.

	£	s.	d.
first this accomptant Chargeth himself wth the rate of 2d. *ob* a pound wch commeth	09	05	10
more he chargeth himself of money receaved of Richard King ..	06	16	06
the totall of receipts is ..	£16	02	04
The disburstments as followeth			
Imp payd to Joane Wade 14 moneths at 4s. a moneth	02	16	00
Itt payd to William Coats 5 moneths at 2s. 6d. a moneth ..	00	12	06
Itt payd to William Coats 9 moneths at 3s. a moneth	01	07	00
Itt payd to Richard Deane 14 moneths at 2s. 6d. a moneth ..	01	15	00
Itt payd to Robert Smith 14 moneths at 2s. 6d. a moneth ..	01	15	00
Itt payd to John Hunt 14 moneths at 2s. 6d. a moneth.. ..	01	15	00
Itt payd to Jane Lane 14 moneths at 2s. 6d. a moneth ..	01	15	00
	11	15	06
Itt geaven at sevall times to the poore welch woman	00	08	00
Itt geaven at sevall times to Agnes Smith	00	07	06
Itt geaven at sevall times to Joane Mattock	00	05	06
Itt geaven at sevall times to Robert Smith	00	02	00
Itt geaven at sevall times to Jane Wade	00	05	00
Itt geaven at sevall times to Elizabeth Cook	00	02	00
Itt payd for carring a Cripple to Cribs causway	00	01	00
Itt geaven to William Coats	00	01	00
Itt geaven to a poore gent woman wth a pas and 4 children ..	00	01	00
Itt payd for a warrant for Susan white to put her to St. James prish	00	01	00
Itt for going 3 sev times to St. James to place her there ..	00	03	00
Itt payd for Carring a Cripple to Charlton	00	01	00
Itt payd for keeping of a poore woeman a night and day that had a pas and for carring her away	00	00	08
Itt spent about putting away the millerd	00	02	00
Itt for making the rates and ingrosing the book..	00	04	00
	02	04	08

Page 44.	£	s.	d.
Itt payd for a warrant to put away the Child that was at Robert Morrice and at farnets	00	01	00
Itt for going to the Justice and going 2 sev times about the putting of it away to bristoll	00	02	00
Itt for making mary woods Indentures	00	02	00
Itt payd for a shroud and for buring a poore maid	00	04	00
Itt for going to Sadbury for a warrant to put away the inmates that was at Sherehampton	00	02	06
Itt for a warrant to bring in the new Collectors	00	01	00
my disburstments is ..	£14	12	02

now I Crave allowance for
money that I Could not gather
Mr. Ellis .. .. 7d. *ob*

This being deducted out of my receits there is dew to the psh	01	09	06 *ob*

The accompt of John Hellen one of the Collectors of the poore of prish of Westbury-uppon-trim made the 4th day of May 1663.

This accomptant Chargeth himself wth the rate of 2d. *ob* a pound wch commeth to	09	06	04

The disburstments as followeth

	£	s.	d.
Imp payd to Edward Lansdown for 13 moneths at 4s. a moneth	02	12	00
Itt payd to the Widdow Wood for 13 moneths at 4s. a moneth	02	12	00
Itt payd to Tho: fawkes for 13 moneths at 3s. a moneth ..	01	19	00
Itt payd the Widdow drinckwater 13 moneths at 1s. 6d. a moneth	00	19	06
Itt geaven to Grace Jones in her want	00	05	00
Itt geaven to the Widdow Wickham	00	04	00
Itt geaven to Edward Lansdown	00	03	00
my disburstments is ..	09	01	06
dew unto the prish ..	00	04	10

John Smythe
S. A. Codrington

Richard Davis — church
John Mathews — wardens
Hen Wasborow
Robert White
Tho Adlam

Wee doe nominate and appoint Tho: Wasborow William Arnall and John Baker to serve the Office of Collectors for the yeare ensuing.

Page 45—Blank.

Page 46.

The Accompt of Tho Wasborow one of the Collectors of the poore of the prish of Westbury-uppon-trim made the 14th of April 1664.

	£	s.	d.
This Accomptant Chargeth himself wth a rate of two pence half penny a pound wch commeth unto	08	07	05
The disburstments as followeth			
Imp payd to Joane Wade 12 moneths at 4s. od. a moneth ..	02	08	00
payd to Jane Lane 12 moneths at 2s. 6d. a moneth ..	01	10	00
payd to John Hunt 12 moneths at 2s. 6d. a moneth ..	01	10	00
	05	08	00
Spent when wee went to warne the inmates at Redland ..	00	00	06
payd for making the rates and ingrossing the books ..	00	04	00
payd for a warrant for the new Collectors	00	01	00
Spent when we passed our accompts	00	02	00
	00	07	05
my disburstments	05	15	06
dew to the prish			
more geaven to Jane Wade	00	02	00
more geaven to Elizabeth Cook	00	02	00
now there is dew to the pr. ..	02	07	11

Page 47.

The Accompt of William Arnall one of the Collectors of the poore of the prish of Westbury-uppon-trim made the 14th day of Aprell 1664.

This accomptant Chargeth himself wth a rate of two pence half penny a pound wth commeth unto	09	05	07
The disburstments as followeth			
Imp payd William Coats 12 moneths at 3s. od. a moneth ..	01	16	00
payd to Robert Smith 12 moneths at 2s. 6d. a moneth ..	01	10	00
payd to Richard Deane 12 moneths at 2s. 6d. a moneth ..	01	10	00
payd to Agnes Smith 12 moneths at 1s. od. a moneth ..	00	12	00
	05	08	00
geaven to the poore woeman at the lime Kills at sev times	00	10	00
payd for a payer of shoos for William Coats..	00	04	02
geaven to William Coats at sev times	00	05	00
geaven to Joane Mattock in her sickness	00	03	00
payd for her buriall	00	12	06
more geaven her in her sickness	00	07	00
geaven to Agnes Smith at sev times	00	02	06
	02	04	02
my disburstmen	07	12	02
dew to the prish			
more for carring the book to Sadbury and bringing a warrant	00	02	0?
dew to the prish	£01	11	05

Page 48.

The Accompt of Jo: Baker one of the Collectors of the poore of the prish of Westbury-uppon-trim made the 14th day of Aprell 1664.

	£	s.	d.
This Acomptant Chargeth himself wth the rate of two pence half penny a pound wch commeth to	09	06	04
The disburstments as followeth			
mp payd to Katherene Drinckwater 12 moneths at 1s. 6d. a moneth	00	18	00
payd to Edward Lansdowne 12 moneths at 4s. 0d. a moneth	02	08	00
payd to Widdow Wood 12 moneths at 4s. 0d. a moneth	02	08	00
payd to Thomas ffaux 12 moneths at 3s. 0d. a moneth	01	16	00
payd to the Widdow Wickham 05 moneths at 3s. 0d. a moneth	00	15	00
	08	05	00
geaven to a poor woman wth a pas	00	01	00
geaven at sev times to Edward Lansdowne	00	05	00
geaven to Morrice Baker in his sickness	00	03	00
geaven to Grace Jones	00	03	00
geaven to Katherene Drinckwater	00	01	06
geaven to Thomas ffaux	00	01	06
Widdow Wood	00	01	06
	00	16	06
o: Poyntz — my disburstm	09	01	06
ho Chester — dew to the prish ..	00	04	10 *ob*

we whose names are heare under subscribed doe allow of this accompts

William Steephens } Church
Tho Willis } wardens
Thomas Adlam
Thomas Cuffe

ee doe nominate and appoint to serve the office of Collectors for the yeare ensuing Tho: Atkins Richard Hammans and Richard Spratlee

ow this £4 4s. 2d. wch was in the Collectors hands was deliv to the church-wardens.

Page 49.

A rate made by the inhabitants of the parrish of Westbury for and towards the releef of the poore for this yeare 1664 at the rate of 2d. *ob* a pound as followeth:

		£	sh.	d.	
Imp	Mr. Lock	96	20	00	
	Mr. Walter	81	16	10	*ob*
	Mr. Wasborow	90	18	09	
	William Stephens	90	18	09	
	Mr. Walter	14	02	11	
	Mr. Davis	47	09	10	
	Widdow Wasborow	15	03	01	*ob*
	Mr. Wood	10	02	01	
	Mris. Rutland	04	00	10	
	Mr. Lane	42	08	09	
	Mr. Morgan	30	06	03	
	Robert Wasborow	17	03	06	o
	John England	06	01	03	
	Thomas Adlam	29	06	00	*ob*
	Mris. Avendall	25	05	02	*ob*
	Mr. Wasborow	03	00	07	*ob*
	Robert White	24	05	00	
	Thomas Grant	16	03	04	
	Widdow Hort	17	03	06	*ob*
	Mr. Meredy	25	05	02	*ob*
	Widdow Atkins	25	05	02	*ob*
	Widdow Rumney	18	03	09	
	Mr. Powell	14	02	11	
	Mr. Tompson	11	02	03	*ob*
	Richard Walter	04	00	10	
	Mr. Hort	08	01	08	
	Samuel Sanford	10	02	01	
	Richard Street	05	01	00	*ob*
	Tho: Hort	08	01	08	
	Mris. Beavan	06	01	03	
	Mr. Sampson	12	02	06	
	Widdow Adlam	03	00	07	*ob*
		08	07	05	

Page 50. THE TITHING OF STOKEBISSHOP.

		£	sh.	d.	
mp	Sr. Robert Can	30	06	03	
	Sr. Humphry Hook	70	14	07	
	Sr. Robert Yeomans[1]	40	08	04	
	Mr. Wallis	35	07	03	*ob*
	Mr. Sheremon	38	07	11	
	Mr. Yates	80	16	08	
	Docter Martin	80	16	08	
	Mris. Elizabeth Beavan	54	11	03	
	Mris. Joyce Beavan	38	07	11	
	Mris. yeadeth Beavan	18	03	09	
	William Dimmock	52	10	10	
	Jeorum Cuff	24	05	00	
	Robert White	36	07	06	
	Mris. Rutland	22	04	07	
	Mr. Sampson	02	00	05	
	Mr. Godman	36	07	06	
	Mr. Norris	22	04	07	
	Mr. Gleed	32	06	08	
	Mris. Standfast	20	04	02	
	William Hurtnoll	22	04	07	
	Mr. Hobson	06	01	03	
	Mr. Shore	12	02	06	
	Mris. Haswerd	10	02	01	
	Mr. Husbands	21	04	04	*ob*
	Mr. Brooks	11	02	03	*ob*
	Edward Lewes	02	00	05	
	Mris. Boulton	08	01	08	
	Mr. Hort	26	05	05	
	Mris. Avendall	05	01	00	*ob*
	Mr. Bawldin	08	01	08	
	Richard Willington	08	01	08	
	Tho. Adlam	03	00	07	*ob*
	Hugh Rumney	10	02	01	
	John England	02	00	05	
	Matthew Adlam	02	00	05	
	Mr. Lewes	04	00	10	
	Mr. Saunders	03	00	07	*ob*
		09	05	10	

[1] *See* page 52 of Poor Book.

Page 51. THE TITHING OF SHEREHAMPTON.

	£	sh.	d.	
Imp Mris. Rogers	80	16	08	
Captaine Grummell	40	08	04	
Mris. Bush	40	08	04	
Mr. Holway	15	03	01	*ob*
Widdow Hort	19	03	11	*ob*
William Harris	50	10	05	
Widdow Rome	12	02	06	
Tho: Willis	05	01	00	*ob*
John Mathews	17	03	06	*ob*
Widdow Green	42	08	09	
John Smith	14	02	11	
Widdow Smith	31	06	05	*ob*
Mr. Smether	07	01	05	*ob*
John Stokes	28	05	10	
Mr. Chilton	24	05	00	
Widdow Wasborow	17	03	06	
Widdow Dee	09	01	10	*ob*
Widdow Parker	16	03	04	
Christo: Peacock	21	04	04	*ob*
Richard Lot	14	02	11	
Widdow Heskins	50	10	05	
John Hellen	36	07	06	
Avenhouse	20	04	02	
William Greenfeild	50	10	05	
Mr. Wasborow	36	07	06	
John Smith	02	00	05	
Mr. Mats	16	03	04	
Richard Spratlee	28	05	10	
Mr. Lock	16	03	04	
Mris. Rutland	16	03	04	
Roger Gray	10	02	01	
Widdow Parker	26	05	05	
Morrice Smith	15	03	01	*ob*
John Smith	25	05	02	*ob*
Petre Dee	09	01	10	*ob*
John Berry	14	02	11	
Tho. Herring	11	02	03	
Richard Smith	10	02	01	
John Gunning	04	00	10	

Page 52. THO: ATKINS Collector

The accompt of the Collecter of the poore for the Tithing of Westbury made the 11th day of Aprell 1665.

	£	sh.	d.
This accomptant Chargeth himself wth the rate of two pence half penny a pound wch commeth to	08	07	05
The disburstments as followeth			
Imp payd to Joane Wade 13 moneths at 4s. a moneth ..	02	12	00
payd to John hunt 13 moneths at 2s. 6d. a moneth ..	01	12	06
payd to Jane Lane 15 moneths at 2s. 6d. a moneth ..	01	12	06
geaven to William osborn at sevll times	00	06	00
geaven to Robert Everat at 2 sevll times	00	02	06
geaven to Richard Deane in his sicknes	00	02	00
Disbursted	06	07	6
Dew unto the prish uppon this accompt ..	01	19	11

Sir Robert Yeamans, Bt. (p. 50), equipped in September, 1653, the privateer *The Robert*. He supported Sir Robert Can in 1662 in his struggle with the Bristol Council (*see* above); gave £60, since Bristol's treasury was empty, towards the entertainment of the king and queen in 1663, during which year he was sheriff; and going to Bath, whither the king and queen had returned after the entertainment, he was knighted. He was Mayor of Bristol in 1669, and was so energetic in the persecution of Dissenters, that he brought down upon himself and his supporters the disapproval of the Council. A very severe struggle ensued, and Sir Robert Yeaman was so traduced to the king that he was detained in custody in London, and was not released till April, 1770. On his return to Bristol "soon after his discharge, he was met outside Lawford's Gate by 220 gentlemen on horseback, who cordially welcomed him, and conducted him to his house amidst the cheering of the citizens. The long detention of the mayor evoked still more general sympathy, and on April 20th he was met in a similar manner by 235 horsemen, and had a joyful public reception," while his accuser, Sir John Knight, was obliged to slink away through the back streets to his neighbouring mansion. In 1675 Sir Robert Yeamans took part in a further attack on Dissenters, and in sending some to Newgate Prison. In 1679 he was again in trouble, in conjunction with Sir Robert Can, for denying the existence of the Popish Plot, and was arrested; but on November 13th, appearing at the bar of the House of Commons "to make a humble apology, was discharged on payment of heavy fees."

Page 53. RICHARD HAMMANS, Collector.

The accompt of the Collector of the poore for the tithing of Stokebisshop made the 11th day of Aprell 1665.

	£	sh.	d.
This accomptant Chargeth himself wth the rate of 2d. *ob* a pound wch commeth to	09	05	10
The disbursements as followeth			
Imp payd to William Coats 13 months at 4s. a moneth.. ..	02	12	00
payd to Robert Smith 13 moneths at 2s. 6d, a moneth ..	01	12	06
payd to Richard Deane 13 moneths at 2s. 6d. a moneth ..	01	12	06
payd to Agnes Smith 13 moneths at 2s. 0d. a moneth ..	01	06	00
geaven to William osborne at sevall times	00	04	00
geaven to Richard Deane in his sicknes	00	02	00
geaven to Elizabeth Cook at seavall times	00	04	00
geaven to Robert Smith at sevall times	00	02	00
geaven to William Coats at 2 sevall times	00	01	06
geaven to a poore woeman and 3 children wth a pas ..	00	00	06
geaven to a poore man and woman and child wth a pas ..	00	00	06
spent uppon them that kept Christopher Smith in hold a night and day being taken wth a hue and cry ..	00	03	06
payd for carring away of 3 Cripples and exspences ..	00	01	06
geaven to a poore woeman that was going to the bath ..	00	00	06
geaven to a poore woeman wth 3 children and a pas ..	00	00	06
for making the rates and ingrossing the book	00	04	00
payd for a new auditt book	00	00	08
for going to Thornbury wth the book and for warrant ..	00	02	06
paid for carring of a Cripple and exspences	00	01	00
Disbursted	08	13	00
Dew unto the pish ..	00	12	10

Page 54. RICHARD SPRATLIN, Collector.

'he accompt of the Collector of the poore of the Tithing of Sherehampton made the 11th day of April 1665.

	£	sh.	d.
his accomptant Chargeth himself wth the rate of 2d. *ob* a pound wch commeth to	09	06	04
The disburstments as followeth			
mp payd to Edward Launsdown 13 moneths at 4s. a moneth	02	12	00
payd to Widdow Wood 13 moneths at 4s. a moneth ..	02	12	00
payd to Tho ffaux 13 moneths at 3s. a moneth	01	19	06
payd to Widdow Drinckwater 13 moneths at 1s. 6d. a moneth	00	19	06
:t geaven to Edward Launsdown at sevll times	00	08	00
geaven to the Widdow Woods at sevll times..	00	06	00
geaven to Tho: ffaux at sevll times	00	06	00
geaven to Widdow Drinckwater at sevll times	00	01	06
geaven to Agnes Jones at sevll times	00	03	00
Disbursted ..	09	07	00
Soe it appeareth there is dew unto me..	00	00	08
The whole som of our receipts is	27	19	07

This accompts is seene and allowed by wee whose names are hereunder subscribed

Hen Wasborow
Abell Meredith
Robert Wasborow
Tho Adlam
Anthony hortt
Thomas Willis

10: Chester[1]
hn Smyth

Wee doe nominate and appoint to serve the office of Collectors for the yeare ensuing

Tho: Adlam
Edward Hill
Tho ffar

	£	sh.	d.
Soe it appeareth there is dew to the prish ..	02	12	01

is money that was left in the Collecters was delivd to Tho: Adlams hand onely 8d. wch was payd to Richard Spratlee.

[1] *See* page 55 of Poor Book.

Page 55.—Blank.

Thomas Chester (*see* p. 54) was a Justice of the Peace, and lived at Knowle Park, Glos. "Towards the close of 1646 the parliamentary tribunal charged with inquiring into the value of 'delinquents'' estates, and 'compounding' with the owners for fines in lieu of sequestration, were actively fulfilling their duties," and Thomas Chester escaped with a fine of £1,000, as the Royalists had fired some of his houses. In 1660, Latimer tells us, that the Bristol Council, "taking note of the great number of the cottages lately erected and now erecting outside Lawford's Gate, and conceiving it to tend to the great impoverishment of the city, directed the mayor and city surveyors to confer with Mr. Chester, on whose land the houses were built, for putting a stop to further building. The district, however, soon became the most populous, as it was almost the most disorderly, of the suburbs." This state still in a measure remains; there are in this district about 1,000 dwellers in the common lodging houses each night, and another 1,000 who live in so-called furnished rooms, let at 6d. a night, while the other population is of the poorest sort. When the writer was Assistant Curate and subsequently Vicar of St. Jude's—the area above-mentioned—"outside the gate" was a phrase constantly used by some of the inhabitants when they considered their "rights" were overlooked by the civic authorities, meaning they were unimportant or considered disreputable, and so of no account.

Page 56.

The accompt of Thomas Adlam Collector of the poore for the tithing of Westbury made the 4th day of May 1666.

	£	sh.	d.
first this accomptant Chargeth himself wth the rate of two pence half penny a pound wch commeth to..	08	07	05
more hee Chargeth himself wth money receaved of Edward Hill Collector of the tithing of Stokebisshop..	07	17	00
more hee Chargeth himself wth money receaved of the ould Collectors	02	12	09
totall	18	17	02

The disburstments as followeth

Imp payd to Jeane Wade 13 months at 4s. a moneth	02	12	00
Itt payd to William Coats 13 months at 4s. a month	02	12	00
Itt payd Richard Deane 2 months at 2s. 6d. a month	00	05	00
Itt payd John Hunt 13 months at 2s. 6d. a moneth	01	12	06
Itt payd Robert Smith 13 months at 2s. 6d. a moneth	01	12	06
Itt payd Agnes Smith 13 months at 2s. od. a moneth	01	06	00
Itt payd William Osborne 13 months at 1s. 6d. a moneth ..	00	19	06
	10	19	6
Itt payd for the buring of Richard Deane and for a shroud ..	00	09	06
Itt payd to Richard Spratlee for money layd out the last y̅ ..	00	00	08
Itt spent at the Inn when the ould Collectors past theyr accompts	00	07	00
Itt geaven to Robert Wade at sev times..	00	11	00
Itt geaven to Robert Everat at sev times..	00	08	00
Itt geaven to a poore woeman and 2 children wth a pas ..	00	01	00
Itt geaven to Joane Rumney at sev times..	00	03	00
Itt geaven to a poore woeman that was in labor carring of her away	00	02	00
Itt geaven to the Widdow ffishpall	00	01	00
Itt geaven to Elizabeth Cook	00	01	06
Itt geaven to William Cotten	00	01	00
Itt geaven to the Widdow Weare	00	00	06
Itt geaven to 6 poore people wth a breef	00	01	06
Itt payd for a fox head	00	01	00
Itt geaven to 11 poore people wth a pas	00	01	06
Itt payd to Mr. Davis and Mr. Wasborow for fetching Robert Everat out of Newgate[1]	01	01	09
Itt geaven to a poore woeman wth Child	00	00	06
Itt payd for making of Rates for the Royall Ayd..	00	02	00
Itt payd for a payer of shoes for William Coats	00	03	08
Itt geaven to Welch Joan	00	06	00
Itt spent when the Collectors met..	00	04	00
Itt paid for Carring away Cripples out of Stokebisshops tithing	00	04	00
Itt spent when the prish did meet to Choise officers	00	12	00
Itt geaven to Margaret heskins	00	01	00
Itt spent when the tithing did meet about the Royall Ayd ..	00	07	06
Itt payd to Richard Street for money dew unto him	00	12	06
disbursted	17	05	11
Soe it apeareth there is dew ..	01	12	01

[1] *See* Introduction. Latimer states, "Newgate was rarely free from epidemics, arising from the foulness of the cells," and "was made noisome by the unwholesome

Page 57.

The accompt of Edward Hill Collector of the poore of the tithing of Stokebisshop :

	£	sh.	d.
This accomptant Chargeth himself wth the rate of two pence half penny a pound wch commeth to	09	05	05
Disburstments as followeth			
Imp payd to Thomas Adlam	07	17	00
Itt payd for making the Rates and ingrossing the book ..	00	04	00
disbursted.. ..	08	01	00
I Crave allowance for 5d. of Mathew Adlam. soe it appeareth there is dew ..	01	04	00

The accompt of Thomas far Collector of the poore of Sherehampton.

This accomptant Chargeth himself wth the rate of twopence halfpenny a pound wch commeth to	09	06	04
The disburstments as followeth :			
Imp payd 13 moneths to the poore at 8s. 6d. a moneth	05	10	06
Itt geaven to Margret Cory in her sickness	00	02	00
Itt payd to Tho: faux	00	10	00
Itt payd for house rent for Edward Launsdowne	00	10	00
Itt geaven to the Widdow Drinckwater..	00	02	06
Itt geaven to Tho faux	00	02	06
Disbursted	06	17	06

I Crave allowance for money that I cannot gather

Mary parker .. 10d.

John Smith .. 5d.

This accompts seen and allowed by wee whose names are under subscribed.

Now this being deducted out of my receipts there is dew .. 02 07 07

We doe nominate and appoint to serve the office of Collecters of the poore for the yeare ensuing

Mr. Richard Davis
Mr. Saunders
John Hogkins

John Merifeild }
William Cox } Church Wardens

Tho: Wasborow   Tho: Stephens
Thomas Cuff   Tho Chester

Page 58.

A rate made by the inhabitants of the prish of Westbury-uppon-trim for and towards the releef of the poore for this yeare 1665 at the rate of 2d *ob* a pound, viz. :—

	£	sh.	d.
Imp Mr. Lock	96	20	00
Mris. Walter	81	16	10
Mr. Wasborow	90	18	09
William Stephens	90	18	09
Mr. Davis	47	09	10
Mr. Walter	14	02	11
Widdow Wasborow	15	03	01
Mr. Humphry	10	02	01
Mris. Rutland	04	00	10
Mr. Lane	42	08	09
Mr. Morgan	30	06	03
Robert Wasborow	17	03	06
John England	00	01	03
Tho: Adlam	29	06	00
Mris. Avendall	25	05	02
Mr. Wasborow	03	00	07
Robert White	24	05	00
William Burdges	16	03	04
Mr. Hort	23	04	09
Mr. Meredy	25	05	02
Widdow Atkins	25	05	02
Widdow Rumney	18	03	09
Mr. Powell	14	02	11
Mr. Wells	11	02	03
Richard Walter	04	00	10
Samuel Sanford	10	02	01
Richard Street	05	01	00
Tho: Hort	08	01	08
Mris. Beavan	06	01	03
Mr. Sampson	12	02	06
Widdow Adlam	03	00	07
	08	07	05

Page 59. THE TITHING OF STOKEBISSHOP.

	£	sh.	d.
Imp Sr. Robert Can	30	06	03
Sr. Humphry Hook	70	14	07
Sr. Robert Yeomans	40	08	04
Mr. Wallis	35	07	03
Mr. Sheremon	38	07	11
Mr. Yates	80	16	08
Docter Martin	80	16	08
Mris. Elizabeth Beavan	54	11	03
Mris. Joyce Beavan	38	07	11
Mris. Yeadith	18	03	09
William Dimmock	32	06	08
Jeorum Cuff	24	05	00
Robert White	36	07	06
Mris. Rutland	22	04	07
Mr. Sampson	02	00	05
Mr. Allder	36	07	06
Mr. Norris	22	04	07
Mr. Gleed	52	10	10
Mris. Standfast	20	04	02
William Hurtnoll	22	04	07
Mr. Hobson	06	01	03
Mris. Shore	12	02	06
Mris. Hasewerd	10	02	01
Mr. Husbands	21	04	04
Mr. Brooks	11	02	03
Edward Lewes..	02	00	05
Mris. Boulton	08	01	08
Mr. Hort	26	05	05
Mris. Avendall	05	01	00
Mr. Bawldin	08	01	08
Richard Willington	08	01	08
Tho: Adlam	03	00	07
Hugh Rumney..	10	02	01
John England	02	00	05
Mr. Lewes	04	00	10
Mr. Saunders	03	00	07
	09	05	02

Page 60. THE TITHING OF SHEREHAMPTON.

	£	sh.	d.
Imp Mris. Rogers	80	16	08
Captaine Grummell	40	08	04
Mr. Hollway	55	11	05
Mris. Web	19	03	11
William Harris..	33	06	10
Widdow Rome	12	02	06
Tho. Willis	05	01	00
John Mathews	17	03	06
Widdow Green..	42	08	09
John Smith	14	02	11
Widdow Smith (later insertion)	31	06	05
Mr. Smether	07	01	05
Widdow Stokes	28	05	10
Mr. Chilton	24	05	00
Widdow Wasborow	17	03	06
Petre Dee	18	03	09
Widdow Parker	20	04	02
Widdow Peacock	21	04	04
Richard Lot	14	02	11
Widdow Heskins	50	10	05
John Hellen	36	07	06
Avenhouse	16	03	04
Mr. Wasborow	36	07	06
John Smith	02	00	05
Mr. Mats	16	03	04
Richard Spralee	28	05	10
Mr. Lock	16	03	04
Mr. Dighton	50	10	05
Mris. Rutland	16	03	04
Roger Gray	10	02	01
Widdow Parker	26	05	05
Morrice Smith	15	03	01
John Smith	25	05	02
John Berry	14	02	11
Tho. Herring	11	02	03
Jo. Gunning	04	00	10
Sarah Tayler	07	01	05
John Gush	10	02	01
Richard Smith	10	02	01
	09	05	11

Page 61.

A rate made by the inhabitants of the prish of Westbury-uppon-trim for and towards the releef of the poore for this yeare 1666 at the rate of 2 pence the pound as followeth.

	£	sh.	d.
Imp Mr. Barker	96	16	00
Mr. Wasborow	90	15	00
Mr. Chilton Cook	75	12	06
William Stephens	90	15	00
Mr. Davis	47	07	10
Mr. Walter	12	02	00
Tho: Wasborow	15	02	06
Mr. Humphry	10	01	08
Mris. Rutland	04	00	08
Mr. Lane	42	07	00
Mr. Morgan	30	05	00
Robert Wasborow	17	02	10
John England	06	01	00
Thomas Adlam	29	04	10
Mris. Arendall	25	04	02
Mr. Wasborow	03	00	06
Robert White	24	04	00
William Burdges	16	02	08
Mr. Hort	27	04	02
Mr. Meredith	25	04	02
Widdow Atkins	25	04	02
Widdow Rumney	18	03	00
Mr. Powell	12	02	00
Mr. Wells	11	01	10
Richard Walter	04	00	08
Samuell Sanford	10	01	08
Richard Street	05	00	10
Tho: Hort	08	01	04
Mris. Beavan	06	01	00
Mr. Sampson	12	02	00
Widdow Adlam	03	00	06
William Hedges	04	00	08
	06	14	00

Page 62. THE TITHING OF STOKEBISSHOP.

		£	sh.	d.
Imp	Sr. Robert Can	30	05	00
	Sr. Humphry Hook	70	11	08
	Sr. Robert Yeomans	40	06	08
	Mr. Wallis	35	05	10
	Mr. Sheremon	38	06	04
	Mr. Yates	80	13	04
	Docter Martin	80	13	04
	Mr. Dymer	54	09	00
	Joyce Beavan	38	06	04
	Yeadith Beavan	18	03	00
	William Dimmock	32	05	04
	Jeorum Cuff	24	04	00
	Robert White	36	06	00
	Mris. Rutland	22	03	08
	Mr. Sampson	02	00	04
	Mr. Aldworth	36	06	00
	Mr. Norris	22	03	08
	Mr. Gleed	52	08	08
	Mris. Standfast	22	03	04
	William Hurtnoll	22	03	08
	Mr. Hobson	06	01	00
	Mris. Shore	12	02	00
	Mris. Haswerd	10	01	08
	Mr. Husbands	21	03	06
	Mr. Brooks	08	01	04
	Edward Lewes	02	00	04
	Mris. Boulton	08	01	04
	Mr. Hort Mr. Bubb	26	04	04
	Mris. Avendall	03	00	06
	Mr. Bawldin	08	01	04
	Richard Willington	08	01	04
	Tho. Adlam	03	00	06
	John England	02	00	04
	William Vaughan	04	00	08
	Mr. Saunders	03	00	06
	Hugh Rumney	10	01	08
		07	08	02

Page 63. THE TITHING OF SHEREHAMPTON.

		£	sh.	d.
Imp	Mris. Rogers	80	13	04
	Captaine Grumwell	40	06	00
	Mr. Hollway	55	09	02
	Mr. Harris	33	05	06
	Widdow Rome	12	02	00
	Mris. Web	19	03	02
	Tho. Willis	05	00	10
	Jo. Mathews	17	02	10
	Henry Green	42	07	00
	Jo. Smith	14	02	04
	Widdow Smith	31	05	02
	Mr. Smether	07	01	02
	Widdow Stokes	28	04	08
	Mr. Chilton	24	04	00
	Widdow Wasborow	17	02	10
	Petre Dee	18	03	00
	Widdow Parker	20	03	00
	Widdow Peacock	21	03	06
	Richard Lot	14	02	06
	Widdow Heskins	50	08	04
	John Hellen	26	04	04
	Avenhouse	16	02	08
	Mr. Wasborow	36	06	00
	John Smith	02	00	4
	Mr. Mats	16	02	08
	Richard Spratlee	28	04	08
	Mr. Lock	16	02	08
	Mr. Dighton	50	08	04
	Mris. Rutland	16	02	08
	Roger Gray	10	01	08
	Widdow Parker	26	04	04
	Morrice Smith	15	02	06
	John Smith	25	04	02
	John Berry	14	02	04
	Tho: Herring	11	01	10
	John Gunning	04	00	08
	Sarah Taylor	07	01	02
	John Gush	10	01	08
	Richard Smith	10	01	08
	Gregory Hugh	10	01	08
		07	09	02

Page 64.

[T]he accompt of Mr. Richard Davis one of the Collectors of the poore of the parrish of Westbury-uppon-trim made the two and twenty day of Aprell 1667:

	£	s.	d.
[F]irst this accomptant Chargeth himself wth the rate of two pence a pound wch commeth to	06	14	00
[M]ore he chargeth himself wth fower pounds wch he receaved for half a years rent at Lawfords gate	04	00	00
the totall is	10	14	00
The disburstmens as followeth			
[I]mp payd to Joane Wade 12 moneths at 4s. a moneth	02	08	00
payd to Robert Everatt 12 moneths at 1s. a moneth ..	00	12	00
payd to Jane Lane 12 moneths at 2s. 6d. a moneth ..	01	10	00
payd to Robert Smith 9 moneths at 3s. a moneth	01	07	00
	05	17	00
[I]tt geaven to Robert Smith at sev times..	00	02	00
payd to the Docter for Tho: Wade in his sicknes	01	02	06
geaven to Elizabeth Cook at sev times	00	02	06
payd for provision for the people in green way	00	09	10
geaven to Tho: Wades wife at 8 sev times	00	11	06
payd for a shroud for Robert Smith and buring of him ..	00	07	04
geaven to Robert Wade	00	02	06
payd to Tho Adlam for money that he layd out for the pish	00	04	10
geaven to Welch Joane..	00	01	06
payd for making the Rates and ingrosing the book.. ..	00	04	00
payd for carring away a Cart-load of Cripples and releef ..	00	02	06
	03	11	00
to totall is ..	09	08	00
soe there is dew unto the prish	01	06	00

Page 65.

The accompt of Henry Saunders one of the Collectors of the poore of the parrish of Westbury-uppon-trim made the two and twenty day of Aprell 1667:

	£	s.	
Imp this accomptant Chargeth himself wth the rate of two pence a pound wch commeth to	09	08	02
Itt to William Coats for one moneths pay	00	04	00
Itt to William osberne for one moneths pay	00	01	06
Itt to William osberne for 3 moneths pay	00	04	06
Itt to William Coats for a 11 moneths pay	02	04	00
Itt to William osbern for 8 moneths pay	00	16	00
Itt to John Hunt for 12 moneths pay	01	10	00
Itt to Agnes Smith 12 moneths pay	01	04	00
	06	04	00
Itt payd to Robert Morrice for provision for the house in green way	00	08	06
geaven to Welsh Joane	00	05	00
geaven towards the releef of Tho: Wade	01	00	00
spent looking of the man that had a child borne at the three Marriners and for a warrant	00	03	02
geaven to Osler (?) fishpull	00	01	00
	01	17	08
the totall is	08	01	08

Page 66.

The accompt of Jo: Heskins one of the Collectors of the poore of the prish of Westbury-uppon-trim made the two and twenty day of Aprell 1567:

	£	s.	d.
Imp this accomptant chargeth himself wth the rate of two pence a pound wch commeth to	07	09	02
The disburstments as followeth			
Itt payd to Edward Lansdown 12 moneths at 4s. a months ..	02	08	00
payd to Tho ffaux 12 moneths at 3s. a moneth	01	16	00
payd to Widdow drinckwater 12 moneths at 2s. 6d. ..	01	10	00
Itt geaven to Edward Launsdown and for his house Rent ..	00	19	00
geaven to Jo: Calee	00	03	00
geaven to the Widdow Gunning	00	02	04
geaven to Tho. ffaux	00	03	06
geaven to the Widdow Reed	00	03	02
geaven to the Widdow drinckwater	00	01	06
the totall is	07	06	06
now it appeareth that there is dew to the prish from Mr. Davis	01	08	06
whereof he receaved of Jo: heskins ..	00	02	06

The residue was owing on he accompt
Being 1£ 06s. 00d. out of this
monie hee have paid to Henry
Sanders, due on his acco 13s. 6d.

	sh.	d.
The remainder 2 the new Collector being	12	00

payd when the collectors past their accompt
Wee doe nominate and appoint Robert White
Georg Bennett and Henry Green to serve
the office of Collectors for the yeare ensuing

Hen Wasborow
Anthony Hortt
Tho: Adlam
Gab. Lowe
Tho Chester

Page 67.

A rate made by the Churchwardens and other the inhabytans of the prish of Westbury-uppon-trim for and towards the releef of the poore for this yeare 1667 : at the rate of two pence a pound

		£	s.	d.
Imp	Mr. Barker	96	16	00
	Mr. Wasborow	80	13	04
	Mr. Davis	47	07	10
	Mr. Clutterbook	75	12	06
	William Stephens	90	15	00
	Mr. Walter	12	02	00
	Tho: Wasborow	15	02	06
	William Humphry	10	01	08
	Mris. Rutland	04	00	08
	Mr. Lane	42	07	00
	Mr. Morgan	30	05	00
	Robert Wasborow	17	02	10
	John England	06	01	00
	Tho: Adlam	29	04	10
	Mris. Avendall	25	04	02
	Mr. Wasborow	03	00	06
	Robert White	24	04	00
	William Burdges	16	02	08
	Mr. Hort	26	04	04
	Mr. Meredith	25	04	02
	Anne Atkins	25	04	02
	Jane Rumney	18	03	00
	Mr. Powell	12	02	00
	Mr. Wells	12	02	00
	Richard Walter	04	00	08
	Samuel Sanford	10	01	08
	Richard Street	05	00	10
	Mr. Hort	08	01	04
	Mris. Beavan	06	01	00
	Mr. Sampson	12	02	00
	Widdow Adlam	03	00	06
	Robert Hedges	04	00	08

Page 68. THE TITHING OF STOKEBISSHOP.

	Name	£	sh.	d.
mp	Sr. Robert Can	77	12	10
	Sr. Humphry Hook	70	11	08
	Sr. Robert Yeomans	40	06	08
	Mr. Wallis	35	05	10
	Mr. Sheremon	38	06	04
	Mr. Yates	80	13	04
	Docter Martin	80	13	04
	Mr. Dymer	60	10	00
	Mris. Joyce Beavan	38	06	04
	Mris. yeadith Beavan	18	03	00
	William Dimmock	11	01	10
	Jeorum Cuff	24	04	00
	Mris. Rutland	22	03	08
	Mr. Sampson	02	00	04
	Mr. Alldworth	36	06	00
	Mr. Norris	22	03	08
	Mr. Gleed	66	11	00
	Mr. Standfast	20	03	04
	William Hurtnoll	08	01	04
	Mr. Hobson	06	01	00
	Mris. Shore	12	02	00
	Mris. Haswerd	10	01	08
	Mris. Husbands	21	03	06
	Mr. Brooks	08	01	04
	Edward Lewes	02	00	04
	Mris. Boulton	08	01	04
	Mr. Hort Mris. Bubb	26	04	04
	Mris. Avendall	03	00	06
	Mr. Bawldin	08	01	04
	Richard Willington	08	01	04
	Tho: Adlam	03	00	06
	John England	02	00	04
	William Vaughan	04	00	08
	Mr. Saunders	02	00	04
	Tho: Wallis	10	01	08
	John Barrett	04	00	08

Page 69. THE TITHING OF SHEREHAMPTON.

		£	s.	d.
Imp	Mris. Rogers	80	13	04
	Mris. Grumnell	40	06	08
	Mr. Holloway	55	09	02
	Mris. Web	19	03	02
	William Harris	33	05	06
	Tho: Willis	05	00	10
	Jo: Mathews	17	02	10
	Henry Green and sister	36	06	00
	Widdow Cottrell	06	01	00
	Jo: Smith	14	02	04
	Mr. Smether	07	01	02
	Widdow Stokes	28	04	08
	Mr. Chilton	24	04	00
	Widdow Wasborow	17	02	10
	Petre Dee	18	03	00
	Widdow Parker	20	03	04
	Widdow Peacock	21	03	06
	Richard Lot	14	02	04
	Widdow Heskins	50	08	04
	Jo. Hellen	26	04	04
	Avenhouse	16	02	08
	Mr. Wasborow	36	06	00
	Jo: Smith	02	00	04
	Mr. Mats	16	02	08
	Richard Spratlee	28	04	08
	William Cox	16	02	08
	Mr. Dighton	50	08	04
	Mris. Rutland	16	02	08
	Roger Gray	10	01	08
	Richard Willington	26	04	04
	Morrice Smith	15	02	06
	Jo: Smith	25	04	02
	Jo: Berry	14	02	04
	Tho: Herring	11	01	10
	Widdow Smith and Richard Smith	41	06	10
	Sarah Tayler	07	01	02
	Jo: Cush	10	01	08
	Jo: Berra	12	02	00
	Gregory Pugh	10	01	08
	Widdow Haines	04	00	08

Page 70.

The accompt of Robert White one of the Collectors of the poore of the parrish of Westbury-uppon-trim made the 3 day of Aprell 1668 :

	£	s.	d.
first this accomptant Chargeth himself wth the rate of two pence a pound wch commeth to	06	11	10
more he chargeth himself wth money wch he receaved of the ould collectors	00	12	00
more receaved of Georg bennett	02	00	00
the totall is	09	03	10

The disburstments as followeth

	£	s.	d.
Imp payd to Joane Wade 12 moneths at 4s. a moneth	02	08	00
payd to Jane Lane 12 moneths at 2s. 6d. a moneth ..	01	10	00
payd to Jo: hunt 12 moneths at 2s. 6d. a moneth	01	10	00
payd to Agnes Smith 7 moneths	00	16	06
payd to Ro: Everat 2 moneths	00	09	00
payd for a shroud for Agnes Smith and buring	00	06	06
geaven to Robert Everat in his sicknes	00	01	00
payd for a shroud for Robert Everat	00	05	00
geaven to Tho: Wade in his sicknes	00	10	00
geaven to William Coats in his sickness	00	04	06
geaven to Mergret Smith	00	03	00
geaven to Joane Rumney in her sicknes	00	03	00
geaven to Mergrett Haskins	00	03	00
spent when wee went to the Justice	00	01	06
geaven to Jane Wade for keeping a Child	00	01	00
geaven to the Widdow baker	00	00	06
payd for a warrant	00	00	06
geaven to Elizabeth Cook	00	01	00
my disburstments ..	08	14	00

Soe it appeareth that there is dew to the pissh	00	09	10

Now this 9s. 10d. was payd to the poore the same day.

Page 71.

The accompt of Georg Bennett one of the Collectors of the poore of the parrish of Westbury-uppon-trim made the 3 day of Aprell 1668.

	£	s.	d.
This accomptant Chargeth himself wth the rate of two pence a pound wch commeth to	07	08	08
The disburstments as followeth			
Imp payd to William Coats 12 moneths at 4s. a moneth ..	02	08	00
payd to William osborne 12 moneths at 2s. a moneth ..	01	04	00
payd to Joane Griffin 12 moneths at 1s. a moneth	00	12	00
payd to Robert White	02	00	00
payd for Coals for William Coats	00	03	04
geaven to John Reynolds	00	03	00
payd for making the rates and ingrossing the book ..	00	04	00
geaven to Joane Griffin	00	04	00
payd for a warrant and going to Thornbury	00	03	00
my disburstments ..	07	01	4
Soe it appeareth that there is dew to the prish	00	07	04

now this 7s. 4d. was layd out the same day.

Page 72. 1668.

ꞁhe accompt of Henry Green one of the Collectors of the poore of the parrish of Westbury-uppon-trim made the 3 day of Aprell.

	£	s.	d.
ꞁhis accomptant Chargeth himself wth the rate of two pence a pound wch commeth to	07	09	00

The disburstments as followeth

	£	s.	d.
.mp payd to Edward Launsdown 7 moneths	01	08	00
payd to Mary Lawnsdown 6 moneths	00	12	00
payd to Tho ffaux 13 moneths	01	19	00
payd to Kathern Drinckwater 13 moneths	01	12	06
geaven to Edward Launsdown in his sicknes	00	05	00
geaven to Mergret ffaux for tending of him..	00	05	00
payd for the buring of Edward Launsdown..	00	09	01
payd for Riding to the Justice 2 sev times	00	03	00
payd for rent for Edward Launsdown	00	05	00
for riding to the Justice 2 sev times	00	03	00
payd for 2 warrants	00	01	00
for riding to the Justice to put out Jo: Williams	00	01	06
geaven to Tho: ffaux	00	01	00
geaven to Jo: Callee	00	01	06
geaven to Elnor Reed..	00	01	00
geaven to Kathern Drinckwater	00	00	06
geaven to Mary Lansdown	00	00	06
for going to the Justice about Joseph Gale	00	01	06

:he totall of the disburstments is £21 04 05.

	£	s.	d.
my disburstmens	07	10	01
;oe it appeareth that there is dew to the Collector	00	01	01

:his accompts seen and allowed by wee whose names .re heareunder subscribed.

Vee doe nominate and appoint William Burdges ’etre Muggleworth and Samuell Robins to serve the ffice of Collectors for the yeare ensuing.

Hen Wasborow Church warden
Robert Wasborow
Henry Sandars.
William Harris
Tho Adlam

Gabr Lowe
John Meredith

Page 73. The first of Aprell 1668.

A rate made by the churchwardens and other the inhabitants of the parrish of Westbury-uppon-trim for and towards the releef of the poore for this yeare at the Rate of 2d. a pound.

	£	s.	d.
Imp Mris. Mills and her sisters	96	16	00
Mr. Wasborow	70	13	04
Mr. Davis	46	07	08
Mr. Clutterbook	75	12	06
Mr. Sampson	90	15	00
Mr. Walter	12	02	00
Tho: Wasborow	15	02	06
William Humphry	10	01	08
Mris. Rutland	03	00	06
Mr. Lane	36	06	00
obadiah Web	06	01	00
Mr. Morgan	30	05	00
Robert Wasborow	17	02	10
John England	06	01	00
Tho: Adlam	29	04	10
Mris. Avendall	25	04	02
Mr. Wasborow	03	00	06
Robert White	24	04	00
William Burdges	22	03	08
Mr. Hort	26	04	04
Mr. Meredith	25	04	02
Ane Atkins	25	04	02
Jane Rumny	18	03	00
Mr. Powell	12	02	00
Mr. Wells	12	02	00
Samuell Sanford	10	01	08
Mr. Hort	08	01	04
Mris. Beavan	06	01	00
Mr. Sampson	12	02	00
Widdow Adlam	03	00	06
Robert Hedges..	09	01	06
	06	11	10

Page 74. **THE TITHING OF STOKEBISSHOP.**

	Name	£	sh.	d.
np	Sr. Robert Can	101	16	10
	Sr. Humphry Hook	70	11	08
	Sr. Robert yeomans	40	06	08
	Mr. Wallis	35	05	10
	Mr. Sheremon	38	06	04
	Mr. Yates	80	13	04
	Docter Martin	80	13	04
	Mr. Dymer	60	10	00
	Mris. Joyce Beavan	38	06	04
	Mris. Yeadith Beavan	18	03	00
	William Dimmock	11	01	10
	Mris. Rutland	22	03	08
	Mr. Sampson	02	00	04
	Mris. Alldworth	36	06	00
	Mr. Norris	22	03	08
	Mr. Gleed	66	11	00
	Mr. Standfast	20	03	04
	William Hurtnoll	08	01	04
	Mr. Hobson	06	01	04
	Mris. Shore	12	02	00
	Mris. Haswerd	10	01	08
	Mris. Husbands	21	03	06
	Mr. Brooks	08	01	04
	Edward Lewes	02	00	04
	Mris. Boulton	08	01	04
	Mr. Hort } Mris. Bubb }	26	04	04
	Mris. Avendall	03	00	06
	Mr. Bawldin	08	01	04
	Widdow Wasborrow	08	01	04
	Tho: Adlam	03	00	06
	Jo: England	02	00	04
	Mr. Saunders	02	00	04
	William Vaughan	03	00	06
	Tho: Wallis	10	01	08
	Jo: Barret	04	00	08
		07	06	10

Page 75. THE TITHING OF SHEREHAMPTON.

	£	sh.	d.
Imp Mris. Rogers	80	13	04
Mris. Grumnell	40	06	08
Mr. holloway	55	09	02
Mris. Web	19	03	02
William harris	25	04	02
Tho: Willis	05	00	10
Jo: Mathews	18	03	00
Henry Green	36	06	00
Widdow Cottrell	06	01	00
Jo: Smith	14	02	04
Mr. Smether	07	01	02
Widdow Stokes	28	04	08
Mr. Chilton	24	04	00
Widdow Wasborow	26	04	04
Petre Dee	18	03	00
Widdow Parker	20	03	04
Widdow Peacock	21	03	06
Widdow Lot	14	02	04
Widdow Heskins	50	08	04
Jo: Hellen	26	04	04
Avenhouse	16	02	08
Mr. Wasborow	36	06	00
Jo: Smith	02	00	04
Mris. Mats	16	02	08
Richard Spratlee	28	04	08
William Cox	16	02	08
Mr. Dighton	50	08	04
Mris. Rutland	16	02	08
Roger Gray	10	01	08
Morrice Smith	15	02	06
Jo: Smith	25	04	02
Jo: Berry	14	02	04
Tho: herring	11	01	10
Widdow Smith	31	05	02
Sarah Tayler	07	01	02
Jo: Gush	10	01	08
Samuell Robins	08	01	04
Jo. Berra	12	02	00
Gregory Pugh	10	01	08
Widdow haines	04	00	08
Lord Auston	10	01	08
Morrice Smith	12	02	00
William Peacock	04	00	08

the rate is
£7 9s. 2d.

Page 76.

he accompts of William Burdges and Petre Muggleworth two of the Collectors of the prish of Westbury-uppon-trim made the 13th day of Aprell 1669.

	£	sh.	d.
his accomptants Chargeth themselves wth the rates of two pence the pound wch commeth to	13	18	08
The disburstments as followeth			
mp payd to Joane Wade 13 moneths at 4s. a moneth.. ..	02	12	00
payd to Jane Lane 13 moneths at 2s. 6d. a moneth ..	01	12	06
payd to Joane Jones 13 moneths at 2s. a moneth	01	06	00
payd to Joane Thomas 8 moneths at 4s. a moneth ..	01	12	00
payd to her 3 moneths at 6s. a moneth	00	18	00
payd to her 2 moneths at 2d. a moneth	00	04	00
payd to Jo: Hunt 10 moneths at 2s. 6d. a moneth	01	05	00
payd to Margret Smith 2 moneths at 1s. 6d. a moneth..	00	03	00
payd to her a 11 moneths at 2s. a moneth	01	02	00
	10	14	06
geaven to Jane Lane in her sicknes one to tend her ..	00	04	00
geaven to Elizabeth Cook and at fower sev times.. ..	00	04	00
geaven to Mergret Smith in her sicknes and for tending ..	00	05	00
geaven to Joane Thomas in her sicknes	00	04	00
geaven to Joane Jones in her sickness	00	01	00
geaven to Thomas Wade in his sicknes	00	01	00
geaven to Jane Smith in her sickness	00	01	00
payd for buring Joane Thomas her boy	00	05	00
geaven to Joane Rumney	00	02	00
geaven to Jane Wade	00	02	06
for making the rates and ingrosing the book	00	04	00
geaven to John Reynolds	00	04	04
payd for a warrant and going to Thornbury	00	03	00
	2	3	4
The totall of my disburstments..	12	17	10
Soe it appeareth there is dew to the parrish	01	00	10
payd afterwards for mending the Alms house [1]	00	16	06
more spent at the Inn when the pish met	00	05	00
Soe it appeareth that there is dew to me	00	00	08

[1] *See* Introduction.

Page 77.

The accompt of Samuell Robins one of the Collectors of the poore of the parrish of Westbury-uppon-trim made the 13th day of Aprell 1669.

	£		
This accomptant Chargeth himself wth the rate of two pence the pound wch commeth to	07	09	02

The distburstments as followeth

Imp payd to Tho: faux 13 moneths	01	19	00
payd to Mary Launsdown 7 moneths at 3 shillings ..			
payd to her 6 moneths at 2s. wch is the whole	01	13	00
payd to the widdow Drinckwater 13 moneths	01	19	00
geaven to Widdow Gunning	00	13	00
geaven to Thomas faux	00	04	00
geaven to widdow Drinckwater	00	04	06
geaven to Agnes Smith	00	03	00
geaven to Mary Launsdown	00	04	06
geaven to John Calee	00	04	00
geaven to the Widdow Reed	00	03	08
payd to Roger Bray for money that was left unpayd at the buring of Edward Launsdown	00	01	00
payd to a breef	00	00	04
geaven to the Widdow Drinckwater	00	00	02
	7	9	2

Soe it appeareth that all is disbursted
This accompt seen and allowed by
wee whose names are heare written

Hen Wasborrow
Henry Greene
Churchwardens.

Wee doe nominate and appoint Robert Hedges, John Sampson and Robert Smith to serve the office of Collectors for the yeare ensuing.

Page 78. The 16th of Aprell 1669.

. rate made by the churchwardens and other the inhabytants of the parrish of Westbury-uppon-trim for and towards the releef of the poore for this yeare at the rate of two pence the pound as followeth.

		£	sh.	d.
mp	Mris. Milles and her sisters	96	16	00
	Mr. Wasborow	80	13	04
	Mr. Davis	46	07	08
	Mr. Clutterbook	75	12	06
	Mr. Sampson	90	15	00
	Mris. Walter	12	02	00
	Tho: Wasborow	15	02	06
	William Humphry	10	01	08
	Mris. Rutland	03	00	06
	Mr. Lane	36	06	00
	Obadiah Web	06	01	00
	Mr. Morgan	30	05	00
	Robert Wasborow	17	02	10
	John England	06	01	00
	Mathew Adlam	24	04	00
	John Adlam	05	00	10
	Mris. Arendall	25	04	02
	Mr. Wasborow	03	00	06
	Robert White	24	04	00
	William Burdges	22	03	08
	Mr. Hort	26	04	04
	Mr. Meredith	25	04	02
	Ane Atkins	25	04	02
	Tho: Cuff	18	03	00
	Mr. Powell	12	02	00
	Mr. Wels	12	02	00
	Samuell Sanford	10	01	08
	Mr. Hort	08	01	04
	Mris. Beavan	06	01	00
	Mr. Sampson	12	02	00
	Widdow Adlam	03	00	06
	Robert Hedges	09	07	06
		06	11	10

Page 79. THE TITHING OF STOKEBISSHOP.

		£	sh.	
Imp	Sr. Robert Can..	109	18	02
	Sr. Humphry Hook	70	11	08
	Sr. Robert Yeomans	40	06	08
	Mr. Wallis	35	05	10
	Mr. Sheremon	38	06	04
	Mr. Yates	80	13	04
	Docter Martin	80	13	04
	Mr. Dymer	60	10	00
	Mris. Joyce Beavan	38	06	04
	Mris. Yeadith Beavan	18	03	00
	Mr. Dimmock	11	01	10
	Mris. Rutland	22	03	08
	Mr. Sampson	02	00	04
	Mris. Alldworth	36	06	00
	Mr. Norris	22	03	08
	Mr. Gleed	66	11	00
	Mr. Standfast	20	03	04
	Mr. Hurtnoll	08	01	04
	Mr. Hobson	06	01	00
	Mris. Shore	12	02	00
	Mr. Little	10	01	08
	Mris. Husbands	21	03	06
	Mr. Brooks	08	01	04
	Edward Lewes	02	00	04
	Mr. Criswick	09	01	06
	Mr. Hort	17	02	10
	Mris. Avendall	03	00	06
	Mr. Bawldin	08	01	04
	Charety Wasborow	08	01	04
	Mathew Adlam	03	00	06
	John England	02	00	04
	Mr. Saunders	02	00	04
	William Vaughan	03	00	06
	Stephen Lippet	10	01	08
	John Barrat	04	00	08
		07	06	10

Page 80. THE TITHING OF SHEREHAMPTON.

	£	sh.	d.
Imp Mris. Rogers	80	13	04
Mris. Grumnell	40	06	08
Mrs. Holway	55	09	02
Mris. Web	19	03	02
William Harris	25	04	02
Tho: Willis	05	00	10
John Mathews	18	03	00
Henry Green	36	06	00
Widdow Cottrell	06	01	00
John Smith	14	02	04
Mr. Smether	07	01	02
Widow Stokes	28	04	08
Mr. Chilton	24	04	00
Widdow Wasborow	26	04	04
Petre Dee	18	03	00
Widdow Parker	20	03	04
Widdo Peacock	21	03	06
Widow Lot	14	02	04
Widdow Heskins	50	08	04
John Hellen	26	04	04
Avenhouse	16	02	08
Mr. Wasborow	36	06	00
John Smith	02	00	04
Mris. Mats	16	02	08
Richard Spratlee	28	c4	08
William Cox	16	02	08
Mr. Dighton	50	08	04
Mris. Rutland	16	02	08
Roger Gray	10	01	08
Morrice Smith	15	02	06
John Smith	25	04	02
John Berry	14	02	04
Tho: Herring	11	01	10
Widdow Smith	31	05	02
Sarah Tayler	07	01	02
John Gush	10	01	08
Samuell Robins	08	01	04
John Berra	12	02	00
Gregory Pugh	10	01	08
Widdow Haines	04	00	08
Lord Austin	10	01	08
Morrice Smith	12	02	00
William Peacock	04	00	08
	07	09	02

Page 81.

The Accompt of Robert Hedges one of the Collectors of the poore of the parrish of Westbury-uppon-trim made the 15th day of Aprell 1670:

	£	sh.	d.
This accomptant chargeth himself wth the Rate of 2d. a pound wch commeth to	06	11	10
The disburstments as followeth			
Imp payd to Jeane Wade 9 moneths at 4s. a moneth	01	16	00
payd to Jane Lane 12 moneths at 4s. a moneth	02	08	00
payd to Jane Lane 1 moneth at 2s. 6d. a moneth	00	02	06
payd to Joan Jones 4 moneths at 2s. a moneth	00	08	00
payd for bread for Elizabeth Emree..	00	00	04
geaven to Joane Wade in her sicknes	00	04	00
payd for linnen for Jane Wade	00	05	00
geaven to Tho: Wade in his sicknes..	00	07	00
geaven to Robert Wades wife in her sicknes..	00	07	00
payd for buring Joane wade and her rent	00	01	06
payd for making the rates and ingrosing the book.. ..	00	04	00
geaven to Joane Rumny	00	00	06
the totall is	6	6	00
Soe it appeareth there is dew to the prish..	0	5	6

now this 1s. 6d. is geaven to Jane Wade and
for going to the Justice and for a warrant 2s.
payd to the new Collector .. .. 2s.

Page 82.

The accompt of John Saunson one of the Collectors of the poore of the parrish of Westbury-uppon-trim made the 15 day of Aprell 1670.

	£	sh.	d.
This accomptant chargeth himself with the rate of two pence a pound wch commeth to	07	06	00
The disburstments as followeth			
Imp payd to Joane Jones 9 moneths at 2s. a moneth	00	18	00
payd to Mergret Smith 13 moneths at 2s. a moneth ..	01	06	00
geaven to her in her distres	00	01	00
payd to Joane Rumney 09 moneths at 2s. a moneth ..	00	18	00
payd to Jo: hunt 10 moneths at 2s. 6d. a moneth	01	05	00
Jo Reynolds geaven unto him at sev times..	00	18	00
geaven to Jo White at sev times	01	06	00
geaven to yeadith Morris at sev times	00	08	06
payd for one to tend her	00	02	00
Spent at the Inn when they met about the rates	00	03	00
the totall is ..	07	05	6
Soe there is dew to the prish..	00	00	06

this 6d. is payd to the new Collector.

Page 83.

The accompt of Robert Smith one of the Collectors of the poore of the parrish of Westbury-uppon-trim made the 15th of Aprell 1670.

This Accompt chargeth himself with the rate of two pence a pound wch commeth to	07	09	02

The disbursments as followeth

Imp payd to Tho: faux 13 moneths at 3s. a month	01	19	00
payd to gooddy Gunning 13 months at 3s. a moneth ..	01	19	00
payd to the widdow drinckwater 4 moneths	00	12	00
payd her 9 moneths at 3s. 6d. a moneth	01	11	06
geaven to John Calee..	00	04	00
geaven to the widdow Guning	00	05	00
geaven to Thomas faux	00	04	00
geaven to Ane Smith..	00	05	00
geaven to Elnor Reed..	00	02	06
geaven to the widdow Drinckwater..	00	06	11
geaven to a poore man	00	00	03
the totall is	07	09	02

Soe it appeareth that it is all layd out.

The whole of our recepits is..	21	01	01
The whole of our distburstments is	21	01	01

This accompts seen and allowed by wee
whose names are heareunder subscribed

Hen Wasborow } Church
Henry Green } Wardens
Richard Laine
Anthony Hortt
James Knap

Wee doe nominate and appoint Mathew Adlam
Edward Jochum and John Willis to serve
the office of Collectors for the yeare ensuing.

Joh Lenton
John Meredith.

Page 84. The 20th of Aprell 1670.

A rate made by the Churchwardens and other the inhabitants of the parrish of Westbury-uppon-trim for and towards the releef of the poore for this year at the rate of 2d. a pound as followeth :—

	£	sh.	d.
Imp Mris. Mills and her sisters	96	16	00
Mr. Wasborow	80	13	04
Mr. Davis	46	07	08
Mr. Clutterbook	75	12	06
Mr. Sampson	90	15	00
Mr. Walter	12	02	00
Tho. Wasborow	15	02	06
William Humphry	10	01	08
Mris. Rutland	03	00	06
Mr. Lane	36	06	00
Obadiah Web	06	01	00
Mr. Morgan	30	05	00
Robert Wasborow	17	02	10
John England	06	01	00
Mathew Adlam	24	04	00
John Adlam	07	01	02
Mris. Avendall	25	04	02
Mr. Wasborow	03	00	06
Robert White	24	04	00
William Burdges	22	03	08
Mr. Hort	25	04	02
Mr. Meredith	25	04	02
Ann Atkins	25	04	02
Tho. Cuff	18	03	00
Mr. Powell	12	02	00
Mr. Wells	12	02	00
Samuell Sanford	10	01	08
Mr. Hort	08	01	04
Mris. Beavan	06	01	00
Mr. Sampson	12	02	00
Widdow Adlam	03	00	06
Robert Hedges	09	01	06
	06	11	10

Page 85. The 20th Aprell 1670:

		£	sh.	d.
Imp	Sr. Robert Can..	109	18	02
	Sr. Robert Yeomans	42	07	00
	Mr. Humphry Hook	70	11	08
	Mr. Crump	35	05	10
	Mr. Sheremon	38	06	04
	Mr. Yates	80	13	04
	Docter Martin	80	13	04
	Mr. Dymer	60	10	00
	Mris. Joyce Beavan	38	06	04
	Mris. yeadith Beavan	18	03	00
	Mr. Dimmock	11	01	10
	Mris. Rutland	22	03	08
	Mr. Sampson	02	00	04
	Mris. Alldworth	36	06	00
	Mr. Gleed	66	11	00
	Mr. Tilladam	20	03	04
	Mr. Hurtnoll	08	01	04
	Mr. Hobson	06	01	00
	Mris. Shore	12	02	00
	Mr. Little	10	01	08
	Mris. Husbands	21	03	06
	Mr. Brooks	28	04	08
	Edward Lewes	02	00	04
	Mr. Criswick	09	01	06
	Mr. Hort	17	02	10
	Mris. Avendall	03	00	06
	Mr. Bawldin	08	01	04
	Widdow Wasborow	08	01	04
	Mathew Adlam	03	00	06
	Mr. England	02	00	04
	Mr. Saunders	02	00	04
	William Vaughan	02	00	04
	Stephen Lippett	10	01	08
	Arthur Sawyer	04	00	08
		07	06	10

Page 86.

	£	sh.	d.
Imp Mris. Rogers	80	13	04
Mris. Grumnell	40	06	08
Mr. Hollway	55	09	02
Mris. Web	19	03	02
William Harris	25	04	02
Thomas Willis	05	00	10
John Mathews	18	03	00
Henry Green	36	06	00
Widdow Cottrell	06	01	00
John Smith	14	02	04
Widdow Stokes	28	04	08
Mr. Chilton	24	04	00
Widdow Wasborow	26	04	04
Petre Dee	18	03	00
Widdow Parker	20	03	04
Widdow Lot	14	02	04
Widdow Heskins	50	08	04
Mr. Crismas	26	04	04
Avenhouse	16	02	08
Mr. Wasborow	36	06	00
John Smith	02	00	04
Mr. Mats	16	02	08
Richard Spratlee	28	04	08
William Cox	16	02	08
Mr. Dighton	50	08	04
Mris. Rutland	16	02	08
William Adams	10	01	08
John Smith	25	04	02
Widdow Berry	14	02	04
Tho: Herring	11	01	10
Widdow Smith	31	05	02
Sarah Tayler	07	01	02
Widdow Gush	10	01	08
Samuell Robins	08	01	04
John Barra	12	02	00
Gregory Pugh	10	01	08
Widdow Haines	04	00	08
Lord Austin	10	01	08
Mris. Smether	34	05	08
James Peacock	21	03	06
William Peacock	04	00	08
	07	09	02

Page 87.

The accompt of Mathew Adlam one of the Collectors of the poore of the parrish of Westbury-uppon-trim made the 24th day of Aprell 1671:

	£	sh.	d.
This accomptant Chargeth himself wth the rate of two pence a pound wch commeth to	06	11	10
More he chargeth himself wth two shillings receaved of the ould Collectors	00	02	00
the totall	06	13	10

The disburstments as followeth

Imp payd to Jane Lane 13 moneths at 4s. a moneth	02	12	00
payd to Mergret Smith 13 moneths at 2s. a moneth ..	01	06	00
payd to Elizabeth Cook 13 moneths at 1s. a moneth ..	00	13	00
geaven to William Smith	00	03	06
geaven to Mergret Smith	00	02	00
geaven to Robert Wade	00	03	00
geaven to a poore woeman that was great wth child ..	00	02	06
geaven to John White..	00	02	00
spent when wee went to Cribs to warne the teanaunt ..	00	01	00
spent when we went to take security of Jones and his son for to discharg the parrish of the child..	00	02	06
spent at sev times when the Collectors did meet	00	02	06
geaven to William Cary	00	02	00
spent at another time when the parish did meet	00	02	00
geaven to Mergret Smith another time	00	01	00
	05	15	10
dew to the parrish	00	18	10

Richard Laine
Hen Wasborow
Anthony Hortt

Page 88.

ıe accompt of Edward Jochum one of the Collectors of the poore of the parrish of Westbury-uppon-trim made the 24th day of Aprell 1671 :

	£	sh.	d.
ıis accomptant Chargeth himself wth the rate of two pence a pound wch commeth to	07	06	04

The disburstments as followeth

	£	sh.	d.
ıp payd to John Hunt 13 moneths at 2s. 6d. a month.. ..	01	12	06
payd to Mergret Wade 13 moneths at 2s. 6d. a moneth ..	01	12	06
payd to John Reynolds 13 moneths at 2s. a moneth ..	01	06	00
geaven to John White at sev times	00	10	00
geaven to John Hunt..	00	05	00
geaven to John Reynolds at sev times	00	05	06
spent about the Child that was borne under the hay mow and money that I gave to the woeman..	00	15	01
geaven to yeadith Morrice in her sicknes	00	02	05
payd for making the rates and ingrosing the book.. ..	00	04	00
spent at sev times when the Collectors mett about the parrish business	00	02	06
the totall is ..	06	15	06
Soe it appeareth there is dew	00	10	10

	£	sh.	d.
The whole of our receits is	21	09	04
The whole of our disbursments is	19	19	02
dew to the parrish.. ..	01	10	02

ow this £1 0s. 2d. was payd to the poor for a moneth that was dew to the poor and the week following being 14s. 6d. and 5s. 6d. wch was taken to Henry Green for the poore of Sherehampton and to be payd back the next accompt day.

Page 89.

The accompt of John Willis one of the Collectors of the parrish of Westbury-uppon-trim made the 24 day of Aprell 1671 :

	£	sh.	d.
This accomptant Chargeth himself wth the rate of two pence a pound wch commeth to	07	09	02
The disburstments as followeth			
Imp payd to Tho Vaux 13 moneths at 3s. a moneth	01	19	00
payd to the Widdow Gunning 13 moneths at 3s. a moneth..	01	19	00
payd to the Widdow Drinckwater 3 moneths at 3s. 6d. a moneth	00	10	06
payd for tending and buring of the Widdow Drinckwater..	00	15	11
geaven to the Widdow Gunning at sev times	00	12	00
geaven to Anne Smith	00	02	06
geaven to the Widdow Reed	00	03	00
geaven to Mary Playford	00	02	06
geaven to John By at sev times	00	08	00
geaven to the Widdow Baker at sev times	00	05	00
geaven to John Calee at sev times	00	06	00
geaven to Tho ffaux at sev times	00	04	00
spent when wee met about the parrish busines	00	01	03
	07	08	08
Soe it appeareth dew ..	00	00	06

Richard Laine
Hen Wasborow
Anthony Hortt
James Knap } Churchwardens
Morrice Georg }

Wee doe nominate and appoint Cornelius Jeyn Nicholas Cox Edward Cras to serve the office of Collectors for the poore for the yeare ensuing.

Go Stephens
John Meredith

Page 90. The 12th of Aprell 1671

A rate made by the Churchwardens and other inhabitants of the parrish of Westbury for and towards the releef of the poore for this yeare at the rate of two pence half penny a pound as followeth

	£	sh.	d.
Imp Mris. Mills	96	20	00
Mr. Wasborow	80	16	08
Mr. Davis	46	09	07
Mr. Leaman	75	15	07
Mr. Sampson	90	18	09
Mr. Walter	12	02	06
Tho: Wasborow	15	03	01
William Humphry	10	02	01
Mris. Rutland	03	00	07
Mr. Lane	36	07	06
obadiah Web	06	01	03
Mr. oliff	30	06	03
Robert Wasborow	17	03	06
Mr. England	06	01	03
Mathew Adlam	24	05	00
John Adlam	07	01	05
Mris. Avendall	25	05	02
Mr. Wasborow	03	00	07
Robert White	24	05	00
William Burdges	22	04	07
Mr. Hort	26	05	05
Mr. Meredith	25	05	02
Widdow Atkins	25	05	02
Thomas Cuff	18	03	09
Mris. Powell	12	02	06
Mr. Wells	12	02	06
Samuell Sanford	10	02	01
Mr. Hort	08	01	08
Mris. Beavan	06	01	03
Mr. Sampson	12	02	06
Widdow Adlam	03	00	07
Robert Hedges	09	01	10

Page 91. The 12th of Aprell 1671:

	£	sh.	d.
Imp Sr. Robert Can	109	22	08
Sr. Robert Yeomans	20	04	02
Sr. Humphry Hook	70	14	07
Mr. Crump	35	07	03
Mr. Sheremon	38	07	11
Mr. Yates	80	16	08
Mris. Martin	80	16	08
Mr. Dymer	60	12	06
Mris. Joyce Beavan	38	07	11
Mris. Yeadith Beavan	18	03	09
Mr. Dimmock	11	02	03
Mris. Rutland	24	05	00
Mris. Alldworth	36	07	06
Mr. Gleed	66	13	09
Mr. Tilladam	20	04	02
Mr. Hurtnoll	08	01	08
Mr. Hobson	06	01	03
Mris. Shore	12	02	06
Mr. Little	10	02	01
Mris. Husbands	21	04	04
Mr. Brooks	28	05	10
Edward Lewes	02	00	05
Mr. Criswick	09	01	10
Mr. Hort	17	03	06
Mris. Avendall	03	00	07
Mr. Bawldin	08	01	08
Charety Wasborow	08	01	08
Mathew Adlam	03	00	07
Mr. England	02	00	05
Mr. Blackwell	02	00	05
Mr. Norris	22	04	07
William Vaughan	02	00	05
Stephen Lippett	10	02	01
Arthur Sawyer	04	00	10

Page 92. The 12th of Aprell 1671:

	£	sh.	d.
ıp Mris. Rogers	80	16	08
Mris. Grumnell	40	08	04
Mr. Hollway	55	11	05
Mr. Web	19	03	11
William Harris	25	05	02
Thomas Willis	05	01	00
John Mathews	18	03	09
Henry Green	36	07	06
Widdow Cottrell	06	01	03
John Smith	14	02	11
Widdow Stokes	28	05	10
Mr. Chilton	23	04	09
Widdow Wasborow	26	05	05
Petre Dee	31	06	05
Widdow Parker	20	04	02
Widdow Lot	14	02	11
Widdow Heskins	50	10	05
Mr. Crismas	26	05	05
Avenhouse	16	03	04
Mr. Wasborow	36	07	06
John Smith	02	00	05
Mr. Mats	16	03	04
Richard Spratley	28	05	10
William Cox	16	03	04
Mr. Dighton	50	10	05
Mris. Rutland	16	03	04
William Adams	10	02	01
John Smith	25	05	02
Widdow Berry	14	02	11
Thomas Herring	11	02	03
Widdow Smith	31	06	05
Sarah Tayler	07	01	05
Widdow Gush	10	02	01
Samuell Robins	08	01	08
John Barra	12	02	06
Gregory Pugh	10	02	01
Widdow Haines	04	00	10
Mris. Smether	35	07	03
James Peacock	18	03	09
William Peacock	04	00	10

Page 93.

The accompt of Cornelius Jeine one of the Collectors of the poore of the parrish of Westbury-uppon-trim made the 8th day of Aprell 1672:

	£	sh.	d.
This accomptant Chargeth himself wth the rate of two pence half penny a pound wch commeth to	08	04	09
The disburstments as followeth			
Imp paid to Jane Lane 13 moneths at 4s. a moneth	02	12	00
paid to John hunt 13 moneths at 2s. 6d. a moneth.. ..	01	12	06
paid to Mergret wade 13 mon at 2s. 6d. a moneth	01	12	06
paid to Elizabeth Cook 13 mon at 1s. 0d. a moneth ..	00	13	00
geaven to Mergret Wade in her sicknes	00	04	06
geaven to Kathern Smith in her sicknes	00	01	00
geaven to Agnes White	00	02	00
geaven to Welsh Joane at sevall times	00	04	00
geaven to Elizabeth Cook	00	01	06
geaven to Jane Wade	00	03	00
geaven to Jane Smith in her childrens sicknes	00	02	00
more geaven to her another time	00	01	06
geaven to Alce Rudman	00	02	00
paid for making the Rates and ingrosing the book ..	00	04	00
geaven to Elizabeth Cook	00	00	06
	07	16	00

I Crave allowance for Mr. Abel meredy 5sh. 2d.

	£	sh.	d.
Dew to the parrish ..	00	08	09
		05	02
	£	03	07

Page 94.

ıe accompt of Nicholas Cox one of the Collectors of the poore of the parrish of Westbury-uppon-trim made the 8th day of Aprell 1672.

	£	sh.	d.
ıis accomptant Chargeth himself wth the rate of two pence half penny a pound wch commeth to..	09	03	00

The disburstments as followeth	£	sh.	d.
ıp payd to William Smith 13 mons at 2s. 6d. a moneth ..	01	12	06
payd to Mergret Smith 13 mons at 2s. 6d. a moneth ..	01	12	06
payd to Susan Smith 13 mons at 2s. 0d. a moneth ..	01	06	00
payd to Jo: Reynolds 13 mons at 3s. 0d. a moneth.. ..	01	19	00
geaven to John White at sev times	01	00	00
geaven to John Reynolds at sev times	00	06	00
geaven to William Cary	00	01	00
geaven to Mergret Wade	00	03	06
spent at sev times in the parrish busines	00	03	06
paid for a warrant and going to Thornbury	00	02	06
	08	06	06
Dew to the parrish ..	00	16	06

Page 95.

The accompt of Edward Cras one of the Collectors of the parrish of Westbury-uppon-trim made the 8th day of Aprell 1672.

	£	s.	d.
This accomptant Chargeth himself wth the rate of two pence half penny a pound wch cometh to	09	04	04
The disburstments as followeth			
Imp payd to the Widdow Gunning 13 months at 4s. a month ..	02	12	00
payd to Thomas Vaux 13 months at 3s. a month	01	19	00
payd to Jo: By 13 months at 4s. a month	02	12	00
geaven to the Widdow Gunning at sev times	00	12	00
geaven to John Calee at sev times	00	05	00
geaven to Mary playford at sev times	00	04	00
geaven to Agnes Jones at sev times	00	05	00
geaven to Agnes Smith at sev times..	00	07	00
spent at sev times about the parrish business	00	02	00
payd to the parrish from Sherehampton wch was Receaved of henry Green (?) wch hee borrowed last yeare ..	00	05	06
	09	03	06

	£	s.	d.
our receips is ..	25	0	0
our disburstments is	23	13	9

	£	s.	d.
Dew to the parrish ..	00	00	10
of henry green as above sd	00	05	06
recd of Nicholas Cox ..	00	16	06
recd of henry Jayne ..	00	03	07
	£1	06	05

We doe nominate and appoint Isaac Rumney John Adlam and John Smith to serve the office of Collectors of the poore for the yeare insuing

Richard Laine
Hen Wasborow
Anthony Hortt
Robert White

passed and allowed by us
John Smyth
John Meredith

Page 96. The 12th of Aprell 1672.

rate made by the Churchwardens and other inhabitants of the parrish of Westbury-uppon-trim for and towards the releef of the poore of this yeare at the rate of two pence half penny a pound as followeth

		£	sh.	d.
1p	Mris. Mills	96	20	00
	Mr. Wasborow	80	16	08
	Mr. Davis	46	09	07
	Mr. Leaman	75	15	07
	Mr. Sampson	90	18	09
	Mr. Walter	12	02	06
	Tho: Wasborow	15	03	01
	William Hunmphry	10	02	01
	Mris. Rutland	03	00	07
	Mr. Lane	36	07	06
	Obadiah Web	06	01	03
	Mr. Oliff	30	06	03
	Robert Wasborow	09	01	10
	Mr. England	06	01	03
	Mathew Adlam	24	05	00
	John Adlam	07	01	05
	Mris. Avendall	25	05	02
	Mr. Wasborow	03	00	07
	Robert White	24	05	00
	William Burdges	22	04	07
	Mr. Hort	26	05	05
	Mr. Meredith	25	05	02
	Widdow Atkins	25	05	02
	Thomas Cuff	18	03	09
	Mris. Powell	12	02	06
	Mr. Wells	12	02	06
	Samuell Sanford	10	02	01
	Mrs. Hort	08	01	08
	Mris. Beavan	06	01	03
	Mr. Sampson	12	02	06
	Widdow Adlam	03	00	07
	Robert Hedges	09	01	10
	Samuell Clafell	05	01	00
	William Burdges	01	00	02
	Mathew Adlam	01	00	02
	William Humphries	01	00	02
		08	04	07

Page 97. The 12th of Aprell 1672.

		£	sh.	d.
Imp	Sr. Robert Can	109	22	08
	Sr. Robert yeomans	20	04	02
	Sr. Humphry Hook	70	14	07
	Mr. Crump	35	07	03
	Mr. Sheremon	38	07	11
	Mr. Yates	80	16	08
	Mris. Martin	80	16	08
	Mr. Dymer	60	12	06
	Mris. Joyce Beavan	38	07	11
	Mris. yeadith Beavan	18	03	09
	Mr. Dimmock	11	02	03
	Mris. Rutland	24	05	00
	Mr. Hart	36	07	06
	Mr. Gleed	66	13	09
	Mr. Tilladam	20	04	02
	Mr. Hurtnoll	08	01	08
	Mr. Hobson	06	01	03
	Mris. Shore	12	02	06
	Mr. Little	10	02	01
	Mris. Husbands	21	04	04
	Mr. Brooks	28	05	10
	Edward Lewes	02	00	05
	Mr. Criswick	09	01	10
	Mr. Hort	17	03	06
	Mris. Avendall	03	00	07
	Mr. Bawldin	08	01	08
	Widdow Wasborrow	08	01	08
	Mathew Adlam	03	00	07
	Mr. England	02	00	05
	Mr. Blackwell	03	00	07
	Mr. Norris	22	04	07
	William Vaughan	02	00	05
	Stephen Lippett	10	02	01
	Arthur Sawyer	04	00	10
		09	03	07

Page 98. The 12th Aprell 1672.

	£	sh.	
ıp Mris. Rogers	80	16	08
Richard Grumnell	40	08	04
Mr. Hollway	55	11	05
Mris. Web	19	03	11
William Harris	25	05	02
Tho: Willis	05	01	00
John Mathews	18	03	09
Henry Green	36	07	06
Widdow Cottrell	06	01	03
John Smith	14	02	11
Widdow Stokes	28	05	10
Mr. Chilton	23	04	09
Widdow Wasborow	26	05	05
Petre Dee	31	06	05
Widdow Parker	20	04	02
Widdow Lot	14	02	11
Widdow Heskins	50	10	05
Mr. Crismus	26	05	05
Avenhouse	16	03	04
Mr. Wasborow	36	07	06
John Smith	02	00	05
Mr. Mats	16	03	04
Richard Spratlin	28	05	10
William Cox	16	03	04
Mr. Dighton	50	10	05
Mris. Rutland	16	03	04
William Adams	10	02	01
John Smith	25	05	02
Widdow Berry	14	02	11
Tho: Herring	11	02	03
Widdow Smith	31	06	05
Sarah Tayler	07	01	05
Widdow Gush	10	02	01
Samuell Robins	08	01	08
John Parra	12	02	06
Gregory Pugh	10	02	01
Widdow Haines	04	00	10
Mris. Smether	35	07	03
James Peacock	7½	01	06
William Peacock	06	01	03
William Thring	07	01	05
Henry Green	01½	00	04
	9	05	08

Page 99.

The accompt of Isaac Rumney one of the Collectors of the poore of the parrish of Westbury-uppon-trim made the 14th day of Aprell 1673:

	£	sh.	d.
This accomptant Chargeth himself wth the rate of two pence half penny a pound wch commeth to..	08	04	07
More he chargeth himself wth money receaved of the ould collectors	00	13	00
the totall is ..	08	17	7

The disburstments as followeth

Imp payd John Hunt 12 moneths at three shillings a moneth	01	16	00
payd Jane Lane 12 moneths at fower shillings a moneth..	02	08	00
payd Margret Wade 12 moneths at two shillings sixpence a moneth..	01	10	00
payd Elizabeth Cook 12 moneths at one shilling a moneth	00	12	00
	06	06	00
geaven to William Cary at sevall times	00	12	00
geaven to John Hunt at sevall times..	00	06	00
geaven to Elizabeth Cook	00	01	00
geaven to Jane Lane	00	01	00
payd for a warrant for Henry King..	00	00	06
spent at five sevll sessions	00	05	00
payd for making the Rate and ingrosing the book.. ..	00	04	00
payd for a warrant and going to Thornbury	00	02	00
	01	11	6
layd out in all	07	17	06

I crave allowance for money that I cannot gather

		s.	d.				
Mr. Meredith	..	5	2	dew to the pish ..	01	00	01
Mr. Sampson	..	2	1				

	£	sh.	d.
Soe it appeareth that there is dew to the parrish..	00	12	10

Page 100.

[he accompt of John Adlam one of the Collectors of the poore of the parrish of Westbury-uppon-trim made the 14th day of Aprell 1673.

:his accomptant Chargeth himself wth the rate of two pence half penny a pound wch commeth to..	09	03	07
nore he chargeth himself wth money that he receaved of the ould Collectors	00	13	00
	09	16	07

The disburstments as followeth

mp payd to John Reynolds 12 moneths at three shillings 6 pence a mo	02	02	00
payd to William Smith 12 moneths at two shillings 6 pence a mon	01	10	00
payd to Mergret Smith 12 moneths at two shillings 6 pence a mon	01	10	00
payd to Susan Smith 12 moneths at two shillings a moneth	01	04	00
geaven to John White at sevll times..	01	01	06
geaven to John Reynolds in his sicknes	00	08	00
geaven to Tho: fishpull in his sicknes	00	07	06
geaven to Robert Haskins in his sicknes	00	02	06
geaven to Joane Griffin	00	02	00
geaven to William Cary at sev times..	00	03	00
payd to the Docter for John White child	00	10	00
spent at five sessions	00	04	06
payd for a lodging warrant for the tithing	00	02	06
geaven to Dorethy Playford	00	00	06
layd out in all ..	09	08	00
Soe it appeareth there is dew to the parrish..	00	08	07

	£	sh.	d.
Receaved	27	19	10
layd out	28	02	06

Passed and approved of by us
John Smyth
Christopher Cole [1]

[1] One of the consenting parties to the sale in 1678 of the next presentation but one) Henbury Vicarage. *See* publication of *Deed, etc.* (Arrowsmith) for present writer.

Page 101.

The accompt of John Smith one of the Collectors of the poore of the parrish of Westbury-uppon-trim made the 14th day of Aprell 1673.

	£	sh.	
This accomptant Chargeth himself wth the rate of two pence half penny a pound wch commeth to..	09	05	08

The disburstments as followeth

	£	sh.	d.
Imp payd to John By 12 moneths at fower shillings a moneth	02	08	00
payd to Tho faux 12 moneths at fower shillings a moneth	02	08	00
payd to Widdow Gunning 12 mo: at fower shillings a moneth	02	08	00
payd Ane Smith one moneth..	00	02	00
payd Ane Smith one moneth..	00	04	00
payd Ane Smith 7 moneths at six shillings a moneth ..	02	02	00
payd Mary Playford 7 moneths at two shillings a moneth	00	14	00
geaven to the poore at sevll times	00	06	00
spent at 5 sessions	00	05	00
layd out in all	10	17	00
soe it appeareth there is dew from the parrish	01	11	4
I crave allowance for money that I did not receave ..	00	00	07
so there is dew	01	11	11

Wee doe nominate and appoint Richard Lane Timothy Hallsey Richard Grumnell to serve the office of Collectors for the poore for the yeare Insuing.

	£	s.	d.
Due to John Smyh on his acco: as above	1	11	11
paid him by Jn Adlam 08s. 07d. .. } paid him by Isaac Rumney 12s. 10d. .. }	1	01	05
Rest due to John Smyth =	0	10	06

Richard Laine
Hen Wasborow
Anthony Hortt
Robert White

Page 102. The 12th of Aprell 1673.

rate made by the Churchwardens and other inhabytants of the prish of Westbury-uppon-trim for and towards the releefe of the poore for this yeare at the rate of two pence half penny a pound as followeth.

		£	sh.	d.
np	Mris. Barker	96	20	00
	Mr. Wasborow	80	16	08
	Mr. Davis	46	09	07
	Mr. Leaman	75	15	07
	Mr. Sampson	90	18	09
	Mris. Walter	12	02	06
	Tho: Wasborow	15	03	01
	William Humphries	11	02	03
	Mris. Rutland	03	00	07
	Mr. Lane	36	07	06
	Obadiah Web	13	02	08
	Mr. Oliff	30	06	03
	Robert Wasborow	09	01	10
	John England	06	01	03
	Mathew Adlam	25	05	02
	John Adlam	07	01	05
	Mris. Avendall	25	05	02
	More for Chock lane house	01	00	02
	Mr. Wasborow	03	00	07
	Robert White	24	05	00
	William Burdges	23	04	09
	Mr. Hort	26	05	05
	Mris. Meredith	18	03	09
	Widdow Atkins	25	05	02
	Tho: Cuff	18	03	09
	Mris. Powell	12	02	06
	Mr. Wells	12	02	06
	Samuell Sanford	10	02	01
	Mr. Hort	08	01	08
	John Chesher	04	00	10
	Mris. Beavan	06	01	03
	Mr. Sampson	12	02	06
	Widdow Adlam	03	00	07
	Samuell Clafell	05	01	00
	Robert Hedges	05	01	00
	Richard Hollbrook	04	00	10
		08	05	07

Page 103. The 12th of Aprell 1673.

		£	sh.	d.
Imp	Sr. Robert Can	109	22	08
	Sr. Robert Yeamans	20	04	02
	Sr. Humphry Hook	70	14	07
	Mr. Crump	35	07	03
	Mr. Sheremon	38	07	11
	Mr. Yates	80	16	08
	Mris. Martin	80	16	08
	Mr. Dymer	60	12	06
	Mris. Joyce Beavan	38	07	11
	Mris. Yeadith Beavan	18	03	09
	Mr. Dimmock	11	02	03
	Mris. Rutland	24	05	05
	Mr. Hart	36	07	06
	Mr. Gleed	66	13	09
	Mr. Tilladam	20	04	02
	Mr. Hurtnoll	08	01	08
	Mr. Hobson	06	01	03
	Mris. Shore	12	02	06
	Mr. Little	10	02	01
	Mris. Husbands	21	04	04
	Mr. Brooks	28	05	10
	Edward Lewes	02	00	05
	Mr. Criswick	09	01	10
	Mr. Hort	17	03	06
	Mris. Avendall	03	00	07
	Mr. Bawldin	08	01	08
	Widdow Wasborow	08	01	08
	Mathew Adlam	03	00	07
	Mr. Blackwell	03	00	07
	John England	02	00	05
	Mr. Norris	22	04	07
	Stephen Lippett	10	02	01
	Arthur Sawyer	04	00	10
	William Vaughan	02	00	05
		09	03	07

Page 104. The 12th of Aprell 1673.

	£	sh.	d.
np Mris. Rogers	80	16	08
Richard Grumnell	40	08	04
Mr. Hollway	55	11	05
Mris. Web	19	03	11
William Harris	25	05	02
John Willis	05	01	00
John Mathews	18	03	09
Henry Green	36	07	06
Widdow Cottrell	06	01	03
John Smith	14	02	11
Widdow Stokes	28	05	10
Mr. Chilton	23	04	09
Charety Wasborow	26	05	05
Petre Dee	31	06	05
John Parra	20	04	02
Widdow Lot	14	02	11
William Heskins	50	10	05
Mr. Crismus	26	05	05
Avenhouse	16	03	04
Mr. Wasborow	36	07	06
John Smith	02	00	05
Mr. Mats	16	03	04
Richard Spratlin	28	05	10
William Cox	16	03	04
Mr. Dighton	50	10	05
Mris. Rutland	16	03	04
Mr. Dighton	10	02	01
John Smith	25	05	02
Widdow Berry	14	02	11
Tho: Herring	11	02	03
Widdow Smith	31	06	05
Sarah Tayler	07	01	05
Widdow Gush	10	02	01
Samuell Robins	08	01	08
Mr. Davis	12	02	06
Gregory Pugh	10	02	01
Widdow Haines	04	00	10
Mris. Smether	35	07	03
James Peacock	7½	01	09
William Peacock	06	01	03
William Thring	07	01	05
Petre Dee	31	06	05
	09	05	08

Page 105.

The accompt of Mr. Richard Lane one of the Collectors of the poore of the parrish of Westbury-uppon-trim made the 21th day of Aprell 1674.

	£	sh.	d.
This accomptant Chargeth himself wth the rate of two pence half penny a pound as followeth	08	05	07

The disburstments

	£	sh.	d.
Imp payd John Hunt 3 moneths at 3s. a moneth	00	09	00
more payd him 10 moneths at 4s. a moneth..	02	00	00
payd Jane Lane 13 moneths at 4s. a moneth	02	12	00
payd Margret Wade 13 moneths at 2s. 6d. a moneth ..	01	12	06
payd Elizabeth Cook 13 moneths at 1s. a moneth	00	13	00
payd for a shirt for William Cary	00	03	02
spent when the Child was brought from meer	00	00	06
spent at the petty sessions	00	01	06
geaven to Mergret Wade at sevll times	00	05	06
geaven to Robert Wade	00	02	00
geaven to John Hunt	00	02	06
spent when the Child was brought from	00	00	00
geaven to Welsh Joane	00	03	00
geaven to Jane Smith	00	03	06
geaven to Jane Lane	00	05	06
geaven to William Cary	00	03	00
geaven to Elizabeth Cook	00	02	06
geaven to 3 Seamen that was cast away	00	01	00
geaven to 2 Seamen that was taken by the dutch	00	01	00
geaven to Robert Haskins	00	02	06
geaven to John young of Cribs	00	01	06
geaven to William Cary at 2 sev times	00	05	00
for carring the book to the Justice and for a warrant ..	00	02	06
Payd out ..	09	12	08
I crave allowance for Mr. meredith		03	09
for Mr Jno Sampson		02	01
	9	18	06

due from the parrish to Mr. Lane .. £1 12sh. 11d.

Page 106.

he accompt of Timothy Hallsey one of the Collectors of the poore of the parrish of Westbury-uppon-trim made the 21th day of Aprell 1674.

	£	s.	d.
his accomptant Chargeth himself with the rate of two pence half penny a pound wch commeth to	09	03	07
The distburstments as followeth			
mp payd William Smith 13 moneths at 2s. 6d. a moneth ..	01	12	06
payd Mergret Smith 13 moneths at 2s. 6d. a moneth ..	01	12	06
payd Susan Smith 13 moneths at 2s. 0d. a moneth ..	01	06	00
payd John Reynolds 13 moneths at 3s. 6d. a moneth ..	02	05	06
geaven to Robert Haskins at sevll times	00	05	00
geaven to John White at sevll times	00	10	00
geaven to Elnor Stibbs at sevll times	00	10	00
geaven to William Smith	00	01	00
geaven to Margret Smith	00	01	00
geaven to John Reynolds	00	05	00
payd for signing the rates and charges at the petty sessions and exspences when the child was brought by an order from Meer to our parrish	00	08	11
payd for making the rates and ingrosing the book	00	04	00
	09	01	05

dew from Tymothy halsey to the parrish 2/6.
which is paid to thomas hopkins.

Page 107.

The accompt of Richard Grumnell one of the Collectors of the poore of the parrish of Westbury-uppon-trim made the 21th day of Aprell 1674.

	£	sh.	d.
This accomptant Chargeth himself wth the rate of two pence half penny a pound wch commeth to	09	05	08
The disburstments as followeth			
Imp payd Tho: faux 13 moneths at 4s. a moneth	02	12	00
payd to John By 13 moneths at 4s. a moneth	02	12	00
payd to Ane Smith 9 moneths at 6s. a moneth	02	14	00
payd to Mary Playford 3 moneths at 2s. a moneth ..	00	06	00
payd to her 8 moneths at 2s. 6d. a month	01	00	00
payd to her 2 moneths at 3s. a month	00	06	00
payd one moneth to the Widdow Gunning..	00	04	00
payd for the buring of her	00	11	00
payd to the surgeon and her diett and lodging for Martha Hicks	01	17	00
payd for bread and drinck for the buring of Ane Jones child	00	04	00
payd at the petty sessions and for exspenses going to the Justice 7 times uppon complaints	00	00	00
..	12	06	00

due to Richard Gromnell £3 00sh. 04d.
Wee doe nominate and appoint John Keene Thomas Richardson Henry Weaver to bee overseers of the poore for the yeare Insuing

	£	sh.	d.
our receipts	26	14	10
disburstments	31	00	01

John Meredith
Christopher Cole

pd Ricd Grumnell by his church pay for Robert Smyth	00	08	04
pd him by ditto Smyth the Balance of hiss acco	00	09	00
pd him by And house	00	11	06
pd him by Ricd Davis	00	11	06
	2	00	04
allowed him for paym 1674 for church exspence[1]	1	00	00
	3	00	04

[1] How intimately the church was bound up with the ordinary parochial life will appear from this entry. "Church expenses defrayed out of the Poor Rate" marks how very far we have travelled from those days.

Page 108. The 12th of Aprell 1674.

A rate by the Churchwardens and other inhabitants of the parrish of Westbury-uppon-trim for and towards the releef of the poore for this yeare at the rate of two pence a pound and another rate of three pence a pound as followeth:

		£	sh.	d.
mp	Mris. Barker	96	40	00
	Mris. Wasborow	80	33	04
	Mr. Davis	46	19	02
	the farme of Westbury [1]	50	20	10
	Mr. Leaman	25	10	05
	Mr. Sampson	80	33	04
	Mris. Walter	12	05	00
	Tho Wasborow	15	06	03
	William Humphries	11	04	07
	Mris. Rutland	03	01	03
	Mr. Lane	53	22	01
	obadiah Web	13	05	05
	Mr. oliff	30	12	06
	Robert Wasborow	09	03	09
	John England	06	02	06
	Mathew Adlam	24	10	00
	John.Adlam	07	02	11
	Mris. Avendall	25	10	10
	more for Chok lane	01	00	00
	Mr. Wasborow	03	01	03
	Robert White	24	10	00
	Mr. Burdges	30	12	06
	Mr. Hort	26	10	10
	Mr. Prise	18	07	06
	Tho. Cuff	18	07	06
	for the mill ground	01	00	05
	Mr. Williams	12	05	00
	Mr. Wells	12	05	00
	Samuell Sanford	10	04	02
	Mr. hort	08	03	04
	Mris. Beavan	06	02	06
	Mr. Sampson	12	05	00
	John Chessher	04	01	08
	Widdow Adlam	03	01	03
	Samuel Clafell	05	02	01
	Robert hedges	05	02	01
	Richard shollbrook	04	08	08

£16 6s. 11d.

[1] Part of the possession of Westbury College, and in possession of John Hobhouse (see *Eccles. Hist. of Westbury*, p. 24).

Page 109. The 12th of Aprell 1674.

	£	sh.	d.
Imp Sr. Robert Can..	110	45	10
Sr. Robert Yeomans	20	08	04
Sr. Humphry Hook	70	29	04
Mr. Crump	35	14	07
Mr. Sheremon	38	15	10
Mr. Yates	80	33	04
Mris. Martin	80	33	04
Mr. Dymer	60	25	00
Mris. Joyce Beavan	38	15	10
Mris. Yeadith Beavan	18	07	06
Allderman Blackwell	04	01	08
Mathew Dimmock	11	04	07
Mris. Rutland	22	09	?
Mr. Hart	36	15	00
Mr. Gleed	66	27	06
Mr. Tilladam	20	08	04
Mr. Hartnoll..	08	03	04
Mr. Lewis	06	02	06
Mris. Shore	12	05	00
Mr. Little	10	04	02
Mris. Husbands	21	08	09
Mr. Brooks	28	11	08
Edward Lewes	02	00	10
Mr. Criswick	09	03	09
Mr. Hort	17	07	01
Mris. Avendall	03	01	03
Mr. Bawldin	08	03	04
Widdow Wasborrow	08	03	04
Mathew Adlam	03	01	03
Mr. Norris	22	09	02
Stephen Lippet	10	04	02
Arthur Sawyer	04	01	08
William Vaughan	02	00	10
	18	07	02

Page 110. The 16th of Aprell 1674.

		£	s.	d.
1p	Mris. Rogers	76	31	08
	Richard Grumnell	40	18	08
	Mr. Hollway	40	16	08
	Mris. Web	19	07	11
	William Harris	25	09	0?
	John Willis		?	
20	John Mathews		?	
	Henry Green	42½	17	08
12	John Smith	12	05	10
	Widdow Stokes	28	11	08
	Wirkhouse	15	06	03
	Mr. Edwards	16	06	08
	Widdow Wasborow	26	10	10
	John Barra	20	08	04
43	Petre Dee	43	18	01
	Richard Drichell	58	03	04
	Widdow Lott	14	05	10
	William heskins	54	22	06
	Mr. Crismus	28	11	08
	Avenhouse	16	06	08
	Mr. Wasborow	36	15	00
	Mr. Everat	02	00	09
	John heskins	28	11	08
	William Cox	16	06	08
	Mrs. Dighton	50	20	10
	John Smith	25	10	00
	Widdow Berry	12	05	00
	Tho. herring	11	04	07
	Widdow Smith	31	12	06
	Widdow Jackson	07	02	11
	Widdow Gush	10	04	02
	Samuell Robins	08	03	04
	Mr. Davis	12	05	00
	Mr. Pugh	10	04	02
	Widdow haines	04	01	08
	Mris. Smether	28	11	08
16	James Peacock	16	06	08
	William Peacock	16	02	06
	Mris. Rutland	16	06	08
	Mris. Smether for Clements house	07	02	11
	Mris. Dighton for the Inn	10	04	02

Page 111.

The accompt of John Keene one of the Collectors of the poore of the parrish of Westbury-uppon-trim made the 16th of Aprell 1675.

	£	s.	d.
This accomptant Chargeth himself wth 2 rates one of two pence a pound and the other of three pence a pound wch commeth to	16	06	11

The disburstments as followeth	£	s.	d.
Imp payd to John hunt 4 months at 4s.	00	16	00
more geven to him in his sicknes	00	06	00
payd to Mergret wade 14 moneth at 2s. 6d...	01	15	00
payd to Jane Lane 14 moneths at 5s.	03	10	00
payd to Elizabeth Cook 14 moneths at 1s. 6d.	01	01	00
payd to William Cary 4 moneths at 2s.	00	08	00
payd to William young the whole yeare	04	01	06
the charg about William Cary going sev times to the Justices at Mangersfeild and at Lawfords Gate and to the Justices heer and for hier of horses and for carring of witness and for a surgeon to search his leg	01	11	09
geaven to William Smith in his sicknes	00	10	00
geaven to Susan Smith in her sicknes	00	03	00
geaven to Sarah prenett in her childrens sicknes	00	05	00
geaven to poore people sev times wth Certificats	00	02	00
spent when wee went to Kingsland wth a warrant of disturbances to goe out of the parrish	00	00	06
payd to Mr. Davis money that was dew from the pish ..	00	07	08
payd to Mr. hort money that was dew from the pish ..	00	05	04
payd to Mr. Lane money that was dew from the pish ..	01	02	01
payd for a warrant for Mr. Kingsland	00	01	00
	16	05	10
due from the collector on his acco		01	01
	16	06	11

Richard Lanye.

Page 112.

he accompt of Mr. Thomas Richeson one of the Collectors of the poore of the parrish of Westbury-uppon-trim made the 16th of Aprell 1675.

iis accomptant Chargeth himself wth 2 rates one of two pence a pound and the other of three pence a pound wch commeth to	18	07	02

The disburstments as followeth

ıp payd to John Raynolds 14 moneths at 3s. 6d.	02	09	00
payd to Robert haskins 8 moneths at 2s.	00	16	00
more payd him 5 moneths at 4s.	01	00	00
payd to Kathern Smith 9 moneths at 2s. 6d.	01	2	06
payd her 5 moneths at 4s.	01	00	00
payd to Susan Smith 14 moneths at 2s.	01	08	00
payd to Mergret Smith 9 moneths at 2s. 6d.	01	02	06
payd to William Cary 2 moneths at 8s.	00	16	00
payd to him 7 moneths at 6s.	02	02	00
payd to him 2 weeks	00	03	00
payd to the surgeon for him	01	10	00
geaven to William Cary in his lamenes	00	12	00
geaven to John White..	00	13	00
geaven to John Reynolds	00	05	00
geaven to Elnor Stibbs	00	05	00
geaven to Margret Smith	00	02	06
geaven to Kathern Smith	00	01	00
payd the Cleark for going wth Smiths boy to bristoll 5 sevll times	00	05	00
geaven to Jane Wade sevll times	00	06	00
payd for a shroud and buring of Margret Smith	00	08	06
geaven to Robert haskins	00	03	00
spent when we went to the Justice 2 sevll times about William Cary	00	01	06
spent when I receaved the poors money	00	00	06
payd for carring away Cripples in Westbury and Stoke ..	00	08	00
geaven to Jane Smith	00	01	00
geaven to poore people wth Certificats and passes.. ..	00	06	00
Spent when we went to warne Allexander Kingsland wth a warrant of disturbance	00	00	06
geaven to Elizabeth Cook	00	01	06
pay for haling of William Cary from pitch and pay ..	00	01	06
payd for making the rates and ingrosing the book ..	00	04	00
payd to William Cary 2 weeks	00	03	00
payd for a payer of Stockings and shoos for Smiths boy ..	00	04	04
	18	01	10

due from the collector 5sh. 4d.

Page 113.

The accompt of Henry Weaver one of the Collectors of the poore of the parrish of Westbury-uppon-trim made the 16 Day of Aprell 1675.

This accomptant Chargeth himself wth 2 rates one of two pence a pound and the other of three penc a pound wch commeth to	18	12	06
The disburstments as followeth	£	s.	d.
Imp payd to the poore 10 monts at 11s. a moneth	05	10	00
payd to the poore 4 moneths at 12s. a moneth	02	08	00
payd towards the Auditt	00	10	00
geaven to John Calee in his sicknes..	00	04	00
geaven to poore people wth Certificates	00	03	07
payd for Joane Waters rent..	00	06	00
	09	01	7
I crave allowance for money that I cannot			
gather Richard Grumnell	01	00	00
Widdow Berry	00	00	10
	10	02	05
due from the Collector on this acco	8	10	01
	18	12	06

Richard Davye
Thomas hort
Thomas Cuffe
John Smyth
Henry Greene

William Arnall } Church
John Smith } wardens

our receipts is ..	53	04	06
our disburstments is	45	09	03
left in stock ..	07	15	03

We doe nominate and appoint John Andrews John Barratt and William hiskins to serve the office of overseers of the poore for the yeare ensuing

Go Stephens
John Meredith
Christopher Cole.

Page 114. The 12th of Aprell 1675.

A rate made by the Churchwardens and other inhabytants of the parrish of Westbury-uppon-trim for and towards the releef of the poore for this yeare at the rate of fower pence a pound as followeth :—

	£	s.	d.
Mris. Barker	96	32	00
Mris. Wasborow	80	26	08
Mr. Davis	46	15	04
the farm of Westbury	45	15	00
Mr. Leaman	25	08	04
Mr. Sampson	80	26	08
Mr. Lane	55	18	04
Mr. Prise	31	10	04
Mris. Walter	12	04	00
Tho: Wasborow	15	05	00
William Humphries	11	03	08
Mris. Rutland	03	01	00
Obadiah Web	14	04	08
Mr. Oliff	30	10	00
Robert Wasborow	09	03	00
John England	06	02	00
Mathew Adlam	24	08	00
John Adlam	04	01	04
Mris. Avendall	26	08	08
Mr. Wasborow	03	01	00
William White	24	08	00
Mr. Burdges	30	10	00
Mris. Hort	26	08	08
Tho. Cuff	19	06	04
Mr. Williams	12	04	00
Samuell Sanford	12	04	00
Samuell Sanford for the Inn	10	03	04
Mr. Hort	08	02	08
Mris. Beavan	06	02	00
Mr. Sampson	12	04	00
John Chessher	04	01	04
Widow Adlam	03	01	00
Samuell Clafell	04	01	04
Richard Hollbrook	04	01	04
Robert Hedges	01	00	04
	13	03	04

Page 115. The 12th of Aprell 1675.

	£		
Sr. Robert Can..	110	36	08
Sr. Robert Yeomans	20	06	08
Sr. Humphry Hook	56	18	08
more for the Sea Mills	14	04	08
Mr. Crump	35	11	08
Mr. Sheremon	38	12	08
Mr. Jackson	80	26	08
Mr. Gleed	66	22	00
Mris. Martin	80	26	08
Mris. Dymer	60	20	00
Mris. Joyce Beavan	38	12	08
Mris. yeadith Beavan	18	06	00
Alderman Blackwell	04	01	04
Mathew Dymmock	11	03	08
Mris. Rutland	22	07	04
Mr. Hart	36	12	00
Mr. Tilladam	20	06	08
Mr. Hurtnoll	08	02	08
Mr. Lewes	06	02	00
Mris. Shore	12	04	00
Mr. Little	10	03	04
Mris. Husbands	21	07	00
Mr. Brooks	28	09	04
Edward Lewes	02	00	08
Mr. Criswick	09	03	00
Mr. Hort	17	05	08
Mris. Avendall	03	01	00
Mr. Bawldwin	08	02	08
Widdow Wasborow	08	02	08
Mathew Adlam	03	01	06
Mr. Norris	22	07	04
John Hurn	10	03	04
Arthur Sawyer	04	01	04
Samuell Sanford	02	00	08
John Barratt	02	00	08
William Vaughan	01	00	04
	14	14	08

Page 116. The 12th of Aprell 1675.

		£	s.	d.
	Mris. Rogers	76	15	04
	Richard Grumnell	40	13	04
	Mr. Hollway	40	13	04
	Mris. Web	19	06	04
	William Harris	25	08	04
	John Willis	05	01	08
	John Mathews	20	06	08
	Henry Green	42†	14	02
	John Smith	12	04	00
	Widdow Stokes	28	09	04
	Wirkhouse	15	05	00
	Mr. Edwards	16	05	04
	Widdow Wasborow	26	08	08
	John Barra	20	06	08
	Petre Dee	43	14	04
	Richard Pritchitt	08	02	08
	Widdow Lot	14	04	08
	William Heskins	54	18	00
	Mr. Crismus	28	09	04
	Avenhouse	16	05	04
	Mr. Wasborow	36	12	00
	Mr. Everat	02	00	08
	John Heskins	28	09	04
	William Cox	16	05	04
	Mris. Dighton	50	16	08
	John Smith	25	08	04
	Widdow Berry	12	04	00
	Tho: Herring	11	03	08
	Widdow Smith	31	10	04
	Widdow Jackson	07	02	04
	Widdow Gush	10	03	04
	Samuell Robins	08	02	08
	Mr. Davis	12	04	02
	Mr. Bush	10	03	04
	Widdow Haines	04	01	04
	Mris. Smether	28	09	04
14	James Peacock	16	05	04
	William Peacock	06†	02	02
	Mris. Rutland	16	05	04
	Mris. Smether for Clements house	07	02	04
	Mris. Dighton for the Inn	10	03	04
		14	17	10

Page 117.

The accompt of John Andrews one of the Collectors of the poore of the parrish of Westbury-uppon-trim made the 7th of Aprell 1676.

This accomptant Chargeth himself wth two rates one three pence a pound and the other of a penny a pound wch commeth to	13	03	04
The disburstments as followeth			
Imp payd William Cary 12 moneths at 6d. a moneth	03	12	00
payd Jane Lane 12 moneths at 6d. a moneth	03	12	00
payd Susan Smith 12 moneths at 2s. 6d. a moneth.. ..	01	10	00
payd Elizabeth Cook 12 moneths at 2s. 6d. a moneth ..	01	10	00
payd towards the placing of Georg Wade	00	13	08
payd for a warrant of disturbance and exspences for John hunt	00	01	06
spent when the feafees mett..	00	01	00
geaven to Mary Cotten in her lamenes	00	05	00
spent at Cribbs when we went to disturb the woem ..	00	01	00
payd to John Jefferies for keeping of Nathanell Jones ..	00	10	00
payd for a payer of shoos for him and mending a payer..	00	03	06
geaven to poore people wth passes and Certificates ..	00	06	06
payd to Mr. Lane money that was dew to him	00	04	08
spent at two petty sessions..	00	02	00
geaven to Katherne Boure at sevll times..	00	03	00
geaven to Dorethy Wade towards the keeping the child..	00	05	06
spent when the rates weer made	00	02	00
payd for keeping of wades children 3 weeks	00	09	00
geaven to Jane Wade at sevll times..	00	04	00
payd for keeping them one week 3s. more..	00	03	00
	13	19	4

Due to John Andrews on this accompt now made up = 16s. 00d.

	£	s.	d.
receaved of a drover driving uppon the sabboth day[1]	1	0	0
due to the Seasor ..	0	6	8
there remaineth due ..	0	13	4

now this 13s. and 4d. is payd to the new collectors for to buy Clothes for Jones boy.

[1] *See* Introduction.

Page 118. Barwick.

he accompt of John Barratt one of the Collectors of the poore of the parrish of Westbury made the 7th of Aprell 1676.

	£	s.	d.
his accomptant Chargeth himself wth 2 rates one of three pence a pound and the other a penny a pound wch commeth to	14	14	08
The disburstments as followeth			
np payd to John Raynolds 12 months at 4s. a month.. ..	02	08	00
payd to Margrett wade 4 months 2s. 6d. a moneth.. ..	00	10	00
payd to William Smith 3 moneths 4s. od. a moneth ..	00	12	00
payd to William Smith 3 moneths 6s. od. a moneth ..	00	18	00
payd to Margret haskins 4 moneths 6s. od. a moneth ..	01	04	00
payd to Nicholas Smith 5 moneths 8s. od. a moneth ..	02	00	00
payd to Austin homes 3 moneths 6s. 8d. a moneth ..	01	00	00
payd for buring of Robert haskins..	00	15	03
payd for buring of Kathern Smith..	00	15	00
payd for Carring away Cripples	00	06	00
geaven to John White	00	04	00
geaven to Margret wade	00	04	06
geaven to Nicholas Smith at sevll times	00	06	00
spent at two petty sessions	00	02	00
payd for two warrants	00	02	00
payd for a warrant to take disstres	00	02	06
payd to John White	00	06	06
geaven to John Raynolds	00	03	06
payd to the Docter for Robert Haskins	00	03	06
geaven to Nicholas Smith	00	02	06
payd for making the rates and ingrosing the book.. ..	00	04	00
payd for carring in the book and for a warrant	00	03	00
geaven to Joane Griffin at sevll times	00	03	00
geaven to John White another time..	00	04	00
geaven to William Smith	00	02	06
Elnor Stibbs geaven to her	00	05	00
	13	06	09
Due from John Barratt on this accompt	1	07	11
	14	14	08

ɔw this £1 7s. 11d. was paid to the new Churchwardens and Collectors.

Page 119.

The accompt of William heskins one of the Collectors of the poore of the parrish of Westbury made the 7th of Aprell 1676.

This accomptant Chargeth himself wth 2 rates one of three pen̄ a pound and the other a penny a pound wch commeth to..	14	18	04
payd for the buring of John Williams	00	03	00
geaven to Mary Major and for the haling of her away ..	00	10	00
payd for 3 moneths for keeping John fishpools boy ..	00	18	00
payd to Tho: faux 12 months at 4s. a moneth	02	08	00
payd to Mary Playford 12 months at 4s. a moneth ..	02	08	00
payd to John By 12 months at 4s. a moneth	02	08	00
payd for John Majors house Roome..	00	02	06
geaven to a poore body	00	00	06
geaven to Tho: faux	00	02	00
geaven to John By	00	02	00
geaven to Mary Playford	00	02	00
geaven to John Calee..	00	02	06

These accompts seen and allowed by we whose names are heareunder written (vizt) John Andrews John Barwick Syngeing Accts ?

owing to William heskins ..	05	11	10

now this £5 11s. 10d. was paid to the new Churchwardens and Collectors

Richard Davye — Richard Grumnell, William Arnall } Church wardens
Samuell price
Wathen Adlam
William White
John Adlam

	£	s.	d.
our receits is	42	16	4
our disburstments ..	36	02	07
left in stock .. .. for the new collectors..	06	13	09
and	00	06	00
the whole is ..	06	19	09

We doe nominate and appoint Samuell Prise fraunces Gleed and Richard Jayne to be overseers of the poore for this yeare ensuing.

Page 120. Of William Arnoll and John Barwick.

	£	s.	d.
.n accompt of the Irish goods being distributed the 16 day of November 1675	14	13	04
:mp Jane Lane	00	10	06
Elizabeth Cook	00	08	06
John Raynold	00	10	06
Robert Wade	00	14	00
John White	00	09	00
Susan Smith	00	06	00
William Smith Senor	00	08	00
Mergret Wade	00	08	06
Mergret hobs	00	04	06
Jane Jefferies	00	06	06
William Smith Junor	00	07	06
Joane Griffin	00	08	06
Tho: Prewett	00	05	06
William Cary	00	07	06
Margret haskins	00	06	06
Dorothy Playford	00	08	00
Alce Radman	00	06	00
Ann hawkins	00	06	00
Kathern Boure..	00	06	00
Sarah Pullin	00	06	06
Widdow hunt	00	05	06
Edward Boure	00	02	06
Rummes boy	00	10	00
Nicholas hatter	00	10	00
Tho. fishpull	00	08	06
William Coats	00	08	06
Tho. Wade	00	12	00
Tho. Lippett	00	06	06
Joyce hatter	00	05	06
Jeorum Cuff	00	10	00
Richard Pamer	00	06	06
Elnor Stibbs	00	06	06
William Griffin..	00	06	00
for exspences	00	08	00
	13	00	00

here remaineth dew £1 13s. 04d.

Page 121. Of William Arnoll and John Barwick.

	£	s.	d.
An accompt of the Irish goods being distributed the 17th of September 1675	07	00	00
Imp Jane Lane	00	14	00
Elizabeth Cook	00	05	06
John Raynolds	00	06	00
Robert Wade	00	12	06
Mergret Smith	00	06	06
John White	00	05	00
Mary Cotten	00	04	06
Susan Smith	00	04	06
William Smith senor	00	09	00
Mergret Wade	00	07	00
Mergret hobs	00	02	00
Jane Jefferies	00	05	00
William Smith Junor	00	07	00
Welsh Joane	00	04	00
Sarah Prewett	00	05	06
William Cary	00	05	06
Margrett haskins	00	03	06
Dorothy Playford	00	03	06
Alce Radman	00	05	00
Ann hawkins	00	03	06
Kathern Boure	00	03	00
Sarah Pullin	00	04	06
Widdow Willis	00	06	00
Widdow hunt	00	03	00
Tho: fishpull	00	01	06
	06	17	00
There remaineth dew	00	03	00

now this £1 16s. 4d. is payd towards the keeping of 2 poor Children and for Clothes for them.

Page 122. Of Richard Grumnell and William heskins.

	£	s.	d.
ı accompt of the Irish goods being distributed the 27 day of October 1675	07	18	00
Widdow Reed	00	06	00
Richard Parker	00	11	00
Widdow Parker	00	06	00
John Calee	00	15	00
Widow Baker	00	12	00
Joane Williams	00	07	06
Mary Playford	00	08	00
John By	00	10	00
Widdow Jones	00	09	00
Tho: faux	00	10	00
Henry fishpools	00	05	06
Widdow Reed	00	02	06
Richard Parker	00	05	00
Widdow Parker	00	02	06
John Calee	00	07	00
Widdow Baker	00	07	00
Widdow Williams	00	03	00
Mary playfoord	00	04	00
John By	00	07	00
Tho: faux	00	07	00
Widdow Jones	00	03	00
	07	08	00

ere remaineth dew 10s.

Richard Davye
Samuell Price
Mathew Adlam
John Adlam
William Stephens

ristopher Cole.

Page 123. The 12th of Aprell 1676.

A rate made by the Churchwardens and other inhabytants of the parrish of Westbury-uppon-trim for and towards the releef of the poore for this yeare at the rate of fower pence a pound.

		£	s.	d.
Imp	Mris. Barker	90	30	00
	Mris. Wasborow	80	26	08
	Mr. Davis	46	15	04
	Mr. Geering	60	20	00
	Mr. Leaman	06	02	00
	Mr. Sampson	80	26	08
	Mr. Lane	66	22	00
	Mr. Prise	42	14	00
	Mris. Walter	12	04	00
	Tho. Wasborow	15	05	00
	Mris. Rutland	03	01	00
	obadiah Web	14	04	08
	Mr. Oliff	30	10	00
	Robert Wasborow	09	03	00
	Tho. Prise	06	02	00
	Mathew Adlam	24	08	00
	John Adlam	04	01	04
	Mris. Avendall	06	08	08
	More for Chock lane	01	00	04
	Mr. Wasborow	03	01	00
	William White	24	08	00
	Mris. Burdges	30	10	00
	Mris. Hort	26	08	08
	Tho. Cuff	08	02	08
	Mr. Williams	12	04	00
	Samuell Sanford	12	04	00
	Samuell Sanford for the Inn	10	03	04
	Mr. Hort	08	02	08
	Mris. Beavan	06	02	00
	Mr. Sampson	12	04	00
	John Chessher	04	01	04
	Widdow Adlam	03	01	00
	Samuell Clafell	04	01	04
	Mr. Nicholas	04	01	04
	Mr. Lane [1] for the Colledge	03	01	00
	Mris. Avendall for Cooks house	01	00	04
	Robert Hedges	07	02	04

[1] See *Eccles. Hist. of Westbury*, pp. 17–33.

Page 124. The 12th of Aprell 1676.

		£
ıp	Sr. Robert Can	110
	Sr. Robert yeomans	20
	Sr. Humphry Hook	70
	Mr. Crump	35
	Mr. Sheremon	38
	Mr. Jackson	80
	Mris. Martin	80
	Mr. Gleed	66
	Mris. Dymer	60
	Mris. Joyce Beavan	38
	Mris. yeadith Beavan	18
	Mris. Blackwell	05
	Mathew Dimmock	11
	Mris. Rutland	22
	Mrs. Hart	36
	Mr. Tilladam	20
	Mr. Hurtnoll	08
	Mr. Lewis	06
	Mris. Shore	12
	Mr. Little	10
	Mris. Husbands	21
	Mr. Brooks	28
	Edward Lewes	02
	Mr. Criswick	09
	Mr. Hort	17
	Mris. Avendall	03
	Mr. Bawldin	08
	Widdow Wasborow	08
	Mathew Adlam	03
	Mr. Norris	22
	John Hurn	10
	Arthur Sawer	04
	Samuell Sanford	02
	John Barwick	02
	William Vaughan	01

NOTE.—The numbers of the pages of this register are in a later handwriting: page 124 followed by 126, but no leaf has been torn out; it is the mistake of the enumerator.

Page 126. Aprell the 12th 1676.

	£		
Imp Mris. Rogers	76	25	04
Richard Grumnell	40	13	04
Mr. hollway	40	13	04
Mris. Web	19	06	04
William harris	25	08	04
John Willis	05	01	08
John Mathews	20	06	08
Henry Green	$42\frac{2}{1}$	14	02
John Smith	12	04	00
Arthur White and William White	28	09	04
Wirkhouse	15	05	00
Mr. Edwards	16	05	04
Widdow Wasborow	26	08	08
John Barra	20	06	08
Petre Dee	43	14	04
Richard Pritchett	08	02	08
Widdow Lott	14	04	08
William heskins	54	18	00
Mr. Crismus	28	09	04
Avenhouse	16	05	04
Mr. Wasborow and his teanaunt	36	12	00
Mr. Everatt	02	00	08
John heskins	28	09	04
William Cox	16	05	04
Mris. Dighton	50	16	08
John Smith	25	08	04
Widdow Berry	12	04	00
Tho. herring	11	03	08
Widdow Smith	31	10	04
Widdow Jackson	07	02	04
Widdow Gush	10	03	04
Samuell Robins	08	02	08
Mr. Davis	$12\frac{2}{1}$	04	02
Mr. Bush	10	03	04
Widdow haines	04	01	04
Mris. Smether	35	11	08
James Peacock	14	04	08
William Peacock	$06\frac{2}{1}$	02	02
Mris. Rutland	16	05	04
Mris. Dighton for the Inn	10	03	04

Page 127. The 26th day of Aprell, 1677.

he accompt of Mr. Samuell Prise one of the Collectors of the parrish of Westbury-uppon-trim made.

	£	s.	d.
his accomptant Chargeth himself wth a rate of fower pence a pound wch commeth to	13	03	04
the distburstments as followeth			
np payd to William Cary 10 moneths at 6s. a moneth ..	03	00	00
payd to Jane Lane 14 moneths at 6s. a moneth	04	04	00
payd to Susan Smith 13 moneths at 2s. 6d. a moneth ..	01	12	06
payd to her one moneth	00	04	06
payd to Elizabeth Cook 14 moneths at 2s. 6d. a moneth ..	01	15	00
geaven to William Smith in his daughters sicknes	00	04	00
payd for going wth Isack Rumny to the free schoole ..	00	01	00
payd for a shroud and for buring of William Smith daughter	00	08	00
payd to Mr. Bradway for comming over to bury her ..	00	01	06
payd for going to the Churchward and Collectors to meet	00	01	06
payd for keeping Tho: wades Children 15 weeks	02	12	06
payd for keeping of wades child 2 weeks	00	04	00
payd for going to the Justice wth the book and rates 3 times	00	02	00
payd for making the Indentures for Tho Marsh	00	02	06
payd for bringing away William Jones prentice wth an order from the Justices and for exspences	00	02	06
geaven to Kathern Bour in her sickness and washing her cloths	00	04	06
geaven to ould Smith in the whole year	01	02	00
payd for keeping of wades child one week	00	01	06
payd for keeping of wades child one week	00	02	00
geaven to Susan Smith in her sicknes	00	03	08
geaven to Dorethy Wade	00	02	00
payd for bringing a letter from Mr. Leg of Sadbury ..	00	00	06
payd for making the rates and ingrosing the book	00	04	00
geaven to Kathern Boure	00	02	06
paid for a warrant for the new Collectors	00	01	06
disbosments ..	16	19	08
dew from the parrish ..	3	16	04

Page 128. Barwick.

The accompt of John Barnick one of the Collectors of the poore of the prish of Westbury-uppon-trim made the 26 day of Aprell 1677.

	£	s.	d.
This accomptant Chargeth himself wth the rate of fower pence a pound wch commeth to	14	15	00
the disburstments as followeth			
Imp payd to John Raynolds 14 moneths at 4s. a moneth ..	02	16	00
paid to Nicholas hatter 15 moneths 8s. a moneth	06	00	00
paid to Austin homes 15 moneths 6s. 8d. a moneth ..	05	00	00
paid to William Cary 4 moneths 6s. a moneth	01	04	00
paid to Majors wife 8 moneths 4s. a moneth	01	12	00
geaven to John White at sevll times	00	04	00
geaven to Jeorun Cuff at sevll times	00	04	00
geaven to Nicholas hatter at sevll times	00	03	00
geaven unto 2 poore men	00	01	00
paid for three warrants	00	02	00
paid for Cloths for Jones boy	00	17	08
paid for a Tithing bill	00	03	00
paid for John Raynolds rent	00	06	08
paid for bred for yeadith Boure	00	02	06
geaven to John Raynolds at sev times	00	04	00
geaven to John Raynolds to boy 2 shourtes	00	06	00
geaven to Elizabeth Cox for a roome	00	02	00
disbosments ..	19	07	10
dew from the parrish ..	4	12	10

Page 129.

[The accompt of Richard Jeyne one of the Collectors of the poore of the parrish of Westbury-uppon-trim made the 26 day of Aprell 1677.

	£	s.	d.
[This accomptant Chargeth himself wth a rate of fower pence a pound wch commeth	14	17	10
mp paid to Tho: faux 14 moneths at 4s. a moneth	02	16	00
paid to John By 14 moneths at 4s. a moneth	02	16	00
paid to Mary playford 14 moneths 4s. a moneth	02	16	00
paid to John Calee 14 moneths 1s. 6d. a moneth	01	01	06
paid to Henry fishpoole for 6 moneths pay	01	19	00
paid to Ann Morse 5 moneths at 6s. a moneth	01	10	00
paid to Hannah Roberts 5 moneths 6s. 8d. a moneth ..	01	13	04
paid to Hannah Roberts one week	00	01	04
paid for a warrant of disturbance for Will hart	00	01	00
geaven to Mary Playford at sevll times	00	06	00
geaven to a poore woeman 3 and child with a pas	00	02	00
geaven to 2 poore men wth a pas	00	00	06
spent at monthly meetings and at sessions	00	00	00
paid for the curing of Morris Playford Child	00	10	00
disbosments.. ..	15	12	08

[T]hose accompts examined and allowed by
[w]e whose names are heare under subscribed

dew from the parrish ..	00	14	10

Samuell Sandford } Churchwardens.
William heskins }
Thomas Geering
Thomas Cuff
Henry Greene
William harris

	£	s.	d.
our receipts	42	15	10
the disburstments ..	52	00	02

[W]e doe nominate and appoint to serve the
[o]ffice of overseers for the yeare ensuing
William White
Tho Hopkins for Sr. Robert Can
William Davis.

Page 130. 1677.

Those Remaines in Stooccbo for the use of the poore one accounte of the Eorrishe goods as ffoloweth viz. :—

	£	s.	d.
By moneyes one band ? to Mr. burrit	50	00	00
By moneys to Richard Jayne	10	00	00
By moneys to John hiskings	06	00	00
	66	00	00

Passed by us
John Meredith
Christopher Cole

Page 131. The 10th of Aprell 1677.

A rate made by the Churchwardens and other the inhabytants of the parrish of Westbury-uppon-trim for and towards the releef of the poore for this yeare at the rate of sixpence a pound.

	£	s.	d.
mp Mr. John Knight	90	45	00
Mr. John Lam	80	40	00
Mr. Davis	46	23	00
Mr. Geering	60	30	00
Mr. Leaman	16	08	00
Mr. Sampson	84	40	00
Mr. Lane	66	33	00
Mr. Prise	42	21	00
Mris. Walter	12	06	00
Tho Wasborow	15	07	06
Mris. Rutland	03	01	06
Obadiah Web	14	07	00
Mr. oliff	30	15	00
Joane Wasborow widdow	09	04	06
Mr. Prise	06	03	00
Mathew Adlam	24	12	00
Mris. Avendall	26	13	00
more for Cook and Jones	02	01	00
Mr. Wasborow	03	01	06
William White	24	12	00
Mris. Burdges	30	15	00
Mris. hort	26	13	00
Tho Cuff	08	04	00
Mr. Williams	12	06	00
Samuell Sanford	12	06	00
Mr. hort	08	04	00
Mris. Beavan	06	03	00
Mr. Sampson	12	06	00
John Chessher	04	02	00
John Adlam	04	02	00
Samuell Clafell	04	02	00
Samuell Nicholas	04	02	00
Mr. Lane for the Colledg	03	01	06
Robert hedges	07	03	06
Widdow Adlam	00	01?	06

£3 16s. 6d.

Page 132. The 10th of Aprell 1677.

		£	s.	d.
Imp	Sr. Robert Can	109	54	06
	Sr. Robert Yeomans	20	10	00
	Sr. Humphry Hook	70	35	00
	Mr. Crump	35	17	06
	Mr. Speed	38	19	00
	Mr. Jackson	80	40	00
	Mris. Martin	80	40	00
	Mr. Gleed	66	33	00
	Mris. Dymer	66	30	00
	Mris. Joyce Beavan	38	19	00
	Mris. Yeadith Beavan	18	09	00
	Mris. Blackwell	05	02	06
	Matthew Dimmock	11	05	06
	Mris. Rutland	22	11	00
	Mr. Hart	36	18	00
	Mr. Tilladam	20	10	00
	Mr. Hurtnoll	08	04	00
	Mr. Lewis	06	03	00
	Mris. Shore	12	06	00
	Mr. Little	10	05	00
	Mris. husbands	15	07	06
	Mr. Brooks	30	15	00
	Mr. Criswick	09	04	06
	Mr. hort	17	08	06
	Mris. Avendall	03	01	06
	Mris. Bawldin	08	04	00
	Widdow Wasborow	08	04	00
	Mathew Adlam	03	01	06
	Mr. Norris	22	11	00
	John hurne	10	05	00
	Arthur Sawyer	04	02	00
	Samuell Sanford	02	01	00
	John Barwick	02	01	00
		21	18	06

Page 133. The 10th of Aprell 1677.

	£	s.	d.
np Mris. Rogers	76	38	00
Richard Grumnell	40	20	00
Mr. Hollway	40	20	00
Mris. Web	19	09	06
William harris	25	12	06
John Willis	05	02	06
John Mathews	20	10	00
Henry Green	$42\frac{2}{1}$	21	03
John Smith	12	06	00
William White and Arthur white	28	14	00
Wirkhouse	15	07	06
Jonathan Edwards	16	08	00
Widdow Wasborow	26	13	00
John Barra	20	10	00
Petre Dee	43	21	06
Richard Pritchett	08	04	00
Widdow Lott	14	07	00
William heskins	54	27	00
Mr. Crismus	28	14	00
Avenhouse	16	08	00
Mr. Wasborow	36	18	00
Mr. Everat	02	01	00
John heskins	28	14	00
William Cox	16	08	00
Mris. Dighton	50	25	00
John Smith	25	12	06
Widdow Berry	12	06	00
Tho: herring	11	05	06
Widdow Smith	31	15	06
Widdow Jackson	07	03	06
Widdow Gush	10	05	00
Samuell Robins	08	04	00
Mr. Davis	$12\frac{2}{1}$	06	03
Mr. Bush	10	05	00
Widdow haines	04	02	00
Mris. Smether	35	17	06
James Peacock	14	07	00
William Peacock	$06\frac{2}{1}$	03	03
Mris. Rutland	16	08	00
Mris. Dighton for the Inn	10	05	00

Page 134.

The accompt of William White one of the overseers of the poore of the parrish of Westbury-uppon-trim made the 16 day of Aprell 1678.

	£	s.	d.
This accomptant Chargeth himself wth a rate of six pence a pound wch commeth to	19	15	06
The disburstments as followeth			
Imp paid to Jane Lane one moneth at 6s. a moneth	00	06	00
paid for the buring of her	00	09	00
paid to William Smith 13 moneths at fower shillings a moneth	02	12	00
paid to Susan Smith 13 moneths at fower shillings six pence a moneth	02	18	06
paid to Elizabeth Cook 15 moneths at three shillings a moneth	01	19	00
paid to the widdow Hunt 13 moneths at two shillings a moneth	01	06	00
paid to William Cary nine moneths at six shillings a moneth	02	14	00
paid to William Cary fower moneths at fower shillings a moneth	00	16	00
geaven to William Smith	00	01	00
paid for a warrant of dissturbance and an order to bring the Smith of Cribs away..	00	03	06
paid for keeping of Dorothy wads child 7 moneths at six and fower pence a month	02	04	04
paid for linnen for Kathren Boure	00	03	02
geaven Margret Wade at sevll times in her sicknes ..	00	04	00
geaven to Kathern Boure in her sickness	00	09	02
paid for keeping of Tho wads child	00	02	00
geaven to Margret wade in her sickness	00	08	00
paid for Tiling of Margret wade house and for tile.. ..	02	14	08
paid to Robert wade for going for a bone setter	00	02	00
spent that day that Edward boure bones was set.. ..	00	05	06
paid to the bonesetter..	00	10	00
paid for a chest and shroud for Edward Boure	00	12	00
paid to the Currinor	00	13	04
	21	13	02

Page 135.

	£	s.	d.
paid for one to goe to Sherehapton 2 sevll times	00	01	00
spent when Edward Bowre was buried	00	07	10
paid to Tho: Wasborow when he went to Gloster.. ..	00	18	00
paid for carring away the millerd wth an order	00	02	00
paid to Mr. Prise money that was due to him uppon his accompt	01	01	00
paid to Mathew Adlam for carring away the millerd wth an order	00	04	00
paid to him for Carring away the Smith of Cribs wth an order to Porbury	00	06	00
paid for carring away the millerd wth an order from the sessions	00	04	00
spent at two petty sessions	00	00	00
paid for a warrant for Hester Jones and an order to carry her away	00	03	06
spent when we went away wth her..	00	01	06
paid to william Pitman for comming to John Pulling and for a seer cloth	00	02	00
geaven to John Pullin since he was hurt	00	03	00
paid to Mr. Leaman for comming to Bowre..	00	05	00
paid for haling yeady bowr goods to Wesbury	00	02	00
paid for haling of gooddy Majors goods to Wesb.. ..	00	02	00
	04	02	10
	21	13	02
	25	16	00

	£	s.	d.
now it appeareth that there is dew to William White overseer	06	01	00

Page 136.

The accompt of Thomas Hopkins for Sr. Robert Can one of the overseers of the poore of the parrish of Westbury-uppon-trim made the 16th of Aprell, 1678.

	£	s.	d.
This accomptant Chargeth himself wth the rate of six penc pound wch commeth to	21	18	06

The disburstments as followeth

	£	s.	d.
Imp paid to John Barwick money that was dew to him uppon his accompt	04	12	10
paid Nicholas hatter 13 moneths 8s. a moneth	05	04	00
paid to John Raynolds 13 moneths 6s. a moneth.. ..	03	18	00
paid to Widdow Major 13 moneths 6s. a moneth.. ..	03	18	00
paid to yeady Bowre 7 weeks 3s. 4d. a week	01	03	04
paid to yeady Boure 16 weeks 2s. 6d. a week	02	00	00
paid for keeping Jones boy one moneth	00	06	08
geaven to Margret haskins for tending the Widd Major and for house roome and Lodging	00	04	00
paid for carring her goods and her children..	00	01	00
geaven to her in her sicknes	00	04	06
geaven to Agnes White at sevll times	00	05	00
geaven to Margret haskins in the whole yeare	00	05	00
spent when we went to take bond of Jones..	00	01	06
spent at sevll times when went for the money	00	01	00
spent when we went wth a warrant of dissturbance for the woeman that lay in at Redland and for going to Bristoll to find out the last place of her settlement..	00	01	00
paid for 4 warrants of dissturbance..	00	04	00
paid for 2 orders for Williams and wheeler..	00	05	00
spent at 2 petty sessions	00	0?	00
paid for keeping of 5 sick people all night wch was brought wth a pas out of Kent	00	01	06
geaven to William Smith	00	01	00
geaven to one to goe to Sherehampton	00	00	06
geaven to Nicholas Hatter	00	02	00
paid for Cloaths for Dorethy wads child	00	05	06
paid for one to goe to Bristoll to the bonesetter and for going to pitmans..	00	01	00
spent uppon the bone setter..		00	06
	23	08	10

Page 137.

	£	s.	d.
paid for the buring of Edward Bour and for taking of him up	00	03	06
paid for one to watch wth him a night	00	00	04
paid to Mr. Hort for rent for yeady Bour..	00	07	00
paid to Richard Jaine when he went to Glor	00	01	00
geaven to 7 poore sick people that was brought wth a pas from Westhester	00	00	08
geaven to Robert wade	00	01	00
for making the rates and ingrosing the book	00	04	00
for carring in the book and for a warrant..	00	02	06
paid to the Carpenter for timber and nailes and a daies work about Mergret wades house	00	04	06
geaven to poor people that was brought wth passes from tithing to tithing a whole yeare..	00	01	04
geaven to Kathren Boure in her sicknes	00	03	00
paid for a quarters rent for yeady Boure..	00	04	00
paid for a yeares rent for the Widd Major..	01	00	00
paid to Tho Wasbórow money that he did layd out at Gloster	00	07	00
geaven to pullins wife..	00	01	00
	03	10	04
now it appeereth that there is dew	£	s.	d.
to Tho Hopkins overseer	05	00	08

Page 138.

The accompt of William Harris one of the Collectors of the poore of the parrish of Westbury-uppon-trim made the 16th day of Aprell 1678.

	£	s.	d.
This accomptant Chargeth himself wth the rate of six pence a pound wch commeth to	22	06	09

The disburstments as followeth.

	£	s.	d.
Imp payd to Mary Playford one moneth..	00	05	00
payd to Agnes Jones	00	02	00
payd to Joane Griffin for Ane More	00	06	00
payd to John By	00	04	00
payd to Hanna Roberts	00	06	08
payd to John Caly	00	01	06
payd to Tho: Vaux	00	04	00
the seacond monethly payment commeth to	01	10	02
the third monethly payment commeth to	01	04	02
the fowerth moneths payment commeth to..	01	04	02
geaven to 9 sea men that were cast away..	00	03	00
payd for Cloaths and one quarters keeping for fishpoole	01	05	08
payd for 3 daies diett for Ane More..	00	01	06
payd for the schooling of fishpoole..	00	01	06
	06	19	09
payd to Tho: Vaux 8 moneths at 6s. the moneth	02	08	00
more geaven to Tho Vaux	00	02	00
payd to Mary playfoot 8 moneths at 6s. the moneth ..	02	08	00
geaven to Mary playfoot	00	02	00
payd to John Calee for himself	00	02	00
payd to John Calee for himself and for keeping of Hanna Roberts 8 moneths at 8s. 2d. a moneth..	03	05	04
payd John By 8 moneths at 4s. a moneth..	01	12	00
payd to Lettice Gush for keeping Ane More 11 weeks ..	00	11	00
payd to Joane Thomas for 3 moneths at 7s. a moneth and one moneth at 6s. and one week at 1s. 6d. ..	01	08	06
payd to John Calee for keeping Ane More a week.. ..	00	01	06
geaven to Ane Jones when her daughter was lame.. ..	00	06	00
	17	4	4

Page 139.

payd for one shift and a payer of boddis and a payer of shoos for Ane More	00	08	02
payd for 2 shifts for Hanna Roberts and one payer of shoos and a payer of stockins and mending her shoos	00	04	07
payd for mending of Henry fishpoole Cloaths	00	01	04
payd to Elnor Squier ? for keeping of Henry fishpoole one quarter of a yeare	00	19	06
	01	13	7

Memorand.—That there was due of this accompt to y Parish fro Wm. Harris ye sum of 14s. 8d. of which he paid 5s. to Tho: Wasborow for carrying away of Creeples, by consent of ye Parish.

our receipts.. ..	64	00	03
disbursments ..	73	12	05

We doe nominate and appoint to serve
the office of overseers of the poore for the yeare
ensuing Mr. Ric: Davies Arthur
Sawyer and Richard Pritchett.
These accompts seen and allowed by
we whose names are here under written

John Goldingham Minister of Westbury
Fra Fane [1]
John Meredith
Richard Davies
ffrancis Gleed
Thomas Cuff
Peter Lee
John Adlam
John Hiskins
Mathew Adlam
Samuell price

[1] For some notes on the Fanes, who were patrons of the Westbury Church for 150 years, see *Eccles. Hist. of Westbury*, pp. 63–72.

Page 140. The 26th day of Aprell 1678.

A rate made by the Churchwardens and other inhabytants of the parrish of Westbury-uppon-trim for and towards the releef of the poore for this yeare at the rate of six pence a pound and another rate at three pence a pound as followeth.

			£	s.	d.
Imp	Mr. John Knight	90	03	07	06
	Mr. John Lambe	80	03	00	00
	Mr. Richard Davis	46	01	14	06
	Mr. Thomas Gerring	60	02	05	00
	Mr. Leaman	16	00	12	00
	Mr. John Sampson	80	03	00	00
	Mr. Richard Lane	66	02	09	06
	Mr. Samuell Prise	42	01	11	06
	Mris. Walter	12	00	09	00
	Mris. Rutland	03	00	02	03
	Tho: Wasborow	15	00	11	03
	Mris. Web	14	00	10	06
	Mr. oliff	30	01	02	06
	John England Samuell Clafell	09	00	06	09
	Mr. Prise	06	00	04	06
	Mathew Adlam	24	00	18	00
	Mris. Avendall for Cook and Jones	28	01	01	06
	Mr. Wasborow	03	00	02	03
	Mr. White	24	00	18	00
	Mris. Burdges	30	01	02	06
	Mris. Hort	26	00	19	06
	Tho. Cuff	08	00	06	00
	Mr. Williams	12	00	09	00
	Samuell Sanford	12	00	09	00
	Tho: Hort	08	00	06	00
	Mris. yeadith Beavan	06	00	04	06
	Mr. Sampson	12	00	09	00
	John Chessher	03	00	02	03
	John Adlam	04	00	03	00
	Samuell Clafell	04	00	03	00
	Mr. Nicholas	04	00	03	00
	Mr. Lane for the Colledg	03	00	02	03
	Robert hedges	07	00	05	03
	Widdow Adlam	03	00	02	03

Page 141. The 26th day of Aprell 1678.

		£	£	s.	d.
mp	Sr. Robert Can..	109	04	01	09
	Sr. Humphry Hook	70	02	12	06
	Sr. Robert Yeomans	20	00	15	00
	Mr. Crump	55	01	06	03
	Mr. Speed	38	01	08	06
	Mr. Jackson	80	03	00	00
	Mr. Martin	80	03	00	00
	Mr. Gleed	66	02	09	00
	Mris. Dymer	60	02	05	00
	Mris. Joyce Beavan	38	01	08	06
	Mris. yeadith Beavan	18	00	13	06
	Mris. Blackwell	06	00	04	06
	Mathew Dymmock	11	00	08	03
	Mris. Rutland	22	00	16	06
	Mr. Hart	36	01	07	00
	Mr. Tilladam	20	00	15	00
	Mr. Hurtnoll	08	00	06	00
	Mr. Lewes	06	00	04	06
	Mris. Shore	12	00	09	00
	Mr. Little	10	00	07	06
	Mris. Husbands	16	00	12	00
	Mr. Brooks and Lewis ground	30	01	02	06
	Mr. Criswick	09	00	06	09
	Mr. Hort	17	00	12	09
	Mris. Avendall	03	00	02	03
	Mr. Bawldin or the teanaunts	08	00	06	00
	Widdow Wasborow	08	00	06	00
	Mathew Adlam	03	00	02	03
	Mr. Norris	22	00	16	06
	John hurne	10	00	07	06
	Arthur Sawer	04	00	03	00
	Samuell Sanford	02	00	01	06
	John Barwick	02	00	01	06
			32	19	03

Page 142. The 26th day of Aprell 1678.

		£	£	s.	
Imp	Mris. Rogers	76	02	17	00
	Richard Grumnell	40	01	10	00
	Mr. Hollway	40	01	10	00
	Mris. Web	19	00	14	03
	William Harris	25	00	18	09
	John Willis	05	00	03	09
	John Smith	12	00	09	00
	John Mathews	20	00	15	00
	Henry Green	42½	01	11	10
	William White Arthur White	28	01	01	00
	Wirkhouse	15	00	11	03
	Mr. Edwards	16	00	12	00
	Widdow Wasborow	26	00	19	06
	John Barra	20	00	15	00
	Petre Dee	43	01	12	03
	Richard Pritchett	08	00	06	00
	Widdow Lott	14	00	10	06
	William Heskings	54	02	00	06
	Mr. Crismus	28	01	01	00
	Avenhouse	16	00	12	00
	Mr. Wasborow	36	01	07	00
	Mr. Everatt	02	00	01	06
	John Heskins	28	01	01	00
	William Cox	16	00	12	00
	Mris. Dighton	50	01	17	06
	John Smith	25	00	18	09
	Widdow Berry	12	00	09	00
	Tho: Herring	11	00	08	03
	Widdow Smith	31	01	03	03
	Widdow Jackson	07	00	05	03
	Widdow Gush	10	00	07	06
	Samuell Robins	08	00	06	00
	Mr. Davis	12½	00	09	04
	Mr. Bush	10	00	07	06
	Widdow Haines	04	00	03	00
	Mris. Smether	35	01	06	03
	James Peacock	14	00	10	06
	William Peacock	06½	00	04	10
	Mris. Rutland	16	00	12	00
	Mris. Dighton for the Inn	10	00	07	06
	Tho. Cuff	02	00	01	00

The som is £33 8s. 9d.

Page 143.

he accompt of Richard Davys, one of the overseers of the yeare of the parrish of Westbury-upon-Trym, made the second Day of may 1679.

his Accomptant chargeth himself wth two Rates the one for six pence in the pound the other at three pence in the pound wch amots to..	29	12	06

The disbursments as followeth

pd goodwife Davis for 13 moneths at 6s. 4d.	4	02	04
pd William Cary for 13 moneths at 6s. od.	3	18	00
pd goodwife major for 13 moneths at 6s.	3	18	00
pd Susan Smyth for 13 moneths at 4s. 6d.	2	18	06
pd William Smyth Senor for 13 moneths at 4s.	2	12	00
pd Elizabeth Cooke for 13 moneths at 3/8	1	19	00
pd goodwife hunt for 13 moneths at 2s.	1	06	00
pd francis Yeamans for Daniel Jones Bond		04	06
pd to will Smyth Junor att twice		02	00
pd goodwife draysey for keeping her Sister		04	00
pd to Jerom Cuff at severell tymes		14	00
pd for a shroud and Burying Jn pullin and in sicknes &c.		08	06
pd for Burying a poore woman		02	06
pd Sarah pullin att severall tymes		07	00
pd William Smyth Senor at severall tym		06	00
pd for clothing Edy Bowerys sonn to place him in the free schools at henbury	1	11	06
allowed Mr. Samuell price his two rates on accot of money due to him	2	00	06
pd for warrants and expences		07	00
	27	01	04
Remaynes due to the parrish..	2	11	02
	29	12	06

Page 144.

The accompt of Arthur Sawyer one of the overseers of the poore parrish of Westbury-uppon-trim made the seacond day of May 1679.

	£	s.	d.
This accomptant chargeth himself wth two rates one of six pence a pound the other of three pence the pound wch commeth to	32	19	03
The disburstments as followeth	£	s.	d.
Imp paid to yeadith Boure for one moneth	00	14	00
paid to her for 12 moneths at 10s. a moneth	06	00	00
paid to Nicholas Hatter 13 moneths at 8s...	05	04	00
paid to John Raynolds 13 moneths at 6s...	03	18	00
paid to Mergrett heskins 13 moneths at 3s...	01	19	00
paid to gooddy Chanler in the whole yeare..	01	08	06
geaven to John Pullin in his lamenes	00	08	00
paid to the bone setter for him	00	05	00
paid for a shroud and buring of gooddy bowers child ..	00	04	06
paid for 8 warrants of disturbance..	00	08	00
paid for a warrant of removeall	00	02	06
for expences the whole yeare..	00	04	06
geaven to Dorethy Williams for her sicknes..	00	02	00
geaven to William Smith at sevll times in his sicknes ..	00	09	06
geaven to the Widdow Hawkins at sev times	00	05	00
geaven to Robert wade at two sev times	00	02	06
geaven to Kathern Boure in the whole yeare and for washing her Cloths	00	14	06
geaven to poore people wth passes and Certificates ..	00	03	04
geaven to John white and his family in their sicknes ..	01	00	00
paid for making of 3 deplucates out of the poores book by order of the Deputy Leifteanants..	00	01	06
geaven to Margrett wade in her sicknes and for Coals ..	00	10	06
paid for John Raynolds rent..	00	06	08
paid for a warrant for the father of the child wch was borne uppon the downe and expences..	00	03	00
geaven to hatters wife the Auditt day	00	02	00
geaven to Jeorum Cuff in his sickness	00	02	06
geaven to goody haskins boy in his sicknes..	00	01	00
paid towards the buring of John pullin	00	02	06
paid for making the rates and ingrosing the book.. ..	00	05	00
paid to Mr. Price money that was dew from the pish ..	00	04	06
paid to yeadith Bour 3 weeks pay..	00	04	06
for carring in the book to the Justice and 3 warrants ..	00	03	00
payd the Charges for the woeman that lay in wth a child at Darbies house	02	04	06
	28	04	06
	04	12	3
32 : 19 : 03	32	19	03

Page 145.

'he accompt of Richard Pritchett one of the overseers of the poore of the parrish of Westb-uppon-trim made the seacond day of May 1679.

	£	s.	d.
'his accomptant Chargeth himself wth two rates one of sixpence a pound and the other of three pence a pound wch commeth to	33	08	09
	00	05	08
	33	14	05

The disburstments as followeth	£	s.	
np paid to John Calee 14 moneths at 8s. 2d...	05	14	04
paid to Mary Playford 14 moneths at 6s...	04	04	00
paid to Tho: faux 4 moneths at 6s.	01	04	00
paid to Tho: faux 7 moneths at 3s.	01	01	00
paid to Tho: faux 3 moneths at 4s.	00	12	00
paid to John By 11 moneths at 4s.	02	04	00
paid to Ane More 5 moneths at 7s.	01	15	00
paid to Ane More 3 moneths at 4s.	00	12	00
paid to Ane More 4 moneths at 6s.	01	04	00
paid Ane Drysee at sevll times	01	06	00
paid Mary Hoskins one moneth	00	08	00
geaven to Margrett faux in her sicknes and buring her ..	01	01	00
geaven to Mary Playford in her sicknes	00	12	10
geaven to John By in his sicknes	00	04	00
geaven to Ane More in her sicknes and buring her.. ..	01	05	05
geaven to Mary Hoskins in her sicknes and one to tend her	00	18	00
paid for a payer of shoos for Ane More	00	02	06
paid for Cloaths for Tho Playfoott..	00	15	01
paid for Cloaths for Hannah Roberts	00	11	08
paid for the keeping of Henry ffishpoole	01	19	00
paid for Apparrell for Henry ffishpoole	00	10	06
geaven to Richard Parker in his sicknes	00	10	00
geaven to Joane Baker in her sons sicknes..	00	05	00
geaven to Elnor Reed in her soons sicknes..	00	05	00
geaven to John Calee towards buring his child	00	07	00
paid Ane Draysy	00	01	11
	029	13	03
Remaineth dew to the parish..	04	01	02
	33	14	5

	£	s.	d.
our receipts is	96	06	02
our disburstments is	84	18	07
there remaineth in stock	11	07	07

Page 146.

Wee doe nominate and appoint to serve the
office of overseers for the poore yeare ensuing
Mr. Tho: Gerring Mr. Isaack Dymer
and John Thomas.

The accompts seen and allowed by wee
whose names are heareunder written

Cornelius Jayne +[2] } John Goldingham Minister.[1]
Henry weaver + } their marks Churchwardens.

Jn Knight
1679
Thomas hortt
Mathew Adlam
William White
Thomas Cuff
nic: Veel
John Meredith
Christopher Cole

allowed to Petre Dee uppon my accomp..	01	13	03
allowed to William heskins..	02	00	06
paid to the new Collect this..	00	08	05
	4	01	02

[1] Vicar of Westbury, which at that time was held with Almondsbury, from about 1660 till about 1708.

[2] The two churchwardens were "illiterate."

Page 147. The 15th of Aprell 1679.

A rate made by the inhabytants of the prish of Westbury for and towards the releef of the poore at the rate of six a pound and three pence a pound.

		£	£	s.	d.
mp	Mr. John Knight	90	03	07	00
	Mr. John Lamb	80	03	00	00
	Mr. Richard Davis	46	01	14	06
	Mr. Tho. Gerring	60	02	05	00
	Mr. William Walter	16	00	12	00
	Mr. Sampson	80	03	00	00
	Mr. Richard Lane [1]	75	02	16	03
	Mr. Samuell Prise	42	01	11	06
	Mris. Walter	12	00	09	00
	Mris. Rutland	03	00	02	03
	Tho: Wasborow	15	00	11	03
	Widdow Web	14	00	10	06
	Mr. Oliff	30	01	02	06
	Samuell Clafell	09	00	06	09
	Mathew Adlam	24	00	18	00
	Mris. Avendall	28	01	01	00
	Mr. Wasborow	03	00	02	03
	William White	24	00	18	00
	William Burdges	30	01	02	06
	Widdow Hort	26	00	19	06
	Tho. Cuff	08	00	06	00
	Mr. Williams	12	00	09	00
	Samuell Sanford	09 2/1	00	06	4 2/1 09
	Mr. hort	08	00	06	00
	Mris. Prise	06	00	04	06
	Mr. Sampson	12	00	09	00
	John Chessher	03	00	02	03
	John Adlam	04	00	03	00
	Samuell Clafell	04	00	03	00
	Mr. Nicholas	06 2/1	00	04	10 2/1
	Widdow Adlam	03	00	02	03
	Robert Hedges	07	00	05	03
			29	12	06

[1] Mr. Richard Lane entertained James II and his Queen in 1687. "The Royal Guests ·ere received at Lawford's Gate on September 12th with the accustomed ceremony," writes atimer, "and were conducted to Mr. Lane's Great House at St. Augustine's Back, where a ıxurious banquet was prepared for them, and where the Queen was presented with 100 broad pieces' of gold. Their Majesties returned to Bath the same evening. Their brief isit cost the Corporation no less than £703." Mr. Lane was a sugar merchant, and was [ayor of Bristol in 1688; but on January 13th, by order of His Majesty's Council, and to ırther the promotion of Roman Catholic supremacy, he with others was dismissed from ıe Corporation, and Thomas Day was chosen in his place.

Page 148.	£	£	s.	d.
Ip Sr. Robert Can	109	04	01	09
Sr. Robert yeamans	020	00	15	00
Sr. Robert Southwell [1]	70	02	12	06
Mr. Crump	35	01	06	03
Mr. Speed	38	01	08	06
Mr. Jackson	80	03	00	00
Mr. Martin	80	03	00	00
Mr. Gleed	66	02	09	00
Mr. Dymer	60	02	05	00
Mris. Beavan	38	01	08	06
Mris. Prise	18	00	13	06
Mris. Blackwell	06	00	04	06
Mathew Dimmock	11	00	08	03
Mris. Rutland	22	00	16	06
Mr. Hart	36	01	07	00
Mr. Tilladam	20	00	15	00
Mr. Hurtnoll	08	00	06	00
Mr. Lewis	06	00	04	06
Mris. Shore	12	00	09	00
Mr. Littell..	10	00	07	06
Mris. husbands	16	00	12	00
Mr. Brooks	28	01	02	06
Edward Lewis or the teanant	02	00	00	00
Mr. Criswick	09	00	06	09
Mr. hort	17	00	12	09
Mris. Avendall	03	00	02	03
Mr. Bawldin	08	00	06	00
Widdow Wasborow	08	00	06	00
Mathew Adlam	03	00	02	03
Mr. Norris..	22	00	16	06
John hurn..	10	00	07	06
Arthur Sawyer	04	00	03	00
Samuell Sanford	02	00	01	06
John Barwick	02	00	01	06
		32	19	03

[1] On the death of Sir Robert Hooke, M.P., in October, 1677, and as he was heavily in debt, his trustees began to realise his estate, and in 1680 "disposed of the fine estate at Kingsweston to Sir Robert Southwell." When William III reached Kingroad, on September 6th, 1690, on his return from the Battle of the Boyne, he landed at Kingsweston and stayed the night with Sir Robert Southwell, who at that time was Irish Secretary of State.

Page 149.

	£	£	s.	d.
p Mris. Rogers	76	02	17	00
Mr. hollway	40	01	10	00
Richard Grumnell	40	01	10	00
Mris. Web	19	00	14	03
William harris	25	00	18	09
John Willis	05	00	03	09
John Smith	12	00	09	00
John Mathews or the teunant	20	00	15	00
Henry Green	$42\frac{2}{1}$	02	00	10
William White	14	00	10	06
Arthur White	14	00	10	06
Wirkhouse	15	00	11	03
Jonathan Edwards	16	00	12	00
George Peters	17	00	12	09
Widdow Stokes	09	00	06	09
John Thomas	20	00	15	00
Petre Dee	43	01	12	03
Richard Pritchett	08	00	06	00
Widdow Lot	14	00	10	06
William heskins	54	02	00	06
Mr. Crismus	28	01	01	00
Avenhouse	16	00	12	00
Mr. Wasborow	36	01	07	00
Mr. Everatt	02	00	01	06
John heskins	28	01	01	00
William Cox	16	00	12	00
Mris. Dighton	50	01	17	06
John Smith	25	00	18	09
Widdow Berry	12	00	09	00
Tho. herring	11	00	08	03
Widdow Smith	31	01	03	03
Widdow Jackson	07	00	05	03
Widdow Gush	10	00	07	06
Samuell Robins	08	00	06	00
Mr. Davis	$12\frac{2}{1}$	00	09	04
Mr. Pugh	10	00	07	06
Widdow haines	04	00	03	00
Mris. Smether	35	01	06	03
James Peacock	$14\frac{2}{1}$	00	10	$10\frac{2}{1}$
William Peacock	08	00	04	06
Mris. Rutland	16	00	12	00
Mris. Dighton for the Inn	10	00	07	06
Tho. Cuff	02	00	01	06
		33	18	08

Page 150.

The accompt of Thomas Gerring one of the overseers of the poore of the prish of Westbury-uppon-trim made the 15th day of Aprell 1680.

	£		
This accomptant Chargeth himself wth 2 rates one of six pence a pound and the other of three pence a pound wch commeth to	29	12	06

The disburstments as followeth

Imp paid William Cary 13 moneths at six shillings	03	18	00
paid Gooddy Major 13 moneths at six shillings	03	18	00
paid Susan Smith 13 moneths at shillings 6..	02	18	06
paid William Smith 13 moneths at fower shillings.. ..	02	12	00
paid Elizab Cook 13 moneths at three shillings	01	19	00
gooddy hunt 13 moneths at two shillings..	01	06	00
yeady Boure 13 moneths at six shillings..	03	18	00
for my exspences and horse hire for Riding to 3 the first sessions about the bastard child	01	07	06
for the seacond sessions being out thre daies	01	07	06
paid for Coppy of the order..	00	02	06
paid to Tho Wasborow for going to Stoke to geve notice to them to goe to the sessions..	00	02	06
paid to Mr. Cox the Attorney to plead at the Court ..	00	05	00
paid to Mr. Powell to plead at the Court	00	03	04
paid to Mr. floyd the attorney to draw up the Case to show my Lord Chief Justice..	00	10	00
paid for half a year's Rent for Mary Major..	00	05	00
paid Dorothy Wade for tending of William Bower ..	00	03	00
geaven to William Bower in his sicknes	00	08	00
paid for Tiling part of the almes house	02	10	00
paid John Barwick 13 way of lime about the house and a Rafter	00	10	05
paid to William Atwood wife for keeping the child a 11 weeks at two shillings sixpence a week	01	07	06
paid for Cloths and Stockings and shoos for the child ..	00	16	02
paid Sarah Pull 8 moneths at eight shillings	03	04	00
geaven to William Smith Junor	00	10	00
geaven to Elizabeth Cook	00	00	06
paid Mr. Prise money that was due to him..	01	04	00
paid for a warrant	00	01	06
£ s. d.	35	07	11
dew to me from the parrish.. .. .. 5 15 05			

Page 151.

'he accompt of Isack Dymer one of the overseers of the poore of the prish of Westbury-uppon-trim made the 15th day of Aprell 1680.

	£	s.	d.
his Accomptant Chargeth himself wth 2 rates one of six pence a pound and the other of three pence a pound wch commeth to	32	19	03

The disburstments as followeth

mp paid to gooddy Davis 4 moneths for keeping of wades Child at six shillings fower pence	01	05	04
paid Nicholas hatter 13 moneths at 8s.	05	04	00
paid to John Raynolds 13 moneths at 6s...	03	18	00
paid to Margret hask 13 moneths at 3s.	01	19	00
paid Sara Pullin 13 moneths at 6s...	03	18	00
geaven to gooddy homes in their sicknes..	01	07	06
geaven to the widdow Vaughan	01	08	06
paid towards the Tiling of the Almshouse..	02	10	00
geaven to gooddy Cox the whole yeare	01	06	00
geaven to Robert Bartlutt and his son in their sicknes ..	00	19	06
geaven to Nicholas hatter in his sicknes..	00	07	00
geaven to John White at sevll times	00	10	00
geaven to one in the prish in their want	00	05	00
geaven to John Raynolds	00	01	00
geaven to Katheen Boure	00	02	00
paid John Raynolds rent	00	06	00
paid for making of a pas	00	01	00
paid Mris. Walter for Curing of ould smith..	01	00	00
paid Mr. Prise money that was due to him..	00	10	06
paid for making the rates and ingrosing the book.. ..	00	04	00
geaven to poore people with passes and for carring away a cripple	00	02	00
geaven to Ane hawkins in her sicknes	00	02	06
geaven to three persons with a pas to travell	00	01	00
paid for buring of Dorethy wads Child	01	01	00
geaven to gooddy Davis in the Child sicknes	00	03	00
geaven to goody Vaughan	00	02	06
paid for pulling downe of Vaughan Collage	00	12	03
for Carring away Cripples	00	05	00
£ s. d.			
dew to the pish uppon this accompt .. 3 7 8	29	11	07

Page 152.

The accompt of John Thomas one of the overseers of the poore of the prish of Westbury-uppon-trim made the 15th day of Aprell 1680.

	£	s.	
This accomptant chargeth himself wth two Rates one of six pence a pound and the other of three pence a pound wch commeth to	33	10	03
more he Chargeth himself wth money that he receaved of the ould Collectors	00	08	05
	33	18	08

The disburstments as followeth

Imp paid John Calee 12 moneths at 8s. 2d. a moneth.. ..	04	18	00
paid Mercy Playfoot 7 monet at six shillings	02	02	00
paid Tho Vaux 2 moneths at fower shill	00	08	00
laid out in his sicknes and buriall	01	05	09
paid Ane Draisy 3 moneths at fower shill..	00	12	00
paid Ane West for Ane Draisy Diett 9 moneths	02	14	00
paid Elnor Squier for fishpoole diett half a yeare.. ..	01	19	00
paid Elnor Squier for Tho: Playfoot for 5 moneths and 3 weeks at six shillings..	01	14	06
paid for Cloths for Henry fishpools..	00	06	07
geaven to Tho faux in his sicknes	00	01	05
paid towards the buring of William Reed..	00	02	06
paid for two Caps and a payer of shoos for Calies mac̄ ..	00	02	02
paid for a warrant of the good behavior	00	02	06
geaven to Mary Playfoot in her sicknes	00	10	06
paid for a horse and man to carry Hannah Baker to Almesbury	00	02	00
paid for the Curing Ane Peacocks child	03	00	00
paid for her diett when she lay under the Chiurgery hands	00	17	00
paid towards the buring Mary Winter Child	00	07	00
paid for a payer of stockings for Calies maid	00	00	10
paid for linnen for Cailes maid	00	03	08
geaven to Elizabeth Peere	00	01	08
geaven to a poore Carpenter..	00	00	06
geaven to Mary Playfoot	00	04	06
paid gooddy Michell for enetertaining of a poore woeman in travell	00	06	08
geaven to Calies maid	00	02	04
paid towards the buriell of Mary playfoot..	00	02	00
paid for 4 yards of Cloth for ane draisey	00	05	00
paid to Mary Playfoot	00	00	8

Page 153.

	£	s.	d.
paid for 2 warrants	00	02	00
paid to Petre Dee money that was dew to him	01	12	13
	25	12	00

	£	s.	d.
dew to the pish one this accompt	8	6	8

	£	s.	
our receipts is	96	10	05
our disburstments is ..	90	11	06

We doe nominate and appoint to serve
the office of overseers for the poore for
the yeare ensuing

Mr. John Lambe Petre Dee
Mr. William Martin

These accompts seene and allowed by
wee whose names are heareund subscribed

John Goldingham Curate of Westbury

Fra Fane
Sam Astry [1]

Thomas Cuff
John Reead

	£	s.	d.
Now of this 8 : 6 : 8 was paid to Mr. Gerring in part ..	05	15	05
Wch was dew to him from the parrish			
more paid to Mr. Dymer	02	11	03
	8	6	8
There remaineth dew uppon this accompt..	05	18	08
paid towards the Law about the bastard child	01	00	00
Delivered over to the new Collector Mr. Lamb	04	18	08

[1] See *Eccles. Hist. of Westbury*, pp. 37–42.

Page 154. The 10th of Aprell 1680.

A rate made by the inhabytants of the prish of Westbury for and towards the releef of the poore for this yeare at the rate of six pence a pound as followeth :—

	£	s.	d.
Imp Mr. John Knight	90	45	00
Mr. John Lamb	80	40	00
Mr. Davis	46	23	00
Mr. Gerring	60	30	00
Mr. Walter	16	08	00
Mr. Sampson	80	40	00
Mr. Lane	75	37	06
Mr. Prise	42	21	00
Mris. Walter	12	06	00
Mris. Rutland	03	01	06
Tho. Wasborow	15	07	06
Widdow web	14	07	00
Mr. oliff	30	15	00
Samuell Clafell	09	04	06
Mathew Adlam	24	12	00
Mris. Avendall	28	14	00
Mr. Wasborow Children	03	01	06
William White	24	12	00
William Burdges and teanant	30	15	00
Mris. Hort	26	13	00
Tho. Cuff	08	04	00
Mr. Williams	12	06	00
Samuell Sanford	09$\frac{2}{1}$	04	09
Mr. hort	08	04	00
Mr. Prise	06	03	00
Mr. Sampson	12	06	00
John Chessher	03	01	06
John Adlam	04	02	00
Samuell Clafell	04	02	00
Samuell Nicholas	06$\frac{2}{1}$	03	03
Widdow Adlam	03	01	06
Robert Hedges	07	03	06
	19	15	00

Page 155.

		£	£		
Imp	Sr. Robert Can..	109	2	14	06
	Sr. Robert yeomans	42	1	1	00
	Sr. Robert Southwell	70	1	15	00
	Mr. Crump	35	0	17	06
	Mr. Speed	38	0	19	00
	Mr. Jackson	80	2	00	00
	Mr. Martin	80	2	00	00
	Mr. Gleed	66	1	13	00
	Mr. Dymer	60	1	10	00
	Mris. Beavan	38	0	19	00
	Mr. Prise	18	0	09	00
	Mris. Blackwell	05	0	02	06
	Mr. Dimmock	11	0	05	06
	Mr. Knight	22	0	11	00
	Mr. Hart	36	0	18	00
	Mr. Tilladam	20	0	10	00
	Mr. hurtnoll	08	0	04	00
	Mr. Lewis	06	0	03	00
	Mris. Shore	12	0	06	00
	Mr. Little	10	0	05	00
	Mr. husbands	16	0	08	00
	Mr. Brooks	28	0	14	00
	Edward Lewis and teanant	02	0	01	00
	Mr. Criswick	09	0	04	06
	Mr. hort	17	0	08	06
	Mris. Avendall	03	0	01	06
	Mr. Bawldin	08	0	04	06
	Mris. Stokes and teanant	08	0	04	00
	Mathew Adlam	03	0	01	06
	John hurne	10	0	05	00
	Arthur Sawyer..	04	0	02	00
	Samuell Sanford	02	0	01	00
	John Barwick	02	0	01	00

Page 156.		s.	d.
Imp Mr. Robert Southwell	36	18	00
Mris. Rogers	74	38	00
Mr. Hollway	40	20	00
Richard Grumnell	40	20	00
Mris. Web	19	09	06
William Harris	25	12	06
John Willis	05	02	06
John Smith	12	06	00
John Mathews and teanant	20	10	00
Henry Green	$42\frac{2}{1}$	21	03
William White	14	07	00
Arthur White	14	07	00
Wirkhouse	15	07	06
Jonathan Edwards	16	08	00
Georg Peeters	17	08	00
Widdow Stokes	09	04	06
John Thomas	20	10	00
Peeter Dee	43	21	06
Richard Prichett	08	04	00
Widdow Lott	14	07	00
William Heskins	54	27	00
Mr. Crismus and teanant	28	14	00
Avenhouse	16	09	00
Mr. Everatt	02	01	00
John heskins	28	14	00
William Cox	16	08	00
Mris. Dighton and teanant	50	25	00
John Smith	25	12	06
Widdow Berry	12	06	00
Tho. herring	11	05	06
Widdow Smith	31	15	06
Widdow Jackson	07	03	06
Widdow Gush	10	05	00
Samuell Robins	08	04	00
Mr. Davis	$12\frac{2}{1}$	06	03
Mr. Bush	10	05	00
Widdow haines	04	02	00
Widdow Smether	29	14	06
Robert Smith	06	03	00
James Peacock	14	07	00
William Peacock	$7\frac{2}{1}$	03	03
Mris. Rutland	16	08	00
Mris. Dighton for the Inn	10	05	00
Tho. Cuff	02	01	00

Page 157.

The accompt of Mr. John Lamb one of the overseers of thė poore of the parrish of Westbury-uppon-trim made the 5th day of Aprell 1681.

	£	s.	d.
This accomptant Chargeth himself wth a rate of six pence a pound wch commeth to	19	15	00
more he Chargeth himself wth money receaved of the ould Collectors	05	18	08
	25	13	08
the disburstments as followeth			
Imp payd to William Cary 13 moneths at 6s.	03	18	00
payd to Goodd Major 13 moneths at 6s.	03	18	00
payd to Susan Smith 13 moneths at 4s. 6d...	02	18	06
payd to William Smith 13 moneths at 4s...	02	12	00
payd to bes Cook 13 moneths at 4s...	02	12	00
payd gooddy hunt 13 moneths at 2s.	01	06	00
payd to yeady Boure 13 moneths at 6s.	03	18	00
payd to good Cox 13 moneths at 2s.	01	06	00
payd for charges at Glos: about the bastard child.. ..	01	00	00
payd to Mr. Edwards towards the Law	02	04	06
geaven to Katheren Boure at sevll times	00	11	00
geaven to William Smith at sevll times	00	10	00
geaven to ould William Smith	00	02	00
geaven to gooddy hunt	00	02	06
payd Mary Majors rent one yeare	00	10	00
geaven to Jane Jefferies at sevll times	00	05	00
payd for binding prentice the Child at Sherehamp ..	03	00	00
geaven to Katheren Boure	00	02	00
geaven to poore people wth passes	00	05	00
paid at sevll meetings about parrish business	00	10	00
paid for a warrant to bring in the new Collectors and exspences	00	02	06
The disbursments is ..	31	13	00
	25	13	08
Due from ye pish to Mr. Lambe	05	19	04

The £5 19s. 4d. said to Be Due to Mr. Lambe as above is paid.

p Jonathan Edwards	4	17	09d.
and p mony to Recaved of Collect Deu	1	02	07
	6	00	04

Page 158.

The accompt of Mr. William Martin one of the overseers of the poore of the parrish of Westbury-uppon-trim made the 5th day of Aprell 1681.

	£	s.	d.
This accomptant Chargeth himself wth a rate of six pence a pound wch commeth to	21	18	06

The disburstments as followeth

	£	s.	d.
Imp paid to John Raynolds 13 Moneths at 06s...	03	18	00
paid to gooddy Vaughan 13 moneths at 04s.	02	12	00
paid to gooddy Pullin 07 moneths at 14s...	04	18	00
paid goody Pullin 06 moneths at 12s.	03	12	00
paid goody Haskins 13 moneths at 03s.	01	19	00
paid ould Hatter half a moneth	00	04	00
paid for the Buring of ould hatter..	01	03	04
paid to the parson and Cleark for buring of him.. ..	00	02	06
geaven to gooddy Haskins at sevll times in her sicknes..	00	11	00
geaven to gooddy hatter at sevll times the whole yeare..	01	14	06
geaven to poore Seamen wth passes at sevll times ..	00	05	06
geaven to gooddy homes at sevll times	00	13	00
geaven to John White at sevll times..	00	09	00
paid towards the Child that was bound prentice from Shereh	02	00	00
paid to Mr. Dymer money that he was out the last yeare	00	10	06
paid for Clothes for the Child at pullins	00	12	00
paid for Clothes for playfords boy..	00	04	07
geaven to welsh Joane at sevll times	00	03	00
paid towards buring of Elnor the mid wife	00	05	00
for Charges and exspences about the parrish busines ..	00	18	00
paid John Reynolds rent	00	06	08
The disbursments is	27	09	07
	21	10	06
Due from ye pish to Mr. Martin ..	05	11	01
more paid for harfees boy 5 weeks..	00	11	03
	06	02	04

	£	s.	d.
of wch £6 02s. 04d. he hath Red of Mr. Knight in pt	2	06	04
paid p John Barwick to him ac appears p his accott	3	16	00
	6	02	04

Page 159.

The accompt of Petre Dee one of the overseers of the poore of the parrish of Westbury-uppon-trim made the 5th day of Aprell 1681.

	£	s.	d.
This accomptant Chargeth himself wth a rate of six a pound wch commeth to	22	06	09
The disburstments as followeth	£	s.	d.
Imp paid John Calee 7 moneths at 2s.	00	14	00
paid John Calee 7 moneths at 1s. 6d.	00	10	06
paid Hanna Calee 2 moneths at 6s. 8d.	00	13	04
paid Hanna Calee 12 moneths at 6s...	03	12	00
paid Ane Drayfee 13 moneths at 6s...	03	18	00
paid for keeping of Thomas Plaifool 10 weeks	00	15	00
paid for keeping of fishpoole half a yeare	01	19	00
paid for making a Coat for fishpoole..	00	01	00
paid for stockings and mending of shoos for him.. ..	00	02	00
paid to Joseph Calle for keeping a Child	00	02	06
geaven to poore people	00	03	06
geaven to Joane web to carry her to London	01	00	00
geaven to Davee Web..	00	01	00
paid towards binding the maid prentice at Shereh.. ..	02	08	00
paid to Joane Web for tending of gooddy Hoskings fower months at 10s. a moneth	02	00	00
paid for milk for gooddy Hoskings..	01	05	06
paid for Candels and sope for her	00	06	00
paid for Coale and wood for her	00	04	00
paid for a bed pan and other necessaries	00	04	06
paid for buring of her..	00	10	06
paid for 3 payer of shoos for fishpool and playfoot.. ..	00	04	10
paid for Cloaths for fishpooll..	00	09	06
paid for making the rates and ingrosing the book.. ..	00	04	00
spent when wee bound the maid prentice..	00	02	06
to warne the officers to pas their accomps	00	01	00
	22	06	09
The disbursments is	21	04	02
Due to ye pish ffrm peetre Dee	01	02	07

which sum of £1 : 06 : 06 is paide to Mr. Lambe

The whole recipts is	69	18	11
The disbursments	80	06	09

Wee doe nominate and appoint to searve ye office of overseers of ye poore ffor yeare ensuing Mr. John Knight, Jonathan Edwards and John Barwick. These accounts seene and allowed by us whose names are hereunto subscribed

Richard Davyes

Nic: Veel — Samuell prise

Christopher Cole — Will Davies churchwardens

Thomas Cuffe

Page 160. The 12th of Aprell 1681.

A rate made by the inhabytants of the prish of Westbury-uppon-trim for and towards the releef of the poore for this yeare at the rate of nine pence a pound as follow

	£			
Imp Mr. John Knight	90	03	07	6
Mr. John Lamb	80	03	00	0
Mr. Davis	46	01	14	6
Mr. Gerring	60	02	05	0
Mr. Walter	16	00	12	0
Mr. Sampson	80	03	00	0
Mr. Lane	75	02	16	3
Mr. Prise	42	01	11	6
Mris. Walter	12	00	09	0
Mris. Rutland	03	00	02	03
Tho. wasborow	15	00	11	3
Widdow web	14	00	10	6
Mr. Oliff	30	01	02	6
Samuell Clafell	09	00	06	9
Mathew Adlam	24	00	18	0
Mris. Avendall	28	01	01	0
Sarah Wasborow	03	00	02	3
William white	24	00	18	0
Mr. Burdges	30	01	02	6
Mris. Hort	26	00	19	6
Tho. Cuff	08	00	06	0
Mr. Powell	12	00	09	0
Samuell Sanford	09½	00	06	9
Tho. Hort	08	00	06	0
Mr. Prise	06	00	04	6
Mr. Sampson	12	00	09	0
John Chessher	03	00	02	3
John Adlam	04	00	03	0
Samuell Clafell	04	00	03	0
Samuell Nicholas	06½	00	04	10
Robert Hedges	07	00	03	3
John Wasborow	03	0	02	3

Page 161. The 12th of Aprell 1681.

	£			
Sr. Robert Can..	109	04	09	9
Sr. Robert yeomans	42	01	11	6
Sr. Robert Southwell	70	02	12	6
Sr. Richard Crump [1]	35	01	06	3
Sr. Simon Lewis	06	00	04	6
Mr. Jackson	80	03	00	0
Mr. Martin	80	03	00	0
Mr. Gleed	66	02	09	0
Mr. Dymer	60	02	05	0
Mr. Speed	38	01	08	6
Mris. Joyce Beavan	38	01	08	6
Mr. Prise	18	00	13	6
Mris. Blackwell	05	00	03	9
Mr. Dimmock	11	00	08	3
Mr. Knight	22	00	16	6
Mr. Hart	36	01	07	0
Mr. Tilladam	20	00	15	0
Mr. Hurtnoll	08	00	06	0
Mris. Shore	12	00	09	0
Mr. Dawson	10	00	07	06
Mr. Husbands	16	00	12	00
Mr. Brooks	28	01	01	0
Lewis or teanaunt	02	00	01	6
Mr. Criswick	09	00	06	9
Mr. Hort	17	00	12	9
Mris. Avendall	03	00	02	3
Mr. Bawldin or teanants	08	00	06	0
Widdow Stokes	08	00	06	0
William Self	03	00	02	3
John Hurne	10	00	07	6
Arthur Sawyer	04	00	03	0
Samuell Sanford	02	00	01	6
John Barwick	02	00	01	6

[1] Sir Richard Crump was a chandler, became Mayor of Bristol in 1677, and was elected M.P. for Bristol in 1685. In July, 1687, the Civic Exchequer was so low that the Council determined that the salary of its Members of Parliament " should be paid as the law directs " —sufficiently obscure to mean nothing. For the previous session Sir Richard Crump had been paid £17 13s. 4d., but his colleague, Sir Richard Hart, had received nothing. This resolution was afterwards rescinded.

Page 162. The 12th of Aprell 1681.

		£			
Imp	Sr. Robert Southwell	31	01	03	3
	Mr. Rogers	76	02	17	0
	Mris. Sarah Wasborow	05	00	03	9
	Mr. Hollway	40	01	10	0
	Richard Grumnell	40	01	10	0
	Mris. Web	19	00	14	3
	William Harris	25	00	18	9
	John Willis	05	00	03	9
	John Smith	14	00	10	6
	John Mathews	20	00	15	0
	Henry Green	42	01	11	10
	William White	14	00	10	6
	Arthur White	14	00	10	6
	Wirkhouse	15	00	11	3
	Jonathan Edwards	16	00	12	0
	Georg Peters	17	00	12	9
	Widdow Stokes	09	00	06	9
	John Thomas	20	00	15	0
	Petre Dee	43	01	12	3
	Richard Pritchett	08	00	06	0
	Widd Lott	14	00	10	6
	William heskins	54	02	00	6
	Mr. Crismus or teanant	28	01	01	0
	Avenhouse	16	00	12	0
	John heskins	28	01	07	0
	Mr. Atry	0?	00	03	0
	William Peacock	0?	00	01	6
	William Cox	16	00	12	0
	Mris. Dighton	50	01	17	6
	John Smith	25	00	18	9
	Widdow Berry	12	00	09	0
	Tho: herring	11	00	08	3
	Widdow Smith	31	01	03	3
	Widdow Jackson	07	00	05	3
	Widdow Gush	10	00	07	6
	Samuell Robins	08	00	06	0
	Mr. Davis	12½	00	09	4
	Mr. Bush	10	00	07	6
	Widdow haines	04	00	03	0
	Widdow Smether	35	01	03	0
	James Peacock	14	00	10	6
	Mris. Rutland	16	00	12	0
	Mris. Dighton for the Inn	10	00	07	6
	Tho. Cuff	02	00	01	6

Page 163.

he accompt of Mr. John Knight one of the overseers of the poore of the prish of West-uppon-trim made the 20th day of Aprell 1682.

	£	s.	d.
his accomptant Chargeth himself wth two rates one of six pence a pound and the other three pence a pound wch commeth to	029	12	06
of wch 6 : 14 : 09d. is yet unreceaved.			
np pd Edith Bowry 13 mo att 6s. p mo..	003	18	00
pd Wm. Cary 13 mo att 6s. p mo	003	18	00
pd Mary Major 13 mo at 6s. p mo	003	18	00
pd Wm. Smith 13 mo att 4s. p mo	002	12	00
pd Eliza Cooke 13 mo att 4s. p mo..	002	12	00
pd Goody Hunt 13 mo att 2s. p mo..	001	06	00
pd Shusannah Smith 13 mo att 4s. 06d. p mo	002	18	06
	021	02	06
pd To Wm. Smith at times	000	09	06
pd burying ould Bowryes wife	000	10	00
pd for Seaverall warrants of Removall	000	02	00
pd Mr. Whitlock for Curing Goodman Taffs Legg	000	10	00
pd Mary Majors Rent..	000	05	00
pd Horshire to Stapleton of Stephens his widdowe ..	000	01	00
Given to Seaverall wth Passes et in the whole yeare ..	000	04	06
	023	04	06
To Ballance Receaved In the hands of John Knight The newe accountant	006	08	00

The £6 08s. 00d. was paid Jno Knight

	£	s.	d.
To Wm. Martin for Ball of his acctt.. ..	2	06	04
To Mr. Nicholl 26th May 1682	4	01	08
	6	08	00

Page 164.

The accompt of John Barwick one of the overseers of the poore of the prish of Westbury-uppon-trim made the 20th day of Aprell 1682.

	£	s.	d.
This accomptant Chargeth himself wth two rates one of six pence a pound and the other three pence a pound wch commeth to	32	18	06
Imp paid to good Vaughan 8 moneths at 4s.	01	12	00
paid to good Cox 3 moneths at 2s...	00	06	00
paid to John Raynolds 13 moneths at 6s.	03	18	00
paid to good hatter 13 moneths at 6s.	03	18	00
paid to good pullin 13 moneths at 6s.	03	18	00
paid to her for the Child 13 moneths at 6s...	03	18	00
paid to good haskins 13 moneths at 3s.	01	19	00
paid for harfees boy 13 moneths at 8s.	05	04	00
	24	13	00
paid to Mr. Martin money that was dew to him	03	16	00
paid for carring good Chanler to London..	01	00	00
geaven to good homes the whole yeare	01	00	00
geaven to John White the whole yeare	00	08	00
geaven to Joane Griffin the whole yeare	00	08	06
paid for washing and tending of John Raynolds.. ..	00	04	00
paid John Raynolds rent	00	06	08
paid for a suit of Cloaths for harfees boy	00	09	04
paid for 2 paier of stockins	00	02	06
paid for 2 paier of shoos	00	04	00
paid for a new hatt and mending of cloaths and shoos ..	00	02	10
paid for 2 shirts	00	04	06
paid for carring away Cottens daughter 2 sevll times going to the Justice	00	05	00
geaven to good haskins in her sicknes	00	02	00
geaven to 3 poore people wch had passes	00	01	00
paid for making the the rates and ingrosing the book ..	00	04	00
paid for putting in harfees boy in the free school.. ..	00	03	00
paid toward buring of good Boure..	00	02	00
paid toward the buring of Robert butt	00	03	04
for exspenses sev times going about to warne people for taking in of strangers	00	02	06
geaven to Robert Bartlutt in his sicknes	00	09	06
Paid out uppon the buring of him..	01	00	00
	10	18	10
Due to John Barwick £2 13s. 02d.			
Brought from above ..	24	13	00
	35	11	10

Page 165.

[T]he accompt of Jonathan Edwards one of the overseers of the poore of the prish of Westbury-uppon-trim made the 20th day of Aprell 1682.

	£	s.	d.
[T]his accomptant Chargeth himself wth 2 rates one of six pence a pound and the other three pence a pound wch commeth to	33	10	01

	£	s.	d.
[I]mp paid to John Caly 13 moneths at 4s...	02	12	00
paid to good berry 13 moneths at 6s.	03	18	00
paid for keeping of draysy 13 m at 6s.	03	18	00
	10	08	00
paid to Mathew Lewis for keeping homes child	00	08	08
paid for the buring of the same child	00	08	02
geaven to a poore man wth a pass..	00	00	06
paid for 2 shifts for drasey	00	06	00
paid for a payer of shoos for berries Child..	00	01	06
paid for a warrant and exspences to take Morrice Smith to geve bond to the prish	00	03	00
paid to Mr. Lam money that was dew to him from the prish	04	17	09
for exspences meeting sev times at the Vestry	00	01	00
for exspences going to the Justice wth hann baber ..	00	01	00
paid towards a payer of shoos for draysy	00	01	06
exspences at henbury when Morris Smith gave bond to save the prish harmeless	00	01	00
paid to the tithing man for his exspenses at the Inn uppon Hanna Baber wth the assistance of other men	00	09	10
geaven unto 2 poore woemen..	00	00	10
geaven to John Caly to look remedy for his son being like to loose the use of his arme	01	10	00
geaven to Mary Berry to buy shifts, hosen and shoes and Cloaths	00	10	00
for the Cost of my time and exspences	00	00	00
paid for lodging of John Barrow 2 moneths..	00	12	00
Disbursted ..	20	00	09

	£	s.	d.
[O]ur receipts is	96	01	01
[O]ur disburstments	78	17	01
[R]emaines dew to the pish ..	17	04	00

	£	s.	d.
dew from him to the prish	13	09	04

[W]e doe nominate and appoint to serve [t]he office of overseers for the poore the [y]eare ensuing Samuel Nicholas

William Dawson

John Cook

Page 166.
Those three accompts seene and allowed by us
whose names are heare under written and as followeth

Richard Davye
Sammuell price
Tho: Geering
Isaac Dymer
William Martin
Samuell Nickolas
John Thomas
Henry Greene
William White

	£	s.	d.
Rec the sume of	96	1	1
Disburst ye sume of	78	17	1
Rem to the parish	17	4	0

John Goldingham
Curate of Westbury

Allowed by us
Sam Astry
John Meredith

Page 167. The first of Aprell 1682.

A rate made by the Churchwardens and overseers of the poore of the prish of Westbury-uppon-trim for and toward the releef of the poore for this half yeare at the rate of fower pence a pound ending the nine and twenty day of September next as followeth

	£	£	s.	
Imp Mr. John Knight	90	01	10	00
Mr. John Lamb	80	01	06	08
Mr. Davis	46	00	15	04
Mr. Gerring	60	01	00	00
Mr. Walter	16	00	05	04
Mr. Sampson	80	01	06	08
Mr. Lane	75	01	05	00
Mr. Prise	42	00	14	00
Mris. Walter	12	00	04	00
Mris. Rutland	03	00	01	00
Tho. Wasborow	15	00	05	00
Georg Web	14	00	04	08
Mr. Oliff	30	00	10	00
Samuell Clafell	09	00	03	00
Widdow Adlam	24	00	08	00
Mris. Avendall	28	00	09	04
Mris. Sarah Wasborow	03	00	01	00
William White	24	00	08	00
Mr. Burdges	30	00	10	00
Mris. hort	26	00	08	08
Tho. Cuff	08	00	02	08
Mr. Powell	12	00	04	00
Samuell Sanford	09½	00	03	02
Tho: hort	08	00	02	08
Mr. Prise	06	00	02	00
Mr. Sampson	12	00	04	00
John Chessher	03	00	01	00
John Adlam	03	00	01	00
Richard Horwood	03	00	01	00
Samuell Clafell	04	00	01	04
Samuell Nicholas	06½	00	02	02
Robert Hedges	07	00	02	04
John Wasborow	03	00	01	00
Tho. Wallis	01	00	00	04
		13	08	06

Page 168. The first of Aprell 1682.

		£	s.	d.
Imp	Sr. Robert Can..	109	36	04
	Sr. Robert Yeomans	42	14	00
	Sr. Robert Southwell	76	23	04
	Sr. Richard Crump	35	11	08
	Sr. Simon Lewis	06	02	00
	Mr. Jackson	80	26	08
	Mr. Martin	30	26	08
	Mr. Gleed	66	22	00
	Mr. Dymer	60	20	00
	Mr. Edwards	38	12	08
	Mris. Joyce Beavan	38	12	08
	Mr. Prise	18	06	00
	Mris. Blackwell	05	01	08
	Mr. Dimmock	11	03	08
	Mr. Knight	22	07	04
	Mr. Hart	36	12	00
	Mr. Talladam	20	06	08
	Mr. Hurtnoll	08	02	08
	Mris. Shore	12	04	00
	Mr. Dawson	10	03	04
	Mr. Husbands	16	05	04
	Mr. Brooks	28	09	04
	Lewis or teanant	02	00	08
	Mr. Criswick	09	03	00
	Mr. Hort	17	05	08
	Mris. Avendall	03	01	00
	Mr. Bawldin or teanants	08	02	08
	Widdow Stokes	08	02	08
	William Self	03	01	00
	John Hurne	10	03	04
	Arthur Sawyer	04	01	04
	Samuell Sanford	02	00	08
	John Barwick	02	00	08
	Patrick Browne	04	01	04
		15	00	08

Page 169. The first of Aprell 1682.

			£	s.	d.
	Imp	Sr. Robert Southwell	51	10	04
		Mris. Rogers	76	25	00
		Mris. Sarah Wasborow	05	01	08
		Mr. Hollway	40	13	04
		Richard Grumnell	40	13	04
		Mris. Web	19	06	04
		William Harris	25	08	04
		John Willis	05	01	08
		John Smith	14	04	08
		John Mathews or teanant	20	06	08
		Henry Green	30½	10	02
		Mary Smith Elnor Green	12	04	00
		William White	14	04	08
		Arthur White	14	04	08
		Wirkhouse	15	05	00
		Jonathan Edwards	16	05	04
		Georg Peters	17	05	08
		Widdow Stokes	09	03	00
		John Thomas	20	06	08
		Petre Dee	43	14	04
		Richard Prichett	08	02	08
		Widdow Lott	14	04	08
		William Heskins	54	18	00
		Mr. Crismus	28	09	04
		Avenhouse	16	05	04
		John Heskins	28	09	04
		Mr. Astry	04	01	04
10 0		William Peacock	02	00	08
		William Cox	16	05	04
		Mris. Dighton	50	16	08
		John Smith	25	08	04
		Widdow Berry	12	04	00
		Tho. Herring	11	03	08
		Widdow Smith	31	10	04
		Widdow Jackson	07	02	04
		Widdow Gush	10	03	04
		Samuell Robins	08	02	08
		Mr. Davis	12½	04	02
		Widdow Haines	04	01	04
		Widdow Smether	29	09	08
		Robert Smith	06	02	00
		James Peacock	14	04	08
		Mris. Rutland	10	03	04
0 0		Mr. Dighton	10	03	04
0 0		Tho. Cuff	02	00	08
		Henry Green	02	00	08
		Persevel Reed	01	00	04

Page 170.

The accompt of Samuell Nickells one of the overseares of ye poore of ye parrish of Westbury-upon-Trim and Made ye 20th of Aprill 1683.

	£	s.	d.
ffirst this Accomptant chargeth him selfe with A rate of 4d. in ye pound which comeh	13	08	06
To Monys reseaved of Jonathan Edwards	13	09	04
To Monys Res of Squire Knight	04	01	08
To Monys res of Wasborowes Monys	02	10	00
To Monys Reseaved of one of hallen	10	00	00
	43	09	06

Disbirstments as ffoll	£	s.	d.
pd to Eddy Bowry i munth 6s. p 3 munth 3s. p munth	00	15	00
Good man Cary 3 munthes 6s. p munth	00	18	00
William Smith elder 13 munthes 4s. 6d. p mun.. ..	002	13	06
Sarah gooling 13 munthes 6s. p munth	03	18	00
Elizabeth Cooke 13 munthes 4s. 6d...	02	18	06
Widow Smith 13 munthes 4s. 6d. p munth..	2	18	06
Mary Moior 13 munthes 3s. p munth	01	19	00
Widow hunte 3 munthes 2s. 6d. p munth..	01	12	06
pd To John Barr ffor under collecktor	02	13	00
To John Barwick ffor singing ye poores rate	00	02	06
pd to ould ward of hallen	00	10	00
To pd overseare of ye poore of Sherehampton	03	00	00
Thomas hoskings overseare at twice..	06	00	00
5th of May pd at ye Inne	00	05	08
A man with a passe ye same day	00	00	08
10th of May at ye In and parrish Bynes	00	05	00
ffor . . . . of Williams his 2 witneses ? ..	03	01	06
A woman and 3 children with a pass in July	00	00	09
A good minister and his wife in August	00	01	00
A paire of Bodis ffor Bouy Bowrys daffter..	00	01	08
To haveng poores Rate sined	00	02	06
pay forr and a man witnes also	00	01	06
To carey over Lefe.. ..	34	03	08

NOTE.—This page is the most difficult in the book to transcribe.

Page 171. 1693.

	£	s.	d.
;amuell Nickolls over seaer of ye poore of Westbury-upon-Trime his accompt of dysbust Brought ffrom ye other side	34	03	09
ffor Carring ye Tabell to Bristoll	00	01	00
ffor Binding of Bowrys daghter indentures	03	11	06
William Bowry in his sicknes..	00	02	00
pd Auditt day spent at ye ende	00	15	06
good wiffie wade ye elder	00	01	00
good wiffie wade ye younger being Lame	00	01	00
an owld Man And his wiffe with a passe	00	00	06
pd Jones ye joyner and ye payntor and spent	01	11	00
and gave a cripell with a passe	00	00	06
Muney ye spent at ye End about parrish bisnes	00	06	06
spent r horse hier upon hancocks baster child	00	05	00
gave a Sargant and a ye man to bring Corys master to ye mayor	00	05	00
Eddy Bowry at severall Times in her sicknes	00	02	10
Gave to a poore man with a passe	00	00	06
Goodman Smith the younger in his sicknes..	00	06	06
I crave alowance ffor Sir ffrancis ffane	00	06	08
ffor younge Runly at ye Ende and his Diett	000	02	06
	41	19	03
In the Hands of Mr. Nicholls To Ball	01	10	03
	43	09	06

	£	s.	d.
Iemorand Due by Sr. ffrancis ffane	00	06	08

Wch £1 10s. 3d. paid to Robert fennell

more receaved of John Cook.. .. .. 00 10 07

Page 172.

The accompt of William Dawson, one of the overseers of the poore of the prish of Westbury-uppon-trim made the 20th of Aprell 1683.

	£	s.	d.
first this accomptant chargeth himself a rate of fower pence a pound wch commeth to	15	00	08
more receaved of Mr. Nicholas at 2 sevll times	06	00	00
more receaved of Tho Wasborows money	03	10	00
his disburstments as followeth ..	24	10	08
Imp paid John Raynolds 10 moneths at six shillings	03	00	00
paid to goodd Hatter 10 moneths at six shillings.. ..	03	00	00
paid to her 3 moneths at eight shillings	01	04	00
paid to gooddy Haskins 13 moneths at 3s...	01	19	00
paid to gooddy Homes 13 moneths at 3s...	01	19	00
paid for Harfees boy 13 moneths at 8s.	05	04	00
paid for pullins boy 13 moneths at 6s.	03	18	00
paid for buring of gooddy Davis	00	12	06
paid for washing John Raynolds Clothes	00	08	06
paid for his Rent	00	05	00
paid for 2 horse load of coals for him	00	02	00
geaven to him at 2 sev times..	00	02	00
geaven to Gooddy Griffin in the whole yeare	00	04	00
paid for a Coat for pullins boy	00	04	08
paid for 2 shirts for him	00	02	06
paid for 2 payer of hozen and shoos..	00	03	06
paid for 2 payer of shoos and mending for harfee.. ..	00	05	04
paid for 2 payer of stockings and making 2 shirts ..	00	02	06
paid for making a suit and drawers for him..	00	02	06
paid for stuff for the drawers pockets and buttons.. ..	00	02	04
geaven to John White at sev times..	00	05	06
paid towards the buring of a poore man of Sea Mills ..	00	02	04
paid for Carring away 2 paccell of Criples..	00	01	06
geaven to sev brought by passes from tithing to tithing..	00	01	00
for making the Rates and ingrosing the book	00	04	00
for going sev times about the prish to warne outcommers and exspences	00	02	06
paid towards the buring of John Raynolds..	00	10	00
geaven to the woeman that lay in at haskins	00	05	00
geaven to goodman Davis in his sicknes	00	02	00
geaven to gooddy Haskins	00	01	00
I crave allowance for Sr. ffrances fane	00	06	08
Memorand Due of Sr. ffrn: ffane.. .. .. £ 00 s. 06 d. 08	25	02	10
Recd and allow p. Thom Hopkins..	24	10	08
	00	12	02

Page 173.

The accompt of John Cook one of the overssers of the poore of the prish of Westbury-uppon-trim made the 20th of Aprell 1683.

	£	s.	d.
first this accomptant Chargeth himself wth a rate of fower pence a pound wch commeth to	16	01	00
more receaved of Mr. Martin	07	00	00
more receaved of Mr. Nickolas	03	00	00
The totall is	26	01	00

	£	s.	d.
Imp paid to John Calee 13 months at 4 shillings..	02	12	00
paid for keeping Hannath Robins 13 moneths at 6s. ..	03	18	00
paid for keeping barras boy 13 moneths at 6s.	03	18	00
paid for keeping drasy 13 moneths at 6s.	03	18	00
paid Tho: foord 6 moneths at 8s.	02	08	00
paid him 2 moneths at 6s.	00	12	00
paid him 2 weeks at 1s.	00	02	00
paid to the Docter comming to Tho foord	02	01	07
laid out for John Calee son	00	07	06
geaven to John Calee in his sicknes	00	05	00
geaven to him another time in his want	00	05	00
geaven to Tho: foord at sev times	01	09	00
paid to the Docter for william withers wife..	00	04	02
paid for cloths for Draisy	01	00	00
I Crave allowance for Sr. ffraunces fane	01	02	00
geaven to William Withers in his sicknes	00	05	00
paid for clothes for Draysy	00	10	00
Spent when we had the rate signed	00	01	00
paid for 4 warrants for to take distrese of the quakers ..	00	0?	00
	24	18	03

Memorand Remaines Due of Sr. ffra: ffane .. 1 02 00

£	s.	d.		£	s.	d.
			Rest Due of John Coock is..	01	02	09
00	04	00	from Jeremiah Gush } Taken in Distress p: virtue			
00	03	00	from Hannah Tayler }	26	01	00
			of The Justice Warrant for absenting themselves from			
7			Church[1] wh Seaven Shill: is Distributed to The Poore of the pish accordingly.			

			£	s.	d.
John Thomas	John Lambe	pd . . . Cooke To Tho Hopkins of Due To him as p his Acctt	00	12	02
Robert Hogges	Samuell prise				
Churchwardens		pd To Robert ffennill the . . .	00	10	07
		Tho Knight	01	02	09

1683	£	s.	d.
Receaved the Sum of ..	94	00	02
Disbursted the sum of ..	91	12	10
Due to the prish.. ..	02	07	04

[1] "The Churchwardens are to levy (Stat. 1 Eliz., c. 2) a shilling forfeiture on all such as do not repair to Church on Sundays and holidays."—Blackstone, *Commentaries*, i, 395.

Page 174.
We doe nominate and appoint to serve the office of overseers of the poore for the yeare ensuing

Robert fennell
Richard Stephens
Richard Smith

Allowed by us

Tho Chester

Christopher Cole.

Page 175. The first of Aprell 1683.

rate made by the churchwardens and others of the inhabytans of the prish of Westbury for and towards the releif of the poore for this yeare at the rate of six pence a pound as followeth.

	£		s.	d.
np Sr. ffraunces fane	20	00	10	00
Mr. John Knight	90	02	05	00
Mr. John Lamb	80	02	00	00
Mr. Jackson	46	01	03	00
Mr. Gerring	60	01	10	00
Mr. Walter	16	00	08	00
Mr. Sampson	80	02	00	00
Mr. Lane	75	01	17	6
Mr. Prise	42	01	01	00
Mris. Walter	12	00	06	00
Mris. Rutland	03	00	01	06
Tho. Wasborow	15	00	07	06
Mr. Web	14	00	07	00
Mr. oliff	30	00	15	00
Samuell Clafell	09	00	04	06
Tho Adlam or teanant	24	00	12	00
Mris. Avendall	28	00	14	00
Mris. Sarah Wasborow	03	00	01	06
William White	24	00	12	00
Joseph Burdges	30	00	15	00
Mris. Hort	26	00	13	00
Tho. Cuff	08	00	04	00
Mr. Powell	12	00	06	00
Samuell Sanford	09½	00	04	09
Tho. Hort	08	00	04	00
Mr. Prise	06	00	03	00
Mr. Tison	12	00	06	00
John Chesher	03	00	01	06
John Adlam	03	00	01	06
Richard Horwoad	04	00	02	00
Samuell Clafell	04	00	02	00
Samuell Nicholas	06½	00	03	03
Mr. Cleark	06	00	03	00
Robert Hodges	02	00	01	00
John Wasborow	03	00	01	06
Tho. Wallis	01	00	00	06
804	20	?	07	00

Page 176. The first of Aprell 1683.

		£			
Imp	Sr. Robert Can	109	02	14	6
	Sr. Robert yeomans	42	01	01	0
	Sr. Robert Southwell	70	01	15	0
	Sr. Samuell Austry	11	00	05	6
	Sr. Richard Crump	35	00	17	6
	Sr. Simon Lewis	06	00	03	0
	Mr. Jackson	80	02	00	0
	Mr. Martin	80	02	00	0
	Mr. Gleed	66	01	13	0
	Mr. Dymer	60	01	10	0
	Mr. Edwards	38	00	19	0
	Mris. Joyce Beavan	38	00	19	0
	Mr. Prise	18	00	09	0
	Mris. Blackwell	05	00	02	6
	Mr. Knight	22	00	11	0
	Mr. Hart	36	00	18	0
	Mr. Tilladam	20	00	10	0
	Mr. Hurtnoll	08	00	04	0
	Mris. Shore	12	00	06	0
	Mr. Dawson	10	00	05	0
	Mr. Husbands	16	00	08	0
	Mr. Brooks	28	00	14	0
	Lewis or teanant	02	00	01	0
	Mr. Criswick	09	00	04	06
	Mr. Hort	17	00	08	06
	Mris. Avendall	03	00	01	06
	Mr. Bawldin or teanant	08	00	04	0
	Widdow Stokes	08	00	04	0
	William Self	03	00	01	6
	John Hurne	10	00	05	0
	Arthur Sawyer	04	00	02	0
	Richard Sanford	02	00	01	0
	John Barwick	02	00	01	0
	Patrick Browne	04	00	02	0

Page 177. The first of Aprell 1683.

	£	s.	d.
np Sr. Robert Southwell	31	15	06
Sr. Samuell Austry	04	02	00
Mr. Rogers	78	38	00
Sarah Wasborow	05	02	06
Mr. Hollway	40	20	00
Richard Grumnell	40	20	00
Widdow Web	19	09	06
William Harris	25	12	06
John Willis	05	02	06
John Smith	14	07	00
John Mathews or teanant	20	10	00
Henry Green	30½	15	03
Mary Smith and Elnor Green	12	06	00
William White	14	07	00
Arthur White	14	07	00
Wirkhouse	15	07	06
Widdow Edwards	16	08	00
Georg. Peters	17	08	06
Widdow Stokes	09	04	06
John Thomas	20	10	00
Peter Dee	43	21	06
Richard Pritchett	08	04	00
Richard Smith	14	07	00
William Heskins	54	27	00
Mr. Crismus or teant	28	14	00
Avenhouse	16	08	00
Widdow Heskins	28	14	00
William Peacock	02	01	00
William Cox	16	08	00
Mris. Dighton	50	25	00
John Smith	25	08	00
Widdow Berry	12	06	00
Tho: Herring or teanant	11	05	06
Widdow Smith	16	08	00
Tho: Smith	15	07	06
Widdow Jackson	07	03	06
Widdow Gush	10	05	00
Samuell Robins	08	04	00
William Davis	12½	06	03
Mr. Bush	10	05	00
Widdow Haines	04	02	00
Andrew Smether	29	14	06
Richard Smith	06	03	00
James Peacock	14	07	00
Mris. Rutland	16	08	00
Mris. Dighton	10	05	00
Tho: Cuff	02	01	00
Henry Green	02	01	00
Persevell Reed	01	00	06

Page 178.

The accompt of Robert fennell one of the overseers of the poore of the prish of Westbury-uppon-trim made the 5th of Aprell 1684.

	£	s.	d.
first this accomptant chargeth himself wth two rates one of fower pence a pound and the other of two pence a pound wch cometh to	20	07	06
more receaved of the ould Collectors	02	00	10
more receaved of Mr. Martin money	02	10	00
	24	18	04
the disburstments as followeth			
Imp paid to William Smith 13 m at 4s. 6d.	02	18	06
paid to Sarah pulling 13 m at 6s. 0d...	03	18	00
paid Elizab Cook 13 m at 4s. 6d.	02	18	06
paid to Susan Smith 13 m at 4s. 6d...	02	18	06
paid to Mary Major 13 m at 3s. 0d.	01	19	00
paid to gooddy hunt 13 m at 3s	01	19	00
	16	11	06
geaven to gooddy hunt accompt day	00	05	06
geaven to Mary Major the same day..	00	02	00
geaven to William Boure the whole yeare	00	10	00
paid to the bone setter for setting his ribs	00	03	00
geaven to ould smith at sev times	00	06	06
paid gooddy Grant for bring a woeman to bed	00	02	06
geaven to John Jefferies and his wife the whole ye.. ..	00	13	06
spent when I receaved the poore money	00	00	06
paid for 2 payer of shoos and 2 payer of stockins for harfees boy and mending of shoos	00	07	06
paid for a payer of shoos and stockins for pullin	00	02	04
geaven to Ane Tugg	00	02	06
geaven to sev poore people with passes	00	02	00
spent going to sign the poors book	00	01	00
geaven to William Smith Junor	00	05	00
geaven to Dorethy wade	00	02	06
geaven to Robert wade	00	02	06
for signing the book and the warrants	00	02	00
for making the rates and ingrosing the book	00	04	00
paid for the use of ten pounds Gooddy gyllott	00	12	00
paid to Mr. Knight money that he laid out uppon harfees boy	00	10	04
paid towards the publick bridges	00	06	06
paid for mending Tho Tagg house	00	15	02
paid for mending boure house	00	14	06
paid for mending Cooks house	00	06	06
paid for mending of pullins house	00	14	10
	24	06	02

Page 179.

'he accompt of Richard Stephens one of the overseers of the poore of the prish of Westbury-uppon-trim made the 5th of Aprell 1684.

rst this accomptant chargeth himself wth 2 rates one of 4d. a pound and the other of 2d. a pound wch commeth to ..	22	07	06
ɪore receaved of Mr. Martin	06	00	00
	28	07	06

The disburstments

paid for harfee 13 m at 8s.	05	04	00
paid for pullin boy 13 m at 6s.	03	18	00
paid gooddy hatter 13 m at 10s.	06	10	00
paid gooddy homes 13 m at 4s.	02	12	00
paid gooddy haskins 13 m at 4s.	02	12	00
paid goody Vaughan 3 m at 3s.	00	09	00
	21	05	00

geaven to John White at sev times	00	16	00
paid for Cloths for hatter boy	00	11	00
geaven to ould Davis	00	02	00
geaven to gooddy Coats	00	03	06
paid to the Tithing man for releef for Cripples	00	04	06
geaven to the widdow Cuff	00	06	00
paid for Cloaths for pullin boy	00	12	00
geaven to homes at his going away	02	12	00
geaven to Joane Griffin	00	03	06
geaven to gooddy vaughan	00	02	00
geaven to gooddy haskins	00	02	00
spent at sev petty sessions	00	00	00
	26	19	06

Page 180.

The accompt of Richard Smith one of the overseers of the poore of the prish of Westbury-uppon-trim made the 5th of Aprell 1684.

first this accomptant chargeth himself wth 2 rates one of 4d. a pound and the other of 2d. a pound wch commeth to ..	24	01	08
more receaved of Richard Farne	07	03	09
more receaved of Mr. Martin	01	00	00
	32	05	05
paid to John Caly 13 m at 4s...	02	12	00
paid for ane drasy 13 m at 6	03	18	00
paid for playford 13 m at 4	02	12	00
paid for Hanna Roberts 13 m at 6	03	18	00
paid for Barrows boy 13 m at 6	03	18	00
paid for a payer of shoos and stockins for drasy	00	03	04
paid for Cloaths for playford..	00	12	02
paid for a payer of shoos for Han Roberts	00	02	00
geaven to Georg Hoggutt in his sicknes	01	07	03
paid to the Docter for him	00	09	07
paid for the buring of him	01	06	09
paid to the widdow Hoggut 6 m at 6s.	01	16	00
paid for house rent for her	00	11	00
geaven to John Baker in his lameness	00	17	06
paid to the Docter for curing his hand	01	10	00
geaven to Roger Rosser	00	05	00
geaven to Tho: foord	00	02	00
geaven to Bridgett Parker	00	03	00
geaven to Richard parker	00	08	06
paid towards the County bridges	00	06	06
geaven to Mary woods	00	02	00
geaven to Mary Atkins	00	02	00
geaven to John Tomkins	00	02	00
geaven to Joan Baker	00	01	06
geaven to John Shott	00	07	06
I crave allowance for Sr. ffraunces fane	00	03	00
I crave allowance for Richard brittan	00	00	08
I crave allowance for Mr. Reed	00	00	06
	27	17	9

Page 181.

ıe 3 accompts seen and allowed by wee whose names are heare underwritten

ımuell prise

ıo Geering

ıomas Wasborrow

'illiam White

Anthony Ellsworth }
Thomas Smith } Churchwardens.

		£		d.
Receaved the som of	..	85	10	11
disburst the som of	..	79	02	03
dew to the prish ..	..	06	08	08

'e doe nominate and appoint to serve the office of overseer for the poore the yeare ensuing

ıis £6 8s. 8d. was paid to the Churchwarden

Richard Horwood
Edward Hunt
Samuell Child

Allowed by us
Samuel Astry
Tho Chester.

Page 182.

WESTBURY. The first of Aprill 1684.

A Rate made by the Churchwardens and others of the inhabitants of the prish of Westbury-Upon-Trim for and towards the Releife of the poore for the year at the Rate of eight pence A pound as followeth.

	£	s.	d.
Imp Sr. ffrancis ffane for his Tythe	18	12	00
Mrs. Knight £90 her Tythe £4½ all	94½	63	00
Mr. John Lamb	80	53	04
Mr. Jackson £46 his Tythe £2 all	48	32	00
Mr. Geering £40 his Tythe £2 all	42	28	00
Mrs. Turnbridg £20 her Tythe £1 all	21	14	00
Mr. Walter	16	10	08
Mr. Edward Sampson and his brother £79½ their Tythe £3½ all	83	55	04
Mr. Lane £75 his Tythe £2 all	77	51	04
Mr. Price	42	28	00
Mrs. Walter	12	08	00
Mrs. Rutland	03	02	00
Thomas Wasberrow	15	10	00
Mr. George Webb	14	09	04
Mr. Cliff	30	20	00
Samuell Clafell	09	06	00
Thomas Adlam or Tenant	24	16	00
Mrs. Avendell	28	18	08
Mrs. Sarah Wasberrow	03	02	00
Mr. William White	24	16	00
Joseph Burges £30 his Tythe £1½ all	31½	21	00
Mrs. Hort	20	17	04
Thomas Cuffe	08	05	04
Mr. Powell £12 his Tythe £½ all	12½	08	04
Samuell Sandford	09½	06	04
Thomas Hort	08	05	04
Mr. Price	06	04	00
Mr. Tyson	12	08	00
John Chessheir..	03	02	00
John Adlam	02	01	04
Richard Horwood	03	02	00
Samuell Nicholas	07	04	08
Samuell Claffell	04	02	08
Mr. Clarke	06	04	00
Robert Hodges	01	00	08
John Wasberrow	03	02	00
Thomas Wallis	01	00	08
Giles Nurse halfe A pound	00½	00	04
	27	ii	08

Page 183.
STOAKBISHOPP. The first of Aprill 1684

		£	s.	d.
Imp Sr. ffrancis ffane for his Tythe	.. ..	13	08	08
Sr. Robert Cam	£109 for his Tythe £5 all	114	76	00
Sr. Robert yeamans	£42 his Tythe £02 all	044	29	04
Sr. Robert Southwell	.. ..	70	46	08
Sr. Samuell Astry	.. ..	11	07	04
Sr. Richard Crumpe	£35 his Tythe £02 10s. all ..	37½	25	00
Sr. Symon Lewis	.. ..	06	04	00
Mr. Jackson	£80 his Tythe £04 all	84	56	00
Mr. Martin	£80 his Tythe £4 all	84	56	00
Mr. Gleed	.. ..	52	34	00
Mr. Kirk	£14 his Tythe ½ a £ all	14½	09	08
Mr. Dymer	£60 his Tythe £4½ all	64½	43	00
Mr. Edwards	£38 his Tythe £01½ all	39½	26	04
Mrs. Joyce Beavan	.. ..	38	25	04
Mr. Price	£18 Tythe ½ a £ all..	18½	12	04
Mrs. Blackwell	.. ..	05	03	04
Mrs. Knight	.. ..	22	14	08
Mr. Hart	£36 Tythe £01½ all..	37½	25	00
Mr. Tiladam	.. ..	20	13	04
John Hurtnell	.. ..	08	05	04
Mrs. Shore	£12 Tythe ½ a £ all	12½	08	04
Mr. Dawson	£10 Tythe ½ a £ all	10½	07	00
Mr. Husbands	.. ..	16	10	08
Mr. Brookes	£28 Tythe £01 all	29	19	04
Edward Lewis or Mr. Brookes	.. ..	02	01	04
Mr. Creswick	.. ..	09	06	00
Mr. Hort	.. ..	17	11	04
Mr. Bauldin	.. ..	08	05	04
Mrs. Arendell	.. ..	03	02	00
Widow Stoakes	.. ..	08	05	04
William Selfe	.. ..	03	02	00
John Hurne	.. ..	10	06	08
Arthur Sawyer	£04 his Tythe ½ a £ all	04½	03	00
Samuell Sandford	.. ..	02	01	04
John Barwick	.. ..	02	01	04
Patrick Browne	.. ..	04	02	08
		£30	15	08

Page 184.

SHERHAMPTON. The first of Aprell 1684.	£	s.	d.
Imp Sr. Robert Southwell	31	20	08
Sr. ffrancis ffane for his Tythe	60	40	00
Sr. Samuell Astry	04	02	08
Mrs. Rogers	76	50	08
Sarah Wasberrow	05	03	04
Mr. Hollway	40	26	08
Richard Grumwell	40	26	08
Widow Webb	19	12	08
William Harris	25	16	08
John Willis	05	03	04
John Smith	14	09	04
John Mathews or Tenant	20	13	04
Henry Greene	30½	20	04
Mary Smith and Elnor Green	12	08	00
William White	14	09	04
Arthur White	14	09	04
Wirkhouse	15	10	00
Widow Edwards	16	10	08
George Peters	17	11	04
Widow Stoakes	09	06	00
John Thomas	20	13	04
Peter Dee	43	28	08
Richard Pritchard	08	05	04
Richard Smith	14	09	04
William Heskins now Mr. Martin	54	36	00
Mr. Christmus or Tenant	28	18	08
Avenhouse	16	10	08
Widow Heskins	28	18	08
William Peacock	02	01	04
William Cox	16	10	08
Mrs. Dighton	50	33	04
John Smith	25	16	08
Widow Berry	12	08	00
Thomas Herring or Tenant	ii	07	04
Thomas Smith	16	10	08
Widow Smith	15	10	00
Widow Jackson	07	04	08
Widow Gush	10	06	08
Samuell Robins	08	05	04
Mr. Davies	12½	08	04
Mr. Bush	10	06	08
Widow Haynes	04	02	08
Andrew Smether	29	19	04
Richard Smith	06	04	00
James Peacock	14	09	04
Mrs. Rutland	16	10	08
Mrs. Dighton for the Inn	10	06	08
Thomas Cuffe	02	01	04
Henry Green	02	01	04

Page 185.

VESTBURY.

'he Accompt of Richard Horwood one of the overseers of the poor of the pish of Westbury-upon-Trim made the 4th day of May 1685.

	£	s.	d.
irst the Accomptant Chargeth himselfe wth one rate at 8d. A pound wch cometh unto	27	11	08
[oe Received of Roger Younge £10 he paid in	04	00	00
	31	11	08
The Disburstmts followeth			
mp To old William Smith 14 moneths at 5s. p moneth.. ..	03	10	00
paid Susan Smith 7 m at 04s. 06d. p m	01	11	06
paid Elizabeth Cook 14 m at 04s. 06d. p m..	03	03	00
paid Mary Major 14 m at 03s. p m..	02	02	00
paid for Harvies Boy 14 m at 8s. p m	05	12	00
paid the Widow Hunt 14 m at 3s. p m	02	02	00
paid John Jefferies 3 m at 4s. p m..	00	12	00
paid John Jefferies and his wife 2 m at 05s. p m	00	10	00
paid John Jefferies wife 2 m at 02s. p m	00	04	00
paid Edith Bowre her Son being come to her two m and 3 weeks at 06s. p m	00	16	06
	20	03	00
payd for a Hatt and Stockins for Harvies boy	00	03	00
given Thomas Grant	00	02	06
given to Robert Wade the whole yeare	00	13	06
given to John Jefferies at Sevall tymes before any given monethly	00	05	06
given for the buriall of William Smith Junior	00	12	00
given for the buriall of John White son	00	04	06
given old Bowre at Sevall tymes	00	04	00
payd for Stockings and shoos and a payre of drawes for Harvies boy	00	06	06
payd for the use of £10 to goody Gillett	00	12	00
payd for gray Cloth for a coat for old Smith and makeing it	00	08	01
given to Thomas Wades wife for clothing for her son for Hen: School	00	14	08
paid Edward Jocham for bookes and worke done in ye almeshouse	01	02	00
paid Richard Holbrook for masons work done upon ye almeshouse	00	04	00
given old William Smith at sevall tymes	00	03	00
given to bind out Edith Bowres boy	02	00	00
given to sevall poore people by passes	00	02	06
paid John Grant A moneths dyat for Martha Andrews ..	00	06	00
paid for makeing the rates and ingrossing the book ..	00	04	00
I crave allowance for ye due from Thomas Wallis he being dead	00	00	08
	28	11	05
payd John Claffell wh hee disburst in Receiveing and Sending forward Sevall Cripples	00	06	06

Page 186.

STOAKBISHOPP.

The Accompt of Samuell Childs on of the Overseers of the poore of the pish of Westbury-uppon-Trim made the 4th day of May 1685.

	£	s.	d.
ffirst this accomptant Chargeth himself wth one rate at 8d. A pound wch cometh unto	030	15	08

The disburstmts are as followeth	£	s.	d.
payd goody Hatter 14 moneths at 10s. the moneth ..	07	00	00
payd goody Haskins 14 m at 4s. p m	02	16	00
payd goody Vaughan 14 m at 3s. p m	02	02	00
payd Sarah Pullin 8 m at 12s. p m..	04	16	00
payd Sarah Pullin 6 m at 10s. p m..	03	00	00
payd Joan Griffin 8 m at 02s. p m..	00	16	00
	20	10	00
Given John White for the buriall of his Sonn	00	16	00
given John White in his feeble and poore Condicon ye whole yeare	01	06	06
given Richard ridler being very poore last winter ..	00	13	06
given to the Widow Haskins at sevall tymes being lame..	00	03	06
given to the Releife of poor people by passes	00	02	00
given to John Davies at Sevall tymes	00	02	00
given to Joan Griffin at Sevall tymes before shee came upon monethly pay	00	04	00
payd for Cloth for a Coat for Hatters boy and makeing ..	00	05	06
payd in charges when Sarah Saunders was sent hether by Justices warrant about her bastard child	00	05	06
payd for Shooes and Stockins for ye boy Sarah Pullin keeps	00	03	00
payd William Vaughan for keeping Martha Andrews 10 moneths and a halfe at 6s. p moneths..	03	03	00
payd towards the binding out Edith Bowres Son.. ..	02	00	00
payd for Hatters boy for shoos and Stocking	00	02	06
payd for Shoes for Sarah Pullins boy she keeps	00	01	06
given old goody vaughan	00	01	00
payd for shoos and Stockins for Martha Andrews.. ..	00	03	00
	30	02	06

Page 187.

SHERHAMPTON.

The Accompt of Edmond Hunt one of the overseers of the poore of the pish of Westbury-upon-Trim the 4th Day of May 1685.

	£	s.	d.
ffirst the Accomptant Chargeth himself wth one rate 8d. A pound wch cometh unto	31	10	08
Moe Received of Roger youngs mony	02	00	00
Moe for goods of Edith Williams when shee dyed	02	13	00
	36	09	08

The Disburstmts followeth

	£	s.	d.
Imp paid to John Caly 14 moneths at 4s. p m	02	16	00
paid for keeping Hannah Roberts 6 m at 06s. p m.. ..	01	16	00
paid for Playfoot 13 moneths and A halfe at 4s. p m ..	02	14	00
paid to Mary Hoggett 7 m at 6s. p m [1]	02	09	00
paid to Mary Hoggett 4 m at 4s. p m	00	16	00
paid to Mary Hoggett 3 m at 2s. p m	00	06	00
paid to Ann Draysie 14 m at 6s. p m	04	04	00
paid to John Barree 14 m at 6s. p m	04	04	00
paid to Abigall Parker 12 m at 6s. p m	03	12	00
paid John Baker 3 moneths at 2s. p m	00	06	00
paid to John Baker 5 m at 4s. p m..	01	00	00
given John Baker sevall tymes before he had mly pay ..	00	12	00
paid for Nursing Edith Williams Child 5 m at 8s. p m [1] ..	01	16	00
paid for the burialls of John Guning and Edith Williams..	02	14	00
paid for Abigall Parkers house rent and money gave her..	01	04	06
given to Sisley Lewis in her sicknesse	00	14	00
given to Joan Baker..	00	03	00
paid for Cloaths for Hannah Roberts and makeing her indentures	02	01	06
paid for keeping Hannah Roberts when she came from Bridwell	00	06	00
paid for shoes and Stocking for Playfoot	00	03	02
paid for Edith Williams house rent when shee dyed ..	00	03	06
paid for a petticoat two shifts and payer of bodice stocking and shooes as p note for Ann Draysie	00	15	01
I crave allowance for William Peacock A poor blind man..	00	01	04
	34	17	01

[1] Incorrectly entered by the overseer.

Page 188.

These three Accompts seene and allowed by wee whose names are here under written

	Anthony Ellsworth John ‡ marke Cooke	} Churchwardens.

Richard Lane
John Lambe
Willm Martin
John Smyth
Thomas Smith

	£	s.	d.
Received the Some of ..	98	17	00
Disburst	93	17	06
Due to ye pish	04	19	06

Wee Doe nominate and appoynt to serve the office of overseers of the poore ye yeare ensueing for the Tithing of Westbury

Mr. Samuell Clarke
Mr. Ezechiell Husbands for Stoak Bishop
Thomas Joyner for Sherehampton
Richd Hare
Christopher Cole

Page 189. The ffourth of May 1685.

VESTBURY.

ι rate made by the churchwardens and others of the pish of Westbury-upon-Trim for and towards the Releife of the poore for this yeare at the Rate of eight pence a pound as ffolloweth.

		£	s.	d.
mps	Sr. ffrancis ffane for his Tythe	18	12	00
	Mrs. Knight	94½	63	00
	Mr. John Lambe	80	53	04
	Mr. Jackson	48	32	00
	Mr. Geering	42	28	00
	Mrs. Tunbridg	21	14	00
	Mr. Walter	16	10	08
	Mr. Edward Sampson	75	50	00
	Mr. Ralph Sampson	08	05	04
	Mr. Lane	77	51	04
	Mr. Price	42	28	00
	Mrs. Walter	12	08	00
	Mrs. Rutland	03	02	00
	Thomas Wasberrow	15	10	00
	George Webb	14	09	04
	Mr. Cliff	30	20	00
	Samuell Claffell	09	06	00
	Thomas Adlam or Tenant	24	16	00
	Mrs. Arundle	23	18	08
	Mrs. Susan Wasberrow	03	02	00
	William White	24	16	00
	Joseph Burgis	31½	21	00
	Mrs. Hort	26	17	04
	Thomas Cuff	08	05	04
	Mr. Powell	12½	08	04
	Samuell Sandford	09½	06	04
	Thomas Hort	08	05	04
	Mr. Price	06	04	00
	Mr. Tyson	12	08	00
	John Chessheir	03	02	00
	John Adlam	02	01	04
	Richard Horwood	03	02	00
	Samuell Nicholas	07	04	08
	Samuell Clayfell	04	02	08
	Mr. Clark	06	04	00
	Robert Hodges	01	00	08
	John Wasberrow	03	02	00
	Thomas Wallis or Mr. William Jackson	01	00	08
	Giles Nurse halfe a pound	00½	00	04
		27	11	08

Page 190. The 4th of May 1685.

STOAKBISHOPP.

		£	s.	d.
Imp	Sr. ffrancis ffane for his Tythe	013	08	08
	Sr. Robert Cann	114	76	00
	Sr. Robert yeamans	44	29	04
	Sr. Robert Southwell	70	46	08
	Sr. Samuell Astry	11	07	04
	Sr. Richard Crumpe	37½	25	00
	Sr. Symon Lewis	06	04	00
	Mr. Jackson	84	56	00
	Mr. Martin	84	56	00
	Mr. Gleed	52	34	08
	Mr. Kirk	14½	09	08
	Mr. Dymer	64½	43	00
	Mr. Edwards	39½	26	04
	Mrs. Joyce Beavan	38	25	04
	Mr. Price	18½	12	04
	Mrs. Blackwell	05	03	04
	Mrs. Knight	22	14	08
	Mr. Hart	37½	25	00
	Mr. Tilladam	20	13	04
	John Hurtnell	08	05	04
	Mrs. Shore	12½	08	04
	Mr. Dawson	10½	07	00
	Mr. Husbands	16	10	08
	Mr. Brookes	29	19	04
	Edward Lewis or Mr. Brookes	02	01	04
	Mr. Creswicke	09	06	00
	Mr. Hort	17	11	04
	Mr. Bauldin	08	05	04
	Mrs. Arundell	03	02	00
	Widow Stoakes	08	05	04
	William Selfe	03	02	00
	John Hurne	10	06	08
	Arthur Sawyer	04½	03	00
	Samuell Sandford	02	01	04
	John Barwick	02	01	04
	Patrick Browne	04	02	08
		30	15	08

 The 4th of May 1685.

HEREHAMPTON.

	£	s.	d.
ap Sr. ffrancis ffane for his Tythe	60	40	00
Sr. Robert Southwell	31	20	08
Sr. Samuell Astry	04	02	08
Mrs. Rogers	76	50	08
Mrs. Sarah Wasberrow	05	03	04
Mr. Holway	40	26	08
Richard Grumwell	40	26	08
Mrs. Webb or ye widow Bowre	19	12	08
William Harris	25	16	08
John Willis	05	03	04
John Smith	14	09	04
John Mathewes or tenant	20	13	04
Henry Green	30½	20	04
Mary Smith or Elnor Green	12	08	00
William White	14	09	04
Arthur White	14	09	04
Wirkhouse	15	10	00
Widow Edwards	16	10	08
George Petre	17	11	04
Widow Stoakes	09	06	00
Widow Thomas	20	13	04
Peter Dee	43	28	08
Richard Prichard	08	05	04
Richard Smith	14	09	04
Mr. Martin or Tenant	54	36	00
Mr. Christmus or Tenant	28	18	08
Avenhouse	16	10	08
Widow Heskins	28	18	08
William Peacock	02	01	04
William Cox	16	10	08
Mrs. Dighton late deceased	50	33	04
John Smith	25	16	08
Widow Berry	05	03	04
Sr. Samuell Astry	07	04	08
Thomas Herring or Tenant	11	07	04
Widow Smith	15	10	00
Thomas Smith	16	10	08
Widow Jackson	07	04	08
Widow Gush	10	06	08
Samuell Robins	08	05	04
William Davies	12½	08	04
Mr. Bush	10	06	08
Widow Haynes	04	02	08
Andrew Smether	29	19	04
Richard Smith	06	04	00
James Peacocke estate £4 a yeare is to be taken of and placed to Ann Jones	14	09	04
Mrs. Rutland	16	10	08
Mrs. Dighton for the Inn	10	06	08
Henry Green	02	01	04

Page 192.

WESTBURY.

The Accompt of Mr. Samuell Clarke one of the Overseers of the poore of the pish of Westbury-sup-Trim made the 12th day of Aprill 1686 ffor the Tenemt formerly Higges Tenemt. Dr

	£	s.	d.
To a Rate made at 8d p pound Amounting unto	27	11	08
he is Crede			
By 13 moneths pay to old William Smith at 5s. p m ..	03	05	00
By 13 moneths pay to Bess Cooke at 4s. 6d. p m	02	18	06
By 13 moneths pay to Mary Major at 3s. p m	01	19	00
By 9 moneths ½ pay to Widow Hopkins for Harvies boy at 8s. p moneth	03	16	00
By 13 moneths pay to John Jefferies and his wife at 4s. p m	02	12	00
By 13 moneths pay to Widow Hunt at 3s. p m	01	19	00
By 13 moneths pay for Martha Andrews at 6s. p m ..	03	18	00
	20	07	06
By mony gave old Smith when he was sick and for one to tend him and severall other tymes the yeare	00	10	06
By moe Gave Tho: Tagg being sick and lame in his hand ..	00	05	06
By moe Gave old Bowry in the whole yeare..	00	08	06
By moe payd ye widow Hopkins for Shirts, shooes and mending of Harvies Boyes clothes	00	07	06
By moe pd John Chavell as p his note for sending away poore people and creeples	00	08	00
By moe payd for A yeares interest of Jn Gillets mony ..	00	12	00
By moe Gave John Jefferies and his wife being lame and sick	00	06	06
By moe payd for Clothes and Shooes and Stockins for Martha Andrewes	00	16	08
By more payd towards the binding out Hannah Roberts ..	01	00	00
By moe gave Robert Wades wife at sevall tymes	00	08	00
By moe payd for a weekes dyat for John Andrewes children and sending them home	00	03	04
By moe gave Edith Bowry	00	02	06
By moe payd for makeing the rates and engrossing ye booke	00	04	00
By mo: Given to poor people by passes	00	02	00
I Crave allowance for Giles Nurce	00	00	04
	26	02	10
Rest to Ballance the Accompt ..	01	08	10
	27	11	08

	£	s.	d.	
Ball of this acc is	1	8	10	
pd to buy old ward Lynning	0	7	00	
Rests due	£1	1	10	wch was

payd the next Collector John Hort save onely 01s. pd

Page 193.

;TOAKBISHOPP.

:he Accompt of Mr. Ezechiell Husbands one of the Overseers of ye poore of the pish of Westbury-Upon-Trim made the 12th day of Aprill 1686.

	£	s.	d.
mp the Accomptant Chargeth himselfe wth one rate at 8d. p £ wch cometh unto	030	15	08

The Disburstmts are as ffolloweth	£	s.	d.
Imp pd To Sarah Pullin 13 moneths at 10s p moneth is ..	006	10	00
Item pd to Margaret Haskins 13 moneths at 4s. p moneth..	02	12	00
Payd to Jane Griffin 13 mo at 2s. p moneth..	01	06	00
Payd Goody Hatter 13 moneths at 6s. p moneth	03	18	00
Payd Ned Hatter 12 moneths at 4s. p mo	02	08	00
Payd to Auld Davies 13 mo at 4s. p mo	02	12	00
	19	06	00
Item given Goody Vaughon at severall tymes this yeare ..	00	08	06
Given John White sevall tymes this yeare	01	03	06
Given to John Wasberrow this yeare	00	15	06
Given Mathew Perry his wife being very sick	00	12	06
Given towards the binding out of Hannah Roberts ..	01	00	00
Given to ffishpooles wife being sick	00	02	06
Given Richard Vidler	00	05	00
Given Mrs. Cuff a poore Widow	00	05	00
Payd for A Coat breeches Shifts and otherwayes cloathing the Boy at Sarah Pullins	00	16	08
Payd for Cloathing Ned Hatter in like manner	00	14	02
Given by passes to poore people	00	03	06
Given goody Haskins being sick and lame	00	03	06
Given Auld Davies	00	01	00
I Crave allowance for Patrick Browne	00	02	08
	26	00	00
Rest to Ballance this accompt was payd ye next Collector George Bennet	04	15	08
	30	15	08

Save only 01s. payd ye Justices Clarkes for A warrant to sommon ye sd George Bennet to take to ye office.

Page 194.

SHERHAMPTON.

The Accompt of Thomas Joyner one of the Overseers of the poore of the pish of Westbury-sup-Trim made the 12th day of Aprill 1686.

		£	s.	d.
Impr	the Accomptant Chargeth himselfe wth one Rate at 8d p pound wch cometh unto	31	16	08

The Disburstmts ffolloweth

		£	s.	d.
Impr	payd to John Caly 9 moneths at 4s. p moneth	01	16	00
	Item payd him more 3 mo at 6s. p mo	00	18	00
	Gave to him in his sicknesse	00	02	06
	Payd to John Baker 12 mo at 2s. p mo	01	04	00
	Payd to Abigall Munting 10 mo at 4s p mo	02	00	00
	Payd to Richard Smith for her house rent..	00	10	00
	Payd to Charity Jones for nursing Edith Williams Child one moneth at	00	08	00
	Payd her ii mo and two weeks more at 6s. p mo	03	09	00
	Payd for Clothes for Edith Williams Child..	00	12	00
	Payd to Mary Tomkins 12 mo at 5s. p mo..	03	00	00
	Payd to Elnor Squir for keeping Thos Splayfool 10 mo at 2s. p mo	01	00	00
	Payd for Clothing of him a new suit shirt shooes and Stockings	01	03	00
	Payd for Keeping John Barrow 12 mo at 6s. p mo ..	03	12	00
	Payd to Mary Hoggett 2 mo at 04s. p mo	00	08	00
	Payd for Keeping Hannah Roberts and Clothes for her..	00	19	06
	Payd for the binding her out an apprentice	01	10	00
	Payd for Keeping An Draysy 12 mo at 6s. p mo	03	12	00
	Item Expended in getting out of the pish Charles Turner and bringing him to Bristoll where he was borne ..	00	14	00
	Item Expended in Attending the Justice about Edward Williams his warrant	00	01	06
	Gave him in his sickness	00	04	00
	Payd for Clothing William Peacocks Children	01	00	00
	Payd to Edward Hunt wh remayned due to him last yeare	00	05	00
	Item Expended in attending the Justice about Sisley Lewis warrant	00	02	06
	I Crave allowance for William Peacock being very poore..	00	01	04
	I Crave allowance for wch Tho Everard should pay ..	00	00	08
	Payd for Clothes Shifte Shooes Stockings for Ann Draysie and in all	00	13	04
		29	06	04
	Rest to Ballance the accompt	02	10	04
		31	16	08
	It is ordered to pay out of the ballance to John Baker ..	00	04	00
	Moe to Mary Wood and John Barrow 8s. a piece	0	16	00
		01	00	00

Page 195.

[T]hese Two accompts for ye yeare 1685 and proceedings was pased and allowed of by us whose names are under written this 12th day of Aprill 1686 and the accompts of Samll Clarke and Ezeckiell Husbands.

Samuell Price	Anthony Ellsworth	Churchwardens.
Jo: Lambe	Merke	
Tho Geering	John + Cook	

[T]he preceeding accompt of Thomas Joyner was pased and allowed of By us whose names are here under written this 12th of Aprill 1686 A.D.

Geo Petre Jur	Anthony Ellsworth	Churchwardens.
Willm Stainer	Merke	
Henry Green	John + Cooke	
John Willis		
Thomas Smith		

[W]e Doe nominate and appoynt to serve in the office of overseere of the poor for the yeare ensueing

John Hort for Mrs. Hort for Westbury
George Bennet for Stoke Bishope
John Smith of ye Ivyhouse for Sherhampton

[A]llowed by us

Samuel Astry
Christopher Cole

[A] Rate made by the inhabitants of the pish of Westbury for and towards the Releife of the poore for the yeare 1686 wch is the same by the pounds and everyones Estate the same as in the last yeares Rate 1685 engrossed before the Overseers Accompts above written.

Page 196.

The Amount of John Short one of the overseers of the poore of the pish of Westbury-upon-trim made for this yeare 1686.

	£	s.	d.
Impr The accomptant Chargeth himselfe wth one rate of 8d. p £ wch Cometh unto	27	11	08
More he Recd of Mr. Clarke the last Collector wh was due upon his acco	1	00	10
	£28	12	06

The Disbursmts are as follow

	£	s.	d.
Impr to pd Wm Smith for 12 months and halfe ending the first of Aprill next at 5s. p month is	£ 3	2	6
It to pd Eliza Cooke 12 mo at 4s. 6d. p mo ending 18th Mch last	£ 2	14	0
It to pd Jno Jeffris and wife 12 mo at 4s. p mo	£ 2	08	00
It to pd Mary Major 12 mo at 3s. p mo is	£ 1	16	00
It to pd Mary andrews 6 mo ½ at 10s. p mo beginning the 18th and ending Mrch 21th past..	£ 3	05	00
It to pd widdow Hunt two months at 3 p mo	£..	6	..
It to pd Tho Grant for keeping Martha Andrews 5 weeks is	..	6	6
	£13	18	0
It to gave Mary Major at sevall times in her sicknesse ..	£..	5	6
It to gave Wm. Smith at sevall times in his sicknesse ..	£..	3	6
It to pd for a Coate and hatt and buttons for Wm. Smith	£..	8	5
It to pd for halfe a dozne of faggotts for Ditto Smith ..	⅛..	..	5
It to gave to Robert wade at severall times	£..	9	..
It to gave to Joane Smith in her sicknesse..	£..	1	6
It to pd for the buryall of Joane Smith	£..	11	6
It to gave Mary Radman at sevall times in her sicknesse..	£..	4	6
It to gave to Jno Jeffrey and wife in theire sicknesse ..	£..	6	6
It to pd wth Martha Andrews to Thomas Grant	£ 2	00	0
It to pd for Martha Andrews Indentures and getting ym signed	£..	4	00
It pd for a warrant and bringing Sarah Yates before ye Justice	£..	1	00
It pd for the aparrolling Tho. Wade boy	£..	10	00
It to given to poor Distressed and som by passes.. ..	£..	1	6
It for horse hire and expenses in my journey to old Andrews at Brocktonbury Wiltshire about Jno. Andrews children	£..	13	00
It to pd Interest of Jno. Gillett money as preceited ..	£..	12	00
It to gave Wm Bowry in his Sicknesse	£..	2	00
It to gave to Eliz Bowry at times	£..	2	00
It to pd Jno Harnes towards ye Clearing Rd. Evans out of prison and expense	£..	16	00
It to gave to Ann Bagg at sevall times	£..	13	00
It to gave Robert Hobbs and Wm. wade for loss of times in bringing Joan Cotten before the Justice and removeing her out of ye pish	£..	5	00
It to pd Robert Hobbs for a weekes Diett of Joan Cotton	£..	1	6
It to pd Elnor Druett for tending Ditto Cotton	£..	1	..
It to expenses going before ye Justice sevall times in remoaving Joan Cotton	£..	3	6
It to gave to Margriett Hobbs at sevall times in her sicknesse	£..	5	..
It to pd for the buriiall of Margret Hobbs	£..	11	..
It to pd Joane pearce for tending Mary Major in her sicknesse	£..	2	..
It to pd Sarah Pullin for tending Margrett Hobbs.. ..	£..	1	6

STOOKBISHOPP.

The Accompt of George Bennett one of the Overseers of the poore of the prish of Westbury-upon-Trim made for the yeare 1686.

	£	s.	d.
Impr the Accomptant Chargeth himselfe wth one Rate at 8d. p £ wch cometh unto	030	15	08
Moe he Received of Mr. Husbands the last Collector wh was due upon his Accompt	04	14	08
	35	10	04

The Disburstmts are as followeth	£	s.	d.
Impr To Goody Hatter and ye boy 10 moneths at 10s. p mo ending the 21th of January last is	05	00	00
To Sarah Pullin 12 moneths ½ at 10s, p mo end ye 1st Aprill next	06	05	00
To Margaret Haskins 12 mo: at 4s. p mo end ye 25th of March	02	09	00
To Joan Griffin 12 mo at 2s. p mo end ye 18th of Marsh ..	01	04	00
To John Wasborow 10 mo and ½ at 4s. p mo end ye 1th of Aprill	02	02	00
Moe for the dyat of Ned Hatter 2 mo and ½ at 6s. p mo end ye 1th of Aprill next	00	15	00
	17	15	00
Item disburst in Removeing a bastard child to Wales by order of ye Justice and for hireing man and A nurse to go with it besides myselfe and for of horse and expenses and clothes for ye child and our expences the whole charges I was out is	02	02	06
It Given Old Davies dureing his sickness and tyme of his death	00	11	00
It Disburst upon the buriall of old Davies..	01	00	06
It for Shirts Shooes and Stockins for ye boy at Sarah Pullins	00	07	08
It Given John Wasborow before he came to monethly pay and when he was very sick and weak	00	12	00
It payd for two shirts and paire of stockins and A new bed case for John Wasborow and washing his clothes and toward ye buying of him A Suite of Clothes all is ..	00	17	04
Given Mary Rodman wch came sick into ye pish	00	04	06
Payd Thomas Grant towards ye bindeing out of Martha Andrews and expended then	01	01	06
Given to poor distressed and some by passes	00	02	06
Given to Goody Vaughon at sevall tymes this yeare ..	00	07	00
Given Sarah Pullin being very Lame and bad in her Legg by ye biteing of a Dogg at sevall tymes	00	08	06
pd Elnor Cooke for ye Curring Sarah Pullins Legg ..	00	06	00
It pd for clothing Ned Hatter Coat breeches shirts shooes stockings..	01	06	06
It for a Justice warrant about ye child born at Halseyes and expenses	00	02	00
It Given John White at sevall tymes this yeare and being sick	00	18	06
Given Goody Evans her Husband being in prison and she and her children being in Great want at sevall tymes in mony and Cole	00	14	00
Given to Mathew Penry being in nessessity and his wife sick	00	05	00
It for my horse hire and I expended in my Journey to old Andrews at Brocktonbury in Wiltsheir about Jno Andrews children and expence	00	06	00
It payd towards ye Getting of Richard Evans out of prison and expences	01	01	08
It payd Mr. Dymer for ye bhying of Shirts and clothes for Will Hatter	00	15	00
Given to Goody Haskins towards Cole for fireing.. ..	00	01	00
Given Joan Griffin towards Cole	00	01	00
Given Goody Hatter in ye tyme of her Sickness and at ye tyme of her Death disburst uppon ye buriall of Goody Hatten	00	08	06

Page 198.

SHERHAMPTON.

The Accompt of John Smith one of the Collectors of the poore of the prish of Westbury-upon-Trim made for this yeare 1686.

		£	s.	d.
Impr	The Accomptant Chargeth himselfe wth one Rate at 8d. p £ wch cometh unto	031	16	08
	It Reced of the last Collector Thomas Joyner wh was due	001	09	04
		033	06	00

The Disburstmts are as followeth

		£	s.	d.
Impr	payd to John Cawley 12 moneth at 6s. p mo is	003	12	00
	It pd to John Joans 12 moneths at 6s. p mo	03	12	00
	payd to William Barry 12 mo at 6s. p mo..	03	12	00
	payd to John Cooke 6 mo: at 5s. p mo and 6 mo at 6s. p mo	03	06	00
	payd to Abigall Parker 9 mo at 4s. and 3 mo at 6s. p mo is	02	14	00
	pd to John Baker 12 mo pay at 2s. p mo is	01	04	00
	pd to Elnor Esquire 13 weekes 12d. p week is	00	13	00
	pd for house rent for Abigall Barker 20s. for this yeare and halfe a yeare that was behinde for Last yeare..	01	10	00
	pd for house rent for Edward Williams	00	12	00
	pd for a paire of shooes for Abigall Parkers boy.. ..	00	02	00
	pd to John Cook for clothes for Ann Draysey	00	10	06
	pd for a payre of shooes for Edith Williams her child ..	00	01	02
	Given to Edward Williams in the tyme of his Sicknesse..	00	08	00
	Given to Abigall Parker in the tyme of her Sicknesse ..	00	05	00
	Given to John Baker in the tyme of his sickness.. ..	00	03	00
	Given William Peacock	00	02	00
	Given to poore people by passes	00	01	00
	I Crave allowance for William Peacock	00	01	04
	I Crave allowance for Thomas Everard	00	00	08
	I Crave allowance for Rebecca Brittane..	00	00	08
	payd Richard Jilyne wc was due to him from ye prsh	00	18	00
	payd Thomas Grant of Westbury pipe maker wh Due to him in takeing Martha Andrewes apprentice ..	01	00	00
		24	08	04

	£	s.	d.
Received by ye Rate and the last Overseer of ye poore	33	06	00
Disburst	24	08	04
Rest due to Ballance	08	17	08

William Martin
Will Davis
John Adlam
Thomas Wasborow

Page 199.

	£	s.	d.
Brought over from the Account of John Hort	23	13	10
payd William Jones for ye buriall of John Wade.. ..	00	10	00
I Crave allowance for Giles Nurse	00	00	04
	24	04	02

	£	s.	d.
Received by ye Rate and ye Ballance of ye last Collectors accompt..	28	12	06
Disburst	24	04	02
Rest due to Ballence	04	08	04

	£	s.	d.
wch was payd to Samuell Clavell allowing for ye warrant and Carrying ye booke to be signed Soe that ye whole some payd is..	04	06	04

	£		
Brought over from the Accompt of George Bennett	31	17	10
Received by A Rate and from the Last Collector Mr. Husbands	35	10	04
Disburst as aforesaid	31	17	10
Rest due to Ballance	03	13	06

hese three Accompts seene and
lowed by us
nthony Ellsworth }
ɔhn Cooke } Churchwardens

William Martin
Will Davis
Thomas Wasborow
John Adlam
Tho Berry

/ee doe nominate and appoynt to be overseers for ye poor
ır the yeare ensueing

Samuel Clavell
William Arnold for Mr. Tilladoms Tenem
Abraham Badman

/ee allow this rate
Robert Southwell
Samuel Astry

Page 200.

1687. A Rate made by the churchwardens and overseers of the poore and other Inhabitants of the parish of Westbury-upon-Trim for and towards the reliefe of the poore for the yeare aforesayd after the Rate of six pence p pound as followeth :

		£	s.	£	s.	d.
Imprmis	Sr. Fra: Fane for the Tythe	18		0	09	00
	Mrs. Knight	94	10	2	07	03
	John Lambe Esqr.	80		2	00	00
	Mr. Jackson	48		1	04	00
	Mr. Geering	42		1	01	00
	Mrs. Tunbridge	21		0	10	06
	Mr. Walter	16		0	08	00
	Mr. Edward Sampson	75		1	17	06
	Mr. Ralph Sampson	08		0	04	00
	Mr. Lane	77		1	18	06
	Mr. Price	42		1	01	00
	Mr. Walter	12		0	06	00
	The Executrix of Mrs. Rutland [1]	03		0	01	06
	Thomas Wasborow	15		0	07	06
	George Webb	14		0	07	00
	Mr. Olive	30		0	15	00
	Samuel Clavell	09		0	04	06
	The heirs of Matthew Adlam or the Tenant	24		0	12	00
	Mrs. Arundell	28		0	14	00
	Mrs. Sarah Wasborow	03		0	01	06
	Mrs. William White	24		0	12	00
	Mr. Joseph Burges	31	10	0	15	09
	Mrs. Hort	26		0	13	00
	Thomas Cuffe	08		0	04	00
	Mr. Powell	12	10	0	06	03
	Samuel Sandford	09	10	0	04	09
	Mr. Thomas Hort	08		0	04	00
	Mr. Price	06		0	03	00
	Mr. Tyson	12		0	06	00
	John Cheshire	03		0	01	06
	John Adlam	02		0	01	00
	Richard Horwood	03		0	01	06
	Mrs. Nicholls Widd	07		0	03	06
	Samuel Clavell	04		0	02	00
	Mr. Clark	06		0	03	00
	Robert Hodges	01		0	00	06
	John Wasborow	03		0	01	06
	Mr. William Jackson	01		0	00	06
	Giles Nurse	00	10	0	00	03
	Westbury Rate comes to £ 20 s. 13 d. 09			20	13	09

[1] Mrs. Rutland was the wife of the Vicar of Westbury, who died in 1660. She lost her three sons: one in 1647, another in 1648, and a third in 1674. She finished the remainder of her sad life at Westbury, and by her will, dated March 25th, 1684, left £10 to be distributed to the poor every Good Friday. She also left £50 to procure sermons in the

Page 201.

STOAKBISHOPP.

		£	s.	d.
Impr	Sr. ffrancis ffane for the Tythe	13	06	06
	Sr. Thomas Cann	114	57	00
	The Lady Yeamans	42	22	00
	Sr. Robert Southwell	70	35	00
	Sr. Samuell Astry	11	05	06
	Sr. Richard Crump	37½	18	09
	Sr. Symon Lewis	06	03	00
	Mr. Jackson	84	42	00
	Mr. Martin	84	42	00
	Mr. Gleed	52	26	00
	Mr. Kirk	14½	07	03
	Mr. Dymer	64½	32	03
	Mr. Edwards	39½	19	09
	Mr. Joyce Bevan	38	19	00
	Mr. Price	18½	09	03
	Mr. Blackwell	05	02	06
	Mrs. Knight	22	11	00
	Mr. Hart	37½	18	09
	Mr. Tilladam	20	10	00
	John Hurtnell	08	04	00
	Mrs. Shore	12½	06	03
	Mr. Dawson	10½	05	03
	Mr. Husbands	16	08	00
	Mr. Brookes	29	14	06
	Mr. Brookes for Edward Lewis	02	01	00
	Mr. Creswicke	09	04	06
	Mr. Thomas Hort	17	08	06
	Mr. Bauldin	08	04	00
	Mrs. Arundle	03	01	06
	Widow Stookes	08	04	00
	William Selfe	03	01	06
	John Hurne	10	05	00
	Arthur Sawyer	04½	02	03
	Samuell Sandford	02	01	00
	John Barwick	02	01	00
	William Thomas	04	02	00
	The Some is	23	01	09

Page 202—Blank.

Page 203.

1687. The Accompts of John Clavell one of the overseers of the poore of the parish of Westbury-upon-Trim for the yeare 1687.

	£	s.	d.
Imprimis the Sayd Accomptant chargeth himself with one Rate collected at 6d. p £ which comes to	20	13	09
more received of Mr. John Hort overseer the Last yeare being money remaining in his hand	04	06	04
Received in all	25	00	01

The sayd Accomptant desired allowance for these following disbursments

	£	s.	d.
Imprimis payd William Smyth 13 moneths at 5s. a moneth ..	03	05	00
It payd Eliz: Cook 13 moneths pay at 4s. 6d. a moneth	02	18	06
It payd John Jefferies 10 moneths pay at 4s. a moneth	02	00	00
It payd Mary Major 13 moneths at 3s. a moneth ..	01	19	00
It payd Mary Andrews 2 children 13 moneth pay at 10s. a moneth	06	10	00
It payd Thomas Tagg 13 moneths at 2s. a moneth ..	01	06	00
It payd Robert wade 13 moneths pay at 2s. a moneth	01	06	00
It payd sevrall moneths pay for keeping Margarett Attwood and spent in going to Brockenburrow to . . . . ? with her grandfather	00	16	00
It Layd out for 2 warrants for Patrick Browne and charge in removing of that family	00	06	00
It spent at a meeting of the parish to make the rate ..	00	02	06
It gave William Smyth in his sickness..	00	03	00
It gave severall poore people and disbanded souldiers that came with pass party..	00	05	00
It Layd out for Cloaths and Shoes for Mary Andrews Children	00	10	00
It Layd out at the funerall of Mary Bunwell	00	10	00
It payd Sarah Pullin for attending William Smyth ..	00	02	06
It gave William Bowry in his sickness	00	01	00
It gave John Jefferies in his sickness	00	06	00
It payd for six warrants of disturbance at severall times and for taking distress of those refusing to pay ..	00	06	00
It I crave allowance for what I have not collected of Wm. Prior by rason hee hath taken a poor childe	01	04	00
It I crave allowance for what I have not collected of Giles Nurse	00	00	03
Layed out in all	23	16	09

Page 204.

	£	s.	d.
The Sum Received by John Clavell is	25	00	01
The sum layd out is	23	16	09
Due to the pish to ballance ..	01	03	04
out of which there hath been payd for engrossing the accounts 1s. soe that the sum due to ballance is..	01	02	04
pd Capt. Price towards the Parrish (?) the above Ballance of Jno Clavill	1	2	4
pd him by his own Rate	1	4	0
payd . . . with a . . .	2	6	4

Seen and allowed this acct

Tho Richardson
Willm Staener
Samuell price
Tho Geering

Will Davis
John Adlam
Anthony Ellsworth

Page 205.

STOAKBISHOP.

The Accompt of William Arnold one of the Overseers of the poor of the parish for Mr. Tilladams Tenemt (for this yeare 1687) lately Deceased.

	£	s.	d.
Impr the Accompptant is Charged with one Rate Collected at 6d. p £ wch cometh unto	23	01	09
Moe Received of George Bennet Overseer ye last yeare the money remayned in his hands	03	13	06
The some received	26	15	03

	£	s.	d.
The disburstmts are as ffolloweth.			
Imp to Sarah Pullin and ye boy 13 moneths and ½ at 10s. p mo ending the 13th of Aprill instant 1688 is	06	15	00
Margaret Haskins 13 mos at 4s. p mo end ye 13th of Aprill	02	15	00
Joan Griffin 14 mo at 02s. p mo end ye 13th of aprill ..	01	08	00
Edward Hatter 13 mo ½ at 6s. p mo end ye 13th of aprill ..	04	01	00
John Wasborow 13 mo ½ at 4s. p mo end ye 13th of Aprill..	02	14	00
	17	13	00
payd George Bennet for ye Justice Warrant for ye succeeding overseer	00	01	00
Given ye Clarke to Carrie ye poore booke to be signed by ye Justices	00	00	06
payd for a Coat and breeches and making it for Edward Hatter	00	11	00
payd for two Shirts and two paire of stocking and Shooes for Hatter	00	08	04
payd for the Lodgeing of John Wasborow ye whole yeare 06s. and given being Sick 02s. all is	00	08	00
payd at A prish meeting to make the rate	00	02	06
Spent at another tyme about rates and goeing to ye Justices to have them signed	00	01	00
payd for A Justice warrant and warning William Thomas out of the pish	00	01	06
Spent to warne goody Browne out of ye pish	00	01	00
Given John White at sevall tymes this yeare	00	16	00
Given Goody Vaughon at sevall tymes and being sick by vertue of Sr. Robert Southwells warrant	00	19	06
Given Richard Evans his wife She Lyeing in and now sick like to Dye 10s. 6d. and given one to tend her now in her sicknesse 06s. all	00	16	06
Given the widow Haskins in her sicknesse	00	07	00
payd one to tend her in her sickness..	00	02	06
payd for goody Haskins lodgings before she came to ye almeshouse	00	05	00
Spent in Removeing A woman at Halsies out of ye pish ..	00	01	06
payd for A Justice warrant and spent in removeing Charles Harbatt out of the pish	00	02	06
payd for Stockings and Shooes for ye boy at Sarah Pullins	00	02	06
payd the Coroner that Sate upon ye man killed by ye fall of ye house at gallowes Hill and wh was then spent upon him and ye jury that sate upon him and given that this pish might not be at ye Charge of his buriall	01	01	02
payd for a Justices warrant and to ye Tything man for his labour wth others for the removeing Hester Edwards being very sick to Bedminster and alsoe payd ye Tytheing man wt he was out in sending away Creeples the whole is	00	15	06

Page 206.

	£	s.	d.
Brought over from the other side	24	17	06
given poor distressed Seamen and some there wifes and children Souldiers and others by passes and certificates	00	08	05
Given Jone Griffin being sick..	00	02	00
payd for engrossing the accompts	00	01	00
Moreover this Overseer before his death hoped the pish would consider him as to ye bring and lodgeing of Richard Evans his wife and children for two years to our Lady Day last in the house he payes Sr. Thomas Cann 3s. a yeare his daughter Susan therefore prayes the pish to allow her	00	10	00
Disburst in all	25	18	11

	£	s.	d.
The Some received by William Arnold is	26	15	03
The Some Layd out is	25	18	11
The Some due to ye pish to Ballance this Accompt is	00	16	04
	26	15	03

Seene and allowed these accops by us: ye ballance of this accopt being dew to the parish being 00 16 04

Samuell price
Tho Geering
John Adlam
Will Davis

Tho Richardson }
Willm Stainer } Churchwardens
Anthony Elsworth

Page 207.

1687. The Accompt of Abraham Badman overseer of ye poore of ye tethen of Shearhamton.

	£	s.	d.
Imprimis ye said accompt chargeth himselfe with one rate collected at 6s. p £ which comes to	23	17	6
Mor receaved of John Smith overseer ye last year ye mony ramined in his hands	08	17	8
Reacaved in all	32	15	2
The disbustments are as followeth			
Imprimis to Abigell parker 14 months at 6s. p month	04	04	0
paid John barry 14 months at 6s. p month	04	04	0
payd John cally 2 months at 6s. p month	00	12	0
payd John cally 12 months at 4s. p month	02	08	0
payd Ann williams 14 months at 6s. p month	04	04	0
payd John baker 14 months at 2s. p month	01	08	0
payd Edward williams 10 and ½ at 4s. p month ..	02	02	0
payd Ann draysee 2 months and 4/1 at 5s. p month ..	00	11	3
payd mary farr 10 months at 5s. p month	02	10	0
payd mary farr 1 month at 2s. 6d. p month	00	02	6
payd henry fishpoole 7 months at 5s. p month ..	01	15	0
payd for tending Edward williams when he was sick	00	11	0
payd for making ye rate..	00	01	0
Expences upon parish business..	00	02	0
payd for burieng of ann draysee May ye 3	01	19	6
payd Ann Williams for close and shoes..	00	09	3
July for . . . money for Abigell parker and Edward williams	00	02	0
Mr. goldinham for bering of Ann draysie and John Callys wife	00	03	0
paid for a shirt for Edward williams	00	02	10
paid to John ride for bread and ½ a pound of Sheger and candls	00	01	09
Ann Williams a per of Shues	00	01	03
paid for Abigell parker for Coles	00	01	02
for shues for Abigell parkers children	00	02	08
desember for buring of Edward williams	01	08	2
payd ye coroners fees	00	13	4
payd for two sutes of clos for Abig parker the children	00	17	6
given to poore distresed men	00	01	6
for a . . . ? for Mary far	00	06	0
	31	04	0

Page 208.

	£	s.	d.
brought over from the other side			
ffeabrary the 29th payd ffor House money ffor Edward Williams and Abigall Parker	0	2	00
payd ffor House rent for Edward Willms and Abigall Parker	1	10	00
disbursed in all	32	16	06
Money Received of Mrs. Stockes for ye buriall of her Datur in Lining	1	05	00
John Caly	0	03	00
John Baker	0	02	06
Edward Willms	0	01	06
Abigall Parker	0	06	00
Mary Woods	0	02	00
Willm Peacocke	0	03	06
Bridgat Withers	0	01	06
ffrances foords and old Eiles and Joan Baker and Sisly Lewes	0	05	00
the poore people wch Mis Stokes money pay to ..	1	05	00

	£	s.	d.
The Sum Received by Abr Bodman ..	33	01	08
The Sum Laid out is	32	16	06
The sum dew to ye pish to balance ye accompt ..	00	05	02

Samuell price

Tho Richardson
Willm Stainer
Henry Greene
Geo Petre
Richard Grumnell
John Smyth

llowed by us
Samuell Astry
Jo Dowell

Page 209—Blank.

Page 210.

WESTBURY. The 13th of Aprill 1688.

A rate made by the Churchwardens and others of the pish of Westbury-upon-Trim and towards the reliefe of the poore for this yeare at the Rate of eight pence a pound as followeth.

		£	s.	d.
Impr	Sr. ffrancis Fane for his Tythe	18	12	00
	Mrs. Knight	94½	63	00
	Mr. John Lambe	80	53	04
	Mr. Jackson	48	32	00
	Mr. Geering	42	28	00
	Mrs. Tunbridge	21	14	00
	Mr. Walter	16	10	08
	Mr. Edward Sampson	75	50	00
	Mr. Ralphe Sampson	08	05	04
	Mr. Lane	77	51	04
	Mr. Price	42	28	00
	Mrs. Walter	12	08	00
	Mrs. Rutland	03	02	00
	Thomas Wasborow	15	10	00
	George Webb	14	09	04
	Mr. Doubtin	30	20	00
	Samuell Clavill	09	06	00
	John Adlam	24	14	08
	William Sellfe	02	01	04
	Mrs. Avendall	28	18	08
	Mrs. Sarah Wasborow	03	02	00
	William White	24	16	00
	Mr. Burgis	31½	21	00
	Mrs. Hort	26	17	04
	Thomas Cuff	08	05	04
	Mr. Powell	12½	08	04
	Samuell Sandford	09½	06	04
	Thomas Hort	08	05	04
	Mr. Price	06	04	00
	Mr. Tysan	12	08	00
	John Chessheire	03	02	00
	John Adlam	02	01	04
	Richard Horwood	03	02	00
	Mrs. Nicholas	07	04	08
	Samuell Claffell	04	02	08
	Mr. Clark	06	04	00
	Robert Hodges	01	00	08
	John Wasborow	03	02	00
	Mr. Jackson for Tho: Wallis	01	00	08
	Giles Nurse halfe a pound	00½	00	04
		27	11	08

Page 211.

	£	s.	d.
The Sume disburst by Mr. Hort	27	14	02
Due to the overseer to balance his account	00	02	05

John Adlam
William Martin
John Hurne
Jo Lambe

Page 212.

WESTBURY.

The Account of Mr. Thomas Hort one of the overseer of the poore of this prish for the estate of comb house for this yeare 1688.

	£	s.	d.
Imprs this Accomptant chargeth himselfe with one rate collected at 8 p £ which commeth unto	27	11	08
The disburstments are as followeth	£	s.	d.
Imprs paide to William Smith 13th months at 5s. p moneth ending the 12th of Aprill 1689 is	03	05	00
Item Elizabeth Cook 13 months at 4s. 6d. p month ending the 12th of Aprill	02	18	06
Item Ann Teg 13 months at 4s. p month end the 12 of Aprill	02	12	00
Item Robert Wade 13 months at 2s. p month end the 12 of Aprill	01	06	00
Item Elnor Pamer 11 months at 5s. p month end the 12 of Aprill	02	15	00
Itt Widow Andrews 13 months at 10s. p month end the 15 of Aprill	06	10	00
The Casuall disbursments			
Given to Richard Pamer in his sickness and toward the burying of him	00	13	00
Given to William Bowre in his sicknes	00	05	00
Paid for making the Rates in Parchment and riding to the Justice to signe it	00	03	00
paid to William Jones towards the binding of his Son an Apprentice	02	00	00
paid to Thomas Grant towards the Girle as was left unpaide	01	00	00
paide at a meeting when the Indentures were sealed for Thomas Grants Boy	00	05	00
paide to William Thomas the Tayler for making Close ..	01	01	06
Given to ffrancis Long in her child bed	00	01	00
Capt. Price stopt towards his apprentice in his Pay ..	01	12	00
Spent at a prish meeting	00	04	00
paide to John Clavill for bringing the whores to gaile ..	00	06	00
Given to poore people with passes and certificates ..	00	06	00
Paid for a Justice warrant sommon the next overseer and carrying the book to have it signed by the Justices paid for engrosing it in the book	00	01	06
I crave allowance for Mr. Burgis money I cannot gather	00	01	00
I crave allowance for Giles Nurse and William Selfs money as I cannot Gather	00	01	08
Given to Richard Evans in the time of sickness of his wife and Child	00	04	00
Paid at a prish meeting	00	02	00
The Sume disburst by Mr. Hort is ..	27	14	02

Page 213.

STOAKBISHOP.

The accompt of John Hurne one of the overseer of the poore of this pish for his Estate of his Tenemt of Clack mill for this yeare 1688.

	£	s.	d.
Imprs this Accomptant Chargeth himselfe with one rate collected at 3d. p £ wch cometh unto	30	14	00
Moe Received of the Last yeares Overseers Executrix the money remaynning in hand	00	16	04
The some Received	31	10	04
The disburstmts are as ffolloweth	£	s.	d.
Imprs Margaret Haskins 13 moneths at 4s. p moneth ending the 12th day of Aprill 1689 is	02	12	00
Item John Wasborow 13 mo at 4s. p mo end 12th Aprill	02	12	00
Joan Griffin 13 mo at 02s. p moneth end 12th Aprill alsoe	01	06	00
Sarah Pullin and ye boy 4 mo 3 weeks at 10s. p moneth is	02	07	06
Edward Hatter 5 mo ½ at 06s. p mo is	01	13	00
Sarah pullins boy 5 mo at 4s p mo to Thomas Grant ..	01	00	00
widow Vaughan 6 mo 2s. 06s. p mo is	00	15	00
	12	05	06
Itt spent Hatter running away from his master at severall times	00	06	00
payd for ye Justice warrant for ye succeeding overseer and given to Carrie ye booke for ye Justice to signe it	00	01	06
payd for making ye Rates in parchmt and Riding to ye the Justices to signe it	00	03	00
payd for two suites of clothes for Ned Hatter and Sarah Pullins boye	01	02	00
payd for 4 shirts and 2 hatts for these boyes	00	16	00
payd for two paire of shooes and 2 payre Stockins for these boyes	00	07	08
Given Joan Griffin at sevall tymes this yeare	00	02	00
Given to Sarah Pullin at sevall tymes since she was taken of ye booke	00	17	00
Given ye widow vaughan being weake and feeble this yeare	00	18	06
Given to Goody White at sevall tymes this yeare ..	00	14	06
Given to Goody vidler at sevall tymes this yeare.. ..	00	09	06
payd Thomas Grant towards ye taking Sarah Pullins boy apprentice	02	00	00
Spent when ye pish mett about ye aditt dayes business and about ye bindeing of Sarah Pullins boy.. ..	00	08	00
Spent when ye prish mett about ye rates..	00	02	00
payd for the burying of Richard Evans child	00	06	00
Spent about getting masters for ye boyes above sd and bringing them by others to towne	00	05	00
payd John Bramble ye Smith in money wth Ned Hatter and expences when he was bound	05	05	00
Disburst for two suites of apparell 4 shirts A Hatt 2 payre of shooes and 3 payre of stocking and other nessessary for Ned Hatter when he was bound an apprentice ..	03	04	10
Disburst for A Coat breeches 2 Shirts Stockins and other nessessary for Sarah Pullins boy bound apprentice to Tho Grant	00	18	08
Given Margaret Haskins	00	01	00
Given poore distressed seamen and others their wifes and children by passes and certificates	00	07	06
Spent at sevall tymes and disburst in disturbing John Warner his wife and child one Nuit his wife and children one Bishop his wife and family and one Dorothy Bevan and children	00	07	06
payd for the burying of Richard Vidlers wife	00	06	04
payd for Justice warrant summon ye next overseers and			

Page 214.

	£	s.	d.
The some disburst by John Hurne is	31	16	06
The some Received by him as on ye other side is.. ..	31	10	04
Rest to ballance this accompt	00	06	02
	31	16	06
Due upon the ballance of the account to the overseer six shillings and twopence	00	06	06

John Adlam
William Martin
Thom hort
Thomas Cuff
Jo Lambe

Page 215.

SHEEREHAMPTON.

The account of Thomas Everet one of the Collectors of the poore of the Prish of Westbury-upon-Trim made for this yeare 1688.

	£	s.	d.
mp The accomptant chargeth Himselfe with one rate at 8d. p £ which commeth unto	31	16	08

The disburstmts are as followeth	£	s.	d.
mp Paide to John Cawly 11 months at 4s. p month end the 27th of Aprill 1688 is	02	04	00
Itt Paide to John Cawly one month at 6s. p month end the 27 of Aprill	00	06	00
Itt paide to John Cawly halfe a month	00	03	00
Itt Abigall parker for 13 months at 6s. p month end the same	03	18	00
Itt John Baker 13 months at 2s. p month end the same day	01	06	00
Itt ann Williams 13 months at 6s. p month the same ..	03	18	00
Itt John Barrow 13 months at 6s. p month the same ..	03	18	00
	15	13	00

The Casuall disburstments	£	s.	d.
Paide for two new paire of shoes for John Barrow	00	04	02
paide for two new paire of shoes and mending a paire for John Parker	00	04	08
paide for a new paire of Shoes and mending a paire of shoes for Ann Williams	00	02	04
paide for linning Cloth for Ann Williams	00	03	06
paide for new paire of shoes for Ann Williams	00	02	02
paid Ellin Squire for the Tabling of Harry Fishpoole a quarter of yeare at 1s. 3d. p week	00	17	06
I Gave to four poore men	00	01	06
Paide for linen Cloth for Abigall Parkers children	00	02	06
I gave charity Gale	00	01	06
I gave to Harry Fishpoole	00	01	06
I gave Mary woode	00	02	06
Paide for wollen Cloth for Abigall Parkers children	00	10	00
Itt Paide for the tending of John Cawly in His sickness ..	00	09	00
Itt Paide for the burying of Abigall Parkers Boy	00	10	00
I Gave to Mary Parker in her child bed	00	10	00
I gave to mary wood	00	01	00
Itt for mending a paire of Shoes for Harry Fishpoole ..	00	01	00
Itt Paide to Richard Smith for rent for Abigall Parker ..	00	09	04
Itt Paide for a new paire of shoes for Henry Fishpool ..	00	03	00
Itt Paide for a new paire of shoes for Ann Williams ..	00	02	00
Itt Paide to John Griffin for Harry Fishpoole tabling ..	00	06	00
I Gave to Mary Wood old and feeble	00	10	00
I Gave to Mary Parker in her sickness	00	02	06
I Gave to Ellen Reed	00	02	06
Spent at severall times at Prish meeting	00	06	00

Page 216.

Brought over from the other side.

	£	s.	d.
Gave to Francis Parker	00	01	00
Gave to Mary Woode	00	02	00
Gave to Darkess Parker	00	02	00
Gave to mary Gatkins	00	04	00
Paide for a Justice warrant summon the next overseer and carrying the book to Have it signed by the Justice ..	00	01	06
paide for engrossing it in the book	00	01	00
Gave to John Cawly in his sickness	00	04	00
paide Easter Tuesday..	00	18	00
I crave Allowance for myself and William Peacock for money that I cannot Gather	00	02	00
Itt spent a goeing after Jane Mitchile daughter	00	02	00
The Sum disburst by Thomas Everet is	24	10	08

	£	s.	d.
Rest to ballance this accompt	7	00	00

	£	s.	d.
Paide for William Jones Son towards the binding him Apprentice	02	00	00
Paide to Thomas Wade For the Churchwarden account ..	00	16	03
Paide to Mr. Hurn one of the overseers	00	07	08
Paide to Mr. Hort one of the overseers	00	02	06
	3	6	5
Rest to ballance acct.. ..	3	13	7
To the Clarke..	0	3	0
Rest to ballance	3	10	7

Allowed this account

J. O. Howell

Samuell price

Page 217. The 14th Aprill 1690.

:hoosen officers for ye ensuing yeare as foll

Mr. Samuell Price
Mr. Thomy Alcock } Churchwardens

Mr. Edward Douding
Mr. Joseph Jackson
Mr. William Davis } Overseers of ye poore

t is then agreed yat the last Churchwardens and overseers of ye poore doe bring in and make up yeir accompts on ye 2 May next soe I say ye Second Maij

Richard Lane
Tho: Geering
William Martin
William White
John Hortt
Richard + + Horwods
marke
Thomas Joyner

John Goldingham
Minister.

The . . . . allowed by us but we doe not allow of the Rate of Sherehampton
Tho Chester
Christopher Cole

Page 218.

WESTBURY.

1689. A rate made by the Inhabitants of the Parish of Westbury for and towards the Reliefe of the Poor for the yeare 1689 at 6s. a pound as ffolloweth.

		yearely value. £	s.	s.	d.
Impr	Sr. Francis Fane for the Tythe	18	0	09	00
	Mr. Knight	94	10	47	03
	Mr. Lambe	80	00	40	00
	Mr. Jackson	48	00	24	00
	Mr. Geering	42	00	21	00
	Mrs. Tunbridg	21	00	10	06
	Mr. Walter	16	00	08	00
	Mr. Edward Sampson	75	00	37	06
	Mr. Ralph Sampson	08	00	04	00
	Mr. Lane	78	0	39	00
	Mr. Price	42	0	21	00
	Mrs. Walter	12	0	06	00
	The Heires of Mrs. Rutland	03	0	01	06
	Thomas Wasborow	15	0	07	06
	George Web	14	0	07	00
	Capt. Doubting	30	0	15	00
	Samuell Clavill	09	0	04	06
	The Heirs of Thomas Adlam	24	0	12	00
	Mrs. Avendall	27	0	13	06
	Mrs. Sarah Wasborow	03	0	01	06
	Mr. White	24	0	12	00
	Mr. Burgis widow	31	10	15	09
	Mrs. Hort	26	0	13	00
	Widow Cuff	08	0	04	00
	Mr. Powell	12	10	06	03
	Mr. Samuell Sandford	09	10	04	09
	Mr. Thomas Hort	08	00	04	00
	Mr. Price	06	0	03	00
	Mr. Tysan	12	0	06	00
	John Cheshire	03	0	01	06
	John Adlam	02	0	01	00
	Richard Horwood	03	0	01	06
	Mrs. Nickols	07	0	03	06
	Samuell Clavill	04	0	02	00
	Mr. Clarke	06	0	03	00
	Robert Hodges	01	0	00	06
	John Wasborow	03	0	01	06
	Mr. Jackson for Thomas Wallis deceased	01	0	00	06
	Giles Nurse	00	10	00	03
	The Some is		20	13	09

Page 219.

VESTBURY.

'he account of Robert Fennell one of the Overseers of the Poore of this Parish for Thomas Cuffs widows estate for this yeare 1689

	£	s.	d.
mpr This accomptant chargeth Himself with one rate Collected at 6d. p £ which commeth unto	20	13	09

The Disburstments are as followeth

	£	s.	d.
mp Paid to William Smith 13 months Pay at 5s. p month ending the 11th of Aprill 1690 is..	03	05	00
Paid Elizabeth Cook 13 months Pay at 4s. 6d. a month ending the 11 of Aprill is..	02	18	06
Paid ann Teg 13 months Pay at 4s. a month ending the 11 of Aprill is	02	12	00
Paid Mary Andrews 13 months Pay at 5s. a month ending the 11 of Aprill is..	03	05	00
Paid Robert wade 2 months Pay and a halfe at 2s. a month ending the 3rd of July is :	00	05	00
The Casuall Disburstments ..	12	05	06
mp Paid for making Jack Andrews Indentures..	00	02	06
Paid for 3 Horse loade of Cole for William Smith	00	03	03
Paid for 2 Horse load of Cole for Ann Teg	00	02	02
I Gave to Thomas Prewet in his Lameness	00	03	00
I Gave to William Bowre in his sickness	00	01	00
I Gave to a Poor Creeple the 8th of September	00	01	00
I paid Mr. Elsworth for making the rate	00	02	06
I paid Thomas Grant for the Prentice	02	00	00
I paid for the Apprentice of Jack Andrews	01	10	00
I paid for the use of Sidrack Gillets boys money	00	12	00
I gave to Thomas Hitchins towards the burying of his wife	00	02	06
I gave to a Poore man that was robbed	00	00	06
I gave to two Poore souldiers as came forth of Flanders ..	00	00	06
I gave to William Bowre in the Last time of his sickness ..	00	03	06
I gave to Poore People that came out of Ireland	00	00	06
I paid for a warrant to sommen the next overseer	00	01	00
I paid for carrying the Book to have it signed	00	00	06
I paid for engrosing the account in the Book	00	01	00
I paid for a warrant for Jack Andrews at Easter	00	00	06
I Crave allowance for money that I cannot gather	00	01	00
of John Adlam : I crave allowance for Giles Nurse ..	00	00	03
Gave to two Poor women at the door	00	00	06
Paid to William Smith since his monthly Pay	00	04	06
	18	04	04

Page 220.

The poore rate on ye other side is	20	13	9
disburst for ye Poor as on ye other side	18	4	4
	2	9	5

This Sum is pd to Captn Dowding
the new overseer pd him this 2d.
May 1690

allowed

John Smith	Jos Jackson
William White	Thomas Alcock
Thomas Smith	Samuell price
Richard Jaynes	Will Davis
	Tho Geering

Page 221.

ΓOAKE BISHOPP.

;89. A rate made by the inhabitants of the Parish of Westbury for and towards the reliefe of the Poore for the yeare 1689 at 6d. a pound as followeth.

		yearely value £	s.	s.	d.
npr	Sr. Francis Fane for the Tythe	13	0	06	06
	Sr. Thomas Cann	114	0	17	00
	The Lady Yeamans	44	0	22	00
	Sr. Robert Southwell	70	0	35	00
	Sr. Samuell Astry	11	0	05	06
	Sr. Richard Crump	37	10	18	09
	Sr. Symon Lewis	06	0	03	00
	Mr. Jackson	84	0	22	00
	Mr. Martin	84	0	22	00
	Mr. Gleed	52	0	26	00
	Mr. Kirk	14	10	07	03
	Mr. Dymer	64	10	32	03
	Mr. Edwards	39	10	19	09
	Mrs. Joyce Beavan	38	0	19	00
	Mr. Price	18	10	09	03
	Mrs. Blackwell	05	0	02	06
	Mrs. Knight	22	0	11	00
	Mr. Hart	37	10	18	09
	Mr. Tilladam	20	0	10	00
	The heires of John Hurtnell	08	0	04	00
	Mrs. Shore	12	10	06	03
	Mr. Dawson	10	10	05	03
	Mr. Husbands	16	0	08	00
	Mr. Brookes	29	0	14	06
	Mr. Brookes for Edward Lewis	02	0	01	00
	Mr. Alderman Creswick	09	0	04	06
	Mr. Hort	17	0	08	06
	Mr. Bauldin	08	0	04	00
	Mrs. Avendall	03	0	01	06
	Widow Stoakes	08	0	04	00
	William Self	03	0	01	06
	John Hurne	10	0	05	00
	Arthur Sawyer	04	10	02	03
	Samuell Sandford	02	0	01	00
	John Barwick	02	0	01	00
	William Thomas	04	0	02	00
	The Some is	23	01	09	

STOAKE BISHOP.

The Account of Nicholas Cox one of the overseers of the Poor of this Parish for Mrs. Knights estate for this yeare 1689.

	£	s.	d.
Imp This accomptant chargeth himself with one rate collected at 6d. p £ which commeth unto	23	01	09

The disburstments are as followeth

	£	s.	d.
Paid to John Wasborow 6 months Pay at 4s. a month ending September the 27th is	01	04	00
Paid to Robert Wade 10 months Pay and a halfe at 2s. a month ending the 11th of Aprill 1690 is	01	01	00
Paid to Margaret Haskins 13 months Pay at 4s. a month ending the 11th of Aprill 1690 is	02	12	00
Paid to Joane Griffin 12 months Pay at 2s. a month ending the 4th of APrill 1690 is..	01	06	00
Paid to Sarah Pullin 13 months at 4s. a month ending the same time is	02	12	00
Paid to Goody Vaughan 13 months at 2s. a month ending the same time is	02	08	00
	11	03	00

The Casuall disburstments

	£	s.	d.
Itt Paid James Taint for ffidlers Child	00	08	00
Paid James Taint for ffidlers child another time	00	06	00
Paid William By for ffidlers child	00	06	08
Paid William By for fidlers child	00	06	08
Paid William By and Mary White for nursing fidlers child	00	09	08
Paid William By and Mary White for Nursing	00	14	08
Paid William By and Mary White for Nursing	00	14	08
Paid William By and Mary White for Nursing	00	14	08
Paid William By and Sarah Pullin for Nursing	00	14	08
I Gave to John White..	00	01	00
I Gave to Joane Wild at severall times	00	10	00
I paid for two shirts for ffidlers boy	00	03	9½
I gave to John white at another time	00	02	00
I gave to Joane Wilde at other times	00	13	00
I gave to Alec Bowle	00	02	06
I paid for a Paire of Breeches and stockens for fidlers boy..	00	03	02
I gave to John White at severall times	00	06	00
I gave to Robert Wade for fiering	00	02	00
I paid for a Paire of Shoes for fidler	00	01	08
I paid for making the rate	00	02	06
I paid to Ann Cox for three Weeks Pay	00	09	06
I gave to Deborah challender..	00	04	00
I paid for two shirts for John Walborow	00	04	10
I paid for the Shroud and Coffin and to ye minister ..	00	12	07
I paid Tho: Hopkins	00	03	00
I paid for the tending of John Wasborow	00	02	00
I gave to Goody Vaughan at Severall times	00	05	06
I gave to Alec Downes	00	01	00
I gave to Henry Page at severall times	00	18	06
I paid for cloaths foı the child	00	03	06
I gave at the Doore to those that had Breifes	00	01	08
Itt for expences	00	02	04
I paid to Sarah Pullin..	00	01	06
I paid to Goody vaughon	00	01	00
I paid for a warrant to Sommon the next overseer.. ..	00	01	00
I paid the accounts engrosing in the Book and carrying him to have it signed	00	00	06
I gave John Wasborow in his sickness	00	02	00
I paid for a Paire of Stockens for fidlers Boy	00	[illegible]	[illegible]

Page 223.

	£	s.	d.
I Paid Sarah Pullin	00	01	00
I Paid Goody Vaughon	00	01	00
I Paid Joane Griffin	00	01	00
I Paid Robert Wade	00	01	00
I Paid William By	00	01	08
I Paid Sarah Pulling for nursing	00	04	00
pd Margarett Haskins	00	02	—
pd ye Wido Vaughan	00	02	—
		13	8
Brought from ye other side ..	22	00	11
	24	14	7
The Ballance of this Accompt pd this 2nd of May 1690 to Jos Jackson the new overseer being seaven shillings and two pence		7	2
	23	1	9

ecd	23	19	
aid out	22	14	7
		7	2

Allowed this Accomt by us

Thomas Smith
Richard James

Jos Jackson
Henry Alcock
Samuell price
Will Davis
Edward Dowding
Tho Geering
William White

lemorandum ye Poores
ay for ye Tything Stoke bishop
egins ye 25th Aprell
e Poores pay Westbury ye 4 Aprill

Page 224—Blank.

Page 225.

SHEEREHAMTON.

The account of John Parker one of the overseers of the Poore of this Prish for the yeare 1689.

		£	s.	d.
Impr	This Account Chargeth Himself with one rate at 6d. a Pound which commeth unto	23	16	06
	The Disburstments are as followeth	£	s.	
Impr	Abigall Parker 14 months at 6s. a month is	04	04	00
	Itt to John Baker 14 months at 2s. a month is	01	08	00
	Itt to Ann Williams 14 months at 6s. a month is	04	04	00
	Itt to John Barrow 14 months at 6s. a month is ..	04	04	00
		14	00	00
	The Casuall disburstments			
Impr	I Gave to old Iles in his sickness	00	10	00
	I gave to Mary Atkins in her sickness at severall times ..	00	18	06
	I gave John Baker	00	02	00
	I gave William Peacock at severall times	00	05	00
	I gave to Joane Baker at severall times	00	05	00
	I gave Mary Onion at severall times	00	05	00
	I gave Bridget Parker at severall times	00	05	00
	I gave to William Withers at severall times	00	08	00
	I gave Mary Wood at severall times	00	05	00
	I gave to Elinor Jayne at severall times	00	05	00
	I gave Mary Bowen at severall times	00	03	00
	I gave Frances Foord	00	03	00
	I gave Harry Fishpool at times	00	06	00
	I paid for making the rate	00	02	00
	I added to the Audit money for the Poore..	00	10	06
	I gave to Poore People that traveld with Passes			
Imp	I gave to Henry Gifford	00	01	06
	I gave to Thomas Moorten and his wife	00	06	00
	I gave to two Poore destressed soldiers	00	05	00
	I gave to Mary Loyd and her three Children	00	06	06
	I gave Joseph Millard and his wife..	00	04	00
	I gave Thomas Oliver	00	01	00
	I gave to James Griffin and his wife	00	06	00
	I gave to Thomas Alder and his wife	00	0?	06
	I gave to Charles Mason	00	02	06
	I gave to William James and his wife	00	05	06
	I gave Michael Day	00	02	06
	I gave Robert Harrison his wife and children	00	06	00
	I gave Mary Roberts and her children	00	05	06
	I gave ChristoPher Lane and Robert Tilloson	00	07	00
	I gave to William Right	00	00	06
	I gave to Richard Wade	00	01	06
	I Paid enGrosing the account in the Book and carrying the Book to Have it signed	00	01	06
	Paid for a warrant to Sommon the next overseer.. ..	00	01	00

Page 226.
Alowed by us This acompt of ye other
Side

Geo Petre
Willm Stainer
John Smyth
Richard Grumnell
Thomas Smith

Sept ye 15th
This account allowed ye former
overseer paying to Mr. William Davis
three pounds by us
Tho Chester
Christopher Cole

Page 227.

WESTBURY.

The Account of Edward Dowding one of ye overseers of ye poore of this prish for 1690.

By one rate Collected at 6d. p £ is	20	15	00
By mo recd of Robt ffinell ye Last overseer..	2	09	05
	23	04	05

The disburstmts is as followeth

to Wm Smith 13 mo pay at 5s p mo ending ye 10th Aprill 1691	03	05	00
to Elizabeth Cooke 13 mo pay at 4s. 6d. p mo is	02	18	06
to An tagg 13 mo at 4s. p mo is	02	12	00
to Mary Andrews 13 mo at 5s. p mo is	03	05	00
	12	00	06
to goody Bowry at severall times for her daughter to pay ye doctor	01	05	06
to old tagg at severall times	00	06	06
to poore souldiers at ye door	00	02	00
to a Coat and breeches and a pare of shooes 2 shirts to Jim Smith	01	02	06
to mo gave him in his Sicknes	00	03	00
to ye Buriell of a souldier and bringing from Cribs.. ..	00	12	00
to making ye rates wch a warrant to meet ye Justices for Jno parker to pass his accopt of overseer for 1689 ..	00	03	00
to mo paid when ye Justices met for wine and beer ..	00	13	00
to Mo pd ye Clark for ye use of £10	00	12	00
to olde Bowary in his Sicknes	00	02	00
to Sarah poolling for keeping olde grants aprentic 13 weeks	00	13	00
to a poor woman and two boys at ye door	00	01	06
to mo pd Rob: ffinell for keeping olde Grants Aprentice 8 weeks	00	08	00
to mo pd for Clothing ye Boy	0?	02	04
to Wm Jones in his Sickness at severall times	00	13	06
to Wade for ye Ringers and other expenses wn ye King landed	00	11	03
to severall poore at ye dore at severall times	00	03	06
to old Grante	00	02	06

Page 228.

Brought over from ye other side	20	18	1
to mo pd Mr. Lane ye accopt of Goody palmer	02	00	00
to Wasborow Jocham and Smith and Giles Nurse nt pd ..	00	01	10
to two poore woman of Mr. Jackson Tything	00	01	00
to a poore man at ye dore	00	00	06
	23	01	05

Villiam Martin Allowed by us
Vm White Samuell price
ohn Hortt
ohn Adlam
Thomas Smith
ames Dymer
Vee allow this Accompt and doe Appoint
Ir. Richd Lane overseer for the year
nsuinge Dated the 28 Aprll 1691
Richd Harvey
John Meredith

Page 229—Blank.

Page 230—Blank.

Page 231.

STOKE BISHOP.

The Accompt of Disbursments of Joseph Jackson one of ye overseers of ye parish of Westbury-upon-Trim.

Monthly pay.

Goody Haskins 13 monthes pay 4s. p mo ..	2	12	–			
Sarah Pullen 13 12 ..	7	16	–			
Goody vaughan 13 4 ..	2	12	–			
Robert Wade 13 2 6 ..	1	12	6			
Joane Griffeth 13 2	1	6	–			
Wm By for keeping ffidlers child 7 mo 6s. 8d. ..	2	6	8			
Sam Sandford $1\frac{1}{4}$ ys for Joane Wild house ..	10	–	–	28	05	2

Casuall disbursments

ffor a Hatt ffor ffidlers child	0	1	6			
pd for a warrant to serve overseer	0	1	–			
pd McDowle wife ? parish	0	2	0			
pd Goody Page Husband and wife being sick ..	0	4	–			
pd for a coat petticoat . . . ? frock for Sarah Pullens child	0	12	4			
pd Goody vaughan at severall times	0	5	6			
pd Chandler wife at severall times p order parish and Justice	0	9	–			
pd Goody White at Severall times	0	7	0			
pd Widow Elsworthy p orde Mr. Chest	0	3	–			
pd signing warrant	0	1	–			
pd Goody Haskins at times to buy clohes ..	0	2	–			
pd gave old wade	0	0	6			
I crave allowance for New . . . house ..	0	1	–	2	9	10
				30	15	–

Allowed by us
Samuell price
Tho Geering
William Martin
William White
James Dymer

Page 232.

Received of Nicholas Cox ye old overseer	000	7	2
Received as p ye Rate	23	1	9
	23	8	11
By Ballance	7	6	1
	30	15	–

Wee allow this acct and doe order that ye overseers of ye poore for ye yeare ensuing doe pay unto Joseph Jackson Esqre ye late overseer of ye poore the above ballance being the sum of seven pounds six shill and a penny Edward Jackson is appointed overseer for the yeare ensuing Dated ye 28 Aprill 1691.

Page 233—Blank.

Page 234.

ꟷIEEREHAMTON.

ıe Account of Capt Will Davis one of The overseers of the poore of This parrish for ye yeare 1690.

	£	s.	d.
The accountant chargeth himselfe with a rate amounting to	23	16	06
And money Received of John Parker ye fformer overseer wh was	03	00	00
The disbursments as ffolloweth in all is	26	16	06
ffor wrighting and parchment	00	01	00
payd to Charity Jones for keeping Ann Williams 51 weeks at 1s. 8d. ye week	03	16	06
payd to John Baker for 51 weeks at 6d. ye weeke	01	05	06
payd to Abigall parker for 24 weeks at 18d p the week ..	01	16	00
payd to mary woods for 30 weeks at 1s. ye week began ye 15th of Septembr	01	10	00
payd to goodwife Bye for keeping Ridlars child began ye 7th of November In 1690 to Aprill ye 10th 1691 being 22 weeks at 1s. 8d. ye week	01	16	08
pay for keeping Bareys Boy from ye 18th of Aprill 1690 to the 14th Of ffeauary being forty three weeks at 1s. 6d. ye week	03	04	06
Spent at distributing ye Addiatt money [1]	00	03	00
ffor warents to disturbe John Grimsteed and John Lewes	00	02	00
ffor warents to disturbe John Lewis Charles Wicks and Sarah harris	00	03	00
To sende a sick man away ffrom William Harris his house..	00	02	06
To three Sick souldiers came out of Ireland [2]	00	03	00
To ffrancis parker in Bread and Coles	00	03	00
To Wm withers his wife and three children at severall times	00	03	00
To a payer of Shooes and other Clothes for Ann williams ..	00	08	06
To Mary Atkins in Bread and money at severall Times ..	00	04	00
To money given with Jo Bareye at binding him aprentis ..	06	10	00
To Mr. Ashley for makeing ye Indentures	00	02	06
To charges of ffetching warrants of disturbance and Binding out The Boy	00	10	00
for a warent to bring in the new Colector	0	01	00
for carrying the booke to The Justis..	00	00	06
It comes to	22	06	02

ʼee doe nominate and apoynt To serve the office of overseers for ye poore The yeare Insuing Mr. Richard Lane for the Tithing of Westbury and Mr. Frances dimar for ye Tithing of Stooke bishipp Mr. Georg peeters for ye Tithing of Sherhampton.

[1] Addiatt money=Charity money. Till the present day it is called by some " Audit oney."

Page 234.

Brought from ye other side	22	06	02
To money given to old Iles	00	05	00
To two shirts and other things to Vidlars boy	00	05	00
overrated on Thomas Everatt	00	00	06
To widdow Greene for keeping a sick souldier	00	10	00
To Capt Davis for three sick souldiers	00	12	06
To Rich Hues for fower two days and nights	00	03	00
To Mary Hogget ffor one that died	00	04	00
To Ann Jones for two souldiers	00	03	00
	24	09	02
due to Ballance	02	07	04
	26	16	06

Allowed by us
Samuell price
Tho: Geering
Wm Martin
William White

Wee doe allow of this Accompt and doe appoint Thomas Smith overseer for the yeare ensuinge Dated the 28 Aprill 1691

9 2 Richd Hart
6 2 John Meredith

15 4 pd since ye accot was signed

ffor a warrant to destreyne on Misrs Rogers	00	01	00
ffor Expenses at Laffords gate Apr 28 1691	00	01	06
paide to Thomas Smith ye new overseer May 4 ..	01	07	10

Page 235.

A Rate made by the inhabitants of ye pish of Westbury-upon-Trym for and towards the releife of ye poore at six pence p pound ffor ye yeare 1690.

		£			
	Sr. ffrancis fane for the tyth ..	60 p an	01	10	00
	Sr. Samuell Astry	54	01	07	00
	Sr. Samuell Astry	28	00	14	00
	Sr. Samuell Astry	02	00	01	00
	Misrs. Rogers	76	01	18	00
	phillip Reade or tenant	31	00	15	06
	Misrs. Sarah Wasborow	05	00	02	06
fr. Holloway	Misrs. Holloway	40	01	00	00
35 p anum	Rich. Gromwell	40	01	00	00
	widdow Bowry	19	00	09	06
	Will Harris	25	00	12	06
	John Willis	05	00	02	06
	John Smith pylott yt was	12	00	06	00
	John Mathewes	20	00	10	00
	Widd. Greene..	30 10	00	15	03
	Mary Smith and nell parker.. ..	12 00	00	06	00
	Will White	14	00	07	00
	Mr. Dorney or tenant	14	00	07	00
	Wirkhouse	15	00	07	06
	Widd. Edwards	16	00	08	00
	Mr. George peeters	17	00	08	06
	Widd. Stoaker	09	00	04	06
	Widd. Thomas	20	00	10	00
	Tho. Everatt Shuemaker	08	00	04	00
	Rich. prichard	08	00	04	00
	Rich. Smith	14	00	07	00
	Mr. Chrismas or tenant	28	00	14	00
	Avon House	16	00	08	00
	Thomas Joyner for dightons ..	50	01	05	00
	Widd. Dee	24 10	00	12	03
	Rob. Cornish for Dees	02 10	00	01	03
	Dorothy Dee	05 00	00	02	06
	Ann Cox	01	00	00	06
	Rich. prichard for Dees	01	00	00	06
	John Smith	25	00	12	06
	Tho. Berry	11	00	05	06
	Charity Berry	05	00	02	06
	Thomas Herring or tenant	11	00	05	06
	Widd. Smith	15	00	07	06
	Tho. Smith	16	00	08	00
	Tho. Smith for Berryes	07	00	03	06
	Tho. Smith for peacocks	04	00	02	00
	John Jackson	07	00	03	06
			20	11	09

Page 236.

Widd. Gush	10		00	05	00
Samuell Robins	08		00	04	00
Will Davis	12	10	00	06	03
Gregory Bush..	10	00	00	05	00
Widd. Haynes	04		00	02	00
Edmond Hunt	15		00	07	06
Ann Jones	03		00	01	06
Misrs. Wallcome	08		00	04	00
James Smith	06		00	03	00
Esquire Lewis	16		00	08	00
Mr. Weaver for the Inne	10		00	05	00
Mr. Segwick for Cox	16		00	08	00
Widd. Greene..	02		00	01	00
Mr. Everat of London	02		00	01	00
			03	04	03
			20	11	09
The whole sume is			23	16	00

'age 237.

he Acco of Richard Lane Esqr one of the over Seeres of the poer for ye Parish of Westbury 1691.

Disbursed as ffol

	£	s.	d.
To Wm Smith for 2 monthes pay at 5s. p mo	00	10	—
To charges in Burying him	01	02	—
To Eliza Cooke 13 monthes pay at 4s. 6d. p mo	002	18	06
To Ann Tagg 13 monethes pay at 4s.	02	12	—
To Mary Andrewes 6 moneths and ½ at 5s	01	12	6
To mary Hewitt for Dyet of a Boy and for Shooes &c ..	02	13	1
To Edith Bowerre to goe with her Daughter to Bathe ..	01	10	0
To Richd Holbrooke for Work at ye Almes House 6s. and for time 2s. 9d.	00	08	09
To Capt Timo Payne for taking Jno Andrewes Apprentice £3 and to Mr Richd Yeamans for Binding him 2s. ..	03	02	—
To mony pd Mr. Edwrd ffreeman attorney for Drawing a Receipt for ye Lady yeamans[1] for ye £20 Left p Sr Robt yeams 5s. to a Limner for entering itt on ye Table in the church 4s.	00	09	—
To goodman Grant and his wife both being sick	00	05	—
To Edith Bowerre for her daughter at Severall times ..	00	15	—
To charges in Burying her 17s. moe for a Coffin 5s... ..	01	02	—
To Giles Humberstan for repayring ye almes house ..	00	17	—
To charge of Burying ye Wid Haynes	00	16	04
To Smith for clothes for Tho Andrewes wn put into Henbury Hospitall	00	12	10
To mo gave goodman Prewett 5s. Wm Long 1s.	00	06	00
To Wm Brown at Severall times being long sick	01	10	00
To Edwa Jotham for timber lime and work at ye almes house	01	09	06
To a yeares Rent for goody Palmer to Lady Day 1692 ..	02	00	00
To a Smith for taking Jno Andrewes apprentice	05	—	—
Tho Hopkins for making ye Rate and carrying ye book 18d. and warrant 1s.	00	02	06
	31	14	—
Recd p a rate of 6d. in ye pound Mr. Jackson not paying £1 04s. 6d. Avandall Short 6d. Way 3d. } £ 19 s. 08 d. 06	19	08	9
	£12	05	6
the parish Dr to R. L. to Ballance 14th June 92 Recd Mr. Tho Smith overseerr	02	07	03
	09	18	03
The 6th Dec 1692 pd Mr Wm White p R. Lane to make upp £20 p order of ye Lady Yeamans and for Soe much formerly left the parish p Sr Robt Yeamans Deceased }	10	1	09
Allowed by us	20	—	—

Samuell price
Edward Dowding
William Martin

[1] The inscription runs: "Sr Robert Yeamans Kt and Baronett gave £20 the Proffit hereof to be given to the Poor of this Parish Weekly in Bread for ever."

Page 239.

The Account of Edward Jochem on of ye overseers of ye parrish of Westbury-uppon-Trim in ye Tithing of Stoake Bishopp for ye yeare 1691.

	£	s.	d.
This Accomptant Chargeth himself wth one rat wch cometh to ..	23	1	9

The disburstments are as ffolloweth

Impr payd goody Haskins 13 moneths at 4s. ye moneth which is	02	12	0
Impr payd Sarah pullin for her selfe and ye Girle 3 monets at 12s. p mon	01	16	0
Imp payd Sarah pullin 10 moneths at 10s. ye moneth which is ..	05	0	0
Imp payd ye widow Vaughon 13 months at 4s. ye moneth wh is	02	12	0
Imp payd Robert Wade 13 moneths at 2s. 6d. ye moneth wh is	01	12	6
Imp payd Jane Griffin 13 moneth at 2s. ye moneth wch is ..	01	06	0
Imp payd ye Widow Wild 9 moneths at 8s. ye moneth wch is ..	03	08	0
Imp payd ye Widow Chanler 13 moneth at 2s. ye month is ..	01	06	0
	19	12	6

The chaussell disburstments

Imp payd Mr. Sawyer wch I promised for rent for ye house Ellsworth lived in	01	00	00
Imp ye Widdow Ellsworth at severall Times	00	06	00
Imp payd Davis of Bristoll which I promised him for ye house the Widdow Wild Liveing in now ending at our Lady day	01	00	00
Imp gave the widow Wilde at severall Times	00	09	06
Imp gave Alice Dowle at severall Times	00	05	0
Imp more gave to gody vaughon when she was sick and to buy her a shift	00	8	6
Imp gave to gody White at severall Times	00	04	0
Imp gave gody Bartlett at Times	00	02	0
Imp gave to Ann Cox in the cold Time	00	01	0
Imp payd for making ye rate	00	01	0
Imp given to poore distresed souldiars, seamen and other poore people by passes and certificates	00	05	3
Imp for making ye rates and caring ye booke	00	01	06
Imp for a warrant to bring in the Collectors	00	1	0
Imp for ingroseing the book	00	1	0
	£		
The whole is ..	23	17	9

I crave Alowance for £2 2s. for money
as I cannot Receive of Mr. Jackson
Samuell price William Martin
Edward Dowding

Page 240.

	£	s.	d.
Brought from the other Side disbursmts	23	17	9
for a warrant of Removeall	00	01	00
disburst att ye signing the Book	00	02	00
disburst ..	24	00	09
Recd as p the rate ..	23	01	9
	00	19	00
for wh Mr. Jackson did not pay	02	02	00
the parish Dr to Ed: Jotchan the ballance	3	01	00

Page 241.

SHEEREHAMPTON.

The accounte of Thomas Smith one of The Collectors of The pore of The parrish of Wesbury-uppon-Trim in ye yeare 1691.

And money receved of Captayn davis ye former overseear which was	01	7	10
	£	s.	d.
Imp paid to Ellizabeth By ffor The keeping Vidlers boy six month at 6s. 8d. ye moneth	2	00	0
Imp payd for clothes for Vidlers Boy	00	18	6
Imp payd to John Barker 13 moneths pay at 2s. p month ..	01	06	0
Imp payd Cherity Jones for keeping Ann Williams 13th moneths pay at 6s. p month	03	18	0
Imp payd for makeing a Coat for Ann Williams and buying some clothes and for a payer of shoes..	00	09	6
Imp payd to mary woods 12 moneths pay at 4s. ye moneth ..	02	08	0
Imp payd ffor the Buriall of mary woods..	01	02	0
Imp payd to Richard Jones in his sicknes and gave towards ye buring his child	00	09	0
Imp I gave to Mary Enion towards ye reliefe of she and her child	00	10	0
Imp I gave to Edward Iles and his wiff in theyr sicknes	00	10	6
Imp I gave to John Shoott in his sickness at severall Times ..	00	16	0
Imp payd Towards ye buying a coate for Willm peacocks son ..	00	04	6
Imp I gave to mary Atkins at sevearll times	00	11	0
Imp gave to a poore Mayd as died in Sheerhampton and for buring her	00	06	06
Imp spent at The disbursting of Addiet money	00	02	0
Imp Gave to the woman as Came from Whichchurch	00	01	0
Imp payd for signing ye poores rate	00	01	0
Imp gave to poore peopell as had passes to travell at Times ..	00	07	6
Imp I gave to Abigall parker at severall times	00	12	0
Imp I gave to William Withers at severall Times	00	07	0
Imp I gave to Ellnor Jayne at severall Times	00	07	6
Imp I gave to Jane Baker at severall Times	00	04	0
Imp payd for makeing ye poores rate	00	01	0
Imp for signeing and carrying ye Booke	00	01	6
Imp for a warrant to bring in the new Collector..	00	01	0
Imp I crave allowance for 2s. as Mr Holliway was not to pay ..		02	00
pd for imgroseing ye booke..	00	01	0
	17	18	00

	£	s.	d.
This chargeth himself with on rate ..	23	15	0
By money Rec last dew is	01	07	10
	25	02	10

I charg

Page 242.

Brought from the other side
Wee doe nominate and appoynt to serve the
office of the overseers of the poare of the
Titthing of Wesbury-uppon-Trim
Daniell Weear And Joseph Loyd
for the Titthing of Stoak bishop
and William Stayner for the Titthing
of sheerhampton

	£	s.	d.	£	s.	d.
Brought from the other side ..				17	18	00
To moneys spent marking in the accs				00	05	00
The Rate came to	23	15	00	18	03	00
Rec of Capt Davis	01	07	10			
	25	02	10			
To money dew to the parrish to Balance ..				6	19	10
				25	02	10

Allowed by us
Samuell price
Willm Stainer
Edward Dowding
William Martin

	£	s.	d.
by Money disburst to Thomas Simkinson ..		08	00
Mone disburst is ..		07	07
Mone disburst to Elinor Joyne and Mary Akins		10	00
	1	05	7
ffor My Expence this day ..	0	02	0
Money dew ye parish ..	1	07	7
	5	12	3

We allow of this account and yt
Tho Smith doe pays to Ed Jocham three
pounds one shilling sixpence and ye
rest in his hand to pay to Mr Lane

Tho Chester
John Meredith
Chr Cole

Page 243.

Aprill 18th 1693

officers chosen ffor ye parish of Westbury-upon-Trim ffor ye year ensuing

Mr. William Martin } churchwardens
Edward Hunt }

Mr. James Dymer Stokbishop }
Mr. Geo Peters Shirehampton } Overseers ffor ye poor
Wm Self Westbury }

Page 244—Blank.

Page 245—Blank.

Page 246.

The Acct of Dannel Weare on of ye ovarsears of ye poore of Wesberrye ye 1692.

Disbursted as followeth	£	s.	d.
It pd to Thomas Tagg 13 month paye at 7s. p month	02	12	00
It ,, to Elizebeth Cook nine months paye and a ½ at 7s p mo ..	02	05	09
It ,, to Will Bowary 12 mo paye at 2s. p mo	01	04	00
It to him moore aded 4 mo at 12d. p mo	00	04	00
It to Mary Mejar for Etending Eliz Cook and firing	00	17	06
It to Jon Jeliat for Intrust of money	00	12	00
It to Richard Leane hows rent	002	00	00
It to Tho Hopkins for my rate	00	01	00
Disbursted	09	10	03
Recd ..	26	07	04
balance .	16	11	01

	£	s.	d.
Daniel Weare Chardged himself with one reate at 8d. p £ coming to	27	11	08
I crave elowance for goyes nus ..	00	00	04
now is ..	27	11	04
paid Mr. Jackson ..	01	04	00
now is bal ..	26	07	04

	£	s.	d.
Due to ye parrish from Daniell Weare	16	11	01
Allowance for a warrant to serve the new ovarsear and expence to mete ye parish munday last and to ye Clark for Carying ye book	00	04	00
	16	07	01

April 26 pd By Dan Wear to Joseph Loyd one of ye overseers

Page 247.

The account of Joseph Lloyd one of the overseers of ye poore of ye Parish of Westbury-upon-trim for ye yeare 1692 as follows-eth.

		£	s.	d.
mpr	Payd to Alce Dowle 13 moneths pay at foure shillings p moneth comes to	03	00	00
	It Payd to Robert Wade 13 moneths pay at six shillings p moneth comes to	03	18	00
	It Payd to Sarah Poollen 13 moneths pay at 10s p. moneth comes to..	06	10	00
	It Payd to ye Widd Haskins 13 moneths pay at 4s. p moneth comes to	02	12	00
	It Payd to ye Widd Wilde 13 moneths pay at 8s. p moneth comes to	05	04	00
	It Payd to ye Widd Chanler 13 moneths pay at 2s. p moneth comes to	01	06	00
	It Payd to ye Widd Griffin 13 moneths pay at 2s. p moneth comes to	01	06	00
	It Payd to ye Widd Baham 5 moneths pay at 4s. p moneth and 8 moneths pay at 6s. p moneth comes to ..	03	08	00
692				
uly the 27th	Payd to William White to relieve his mother in her sickness	00	05	00
ugust he 28th	Payd to John White to relieve his sickness	00	05	00
eptember he 9th	Payd to William White towards the buriall of his mother	00	15	00
	Payd to William White more	00	05	00
15th	Payd for two warrants for William White and George Davey to bring them before Justices ..	00	05	00
March he 25th	Payd to Elizabeth Hughs 5 moneths pay at 6s. p moneth and 3 moneths pay at 3s. p moneth cometh to	01	19	00
	Payd for ye Widd Wild one whole years rent ..	02	00	00
		32	18	00

Page 248.

		£	s.	d.
Febr the 24/92	Payd to Mr. Samuel Sandford by ye order of Mr. Samuel Price and Mr. William White both of them being Church-Wardens for this present yeare the sum of	04	00	00
March the 25th	Payd the Widd Ellsworthy's rent	01	00	00
Feb the 9	Spent about ye Widd Cuffs business for going to Justice Cole	00	02	06
	Spent goeing to ye Justice wth ye Widd Barnat and removing of her	00	03	00
	Gave to a poore Seaman haveing a Pass to travail..	00	00	04
	Gave to another Seaman	00	00	06
	It Layd out for the poore Child wch Sarah Pullin keeps to buy her Cloaths	00	14	01
	It Payd for a warrant to remove ye Widd Martin ..	00	03	06
	Gave to ye Widd Vahan	00	02	06
	Gave to ye Widd Vahan	00	01	00
		06	07	05
	The sum over ye other side ..	32	18	06
		39	05	11

	£	s.	d.
Joseph Loyd Chardged himself with on rate at 8d. p £ coms to	30	15	8
Disbursted	39	05	11
Ballance due to him ..	08	19	03

I doe crave allowance for sum of two pounds Sixteen shillings yt I have not received of Mr. Jackson	2	16	00
	11	06	03

	£	s.	d.
Due to me in all	11	06	03
19 Apr 1692 recd from Daniell Weare	5	7	—

Samuel price — William Martin
Joseph Jackson — James Dymer — William White

Page 249.

;HEIERHANTON.

[he Accompt of Willm Stainer one of ye over Seers of ye poore of ye pish of Westbury-upon-trim 1692.

	£	s.	d.
It payd Chareyty Jones 11 mo and ½ for Ann Williams at 6s. p m	3	09	00
It payd John Parker when An Willms boun prentice ..	5	00	00
It a Seute of Cloathers wth Sherts and Shifts	0	18	03
It Layd out ffor Ann Williams when went to John Parker	1	00	09
It John Barker ffor 13 months at 2s. p month	1	06	00
It Mary Atkkins 12 months at 6s. p month..	3	12	00
It Mary Atkkins for Clothers for Her 3 children	1	01	00
It Abill Jaynes children 12 months at 6s. p month.. ..	3	12	00
It payd Tho: Everett ffor a payer of Shewes for Abll Jaynes boyes	0	03	06
It for Abill Jaynes Children for Clothers feaberary.. ..	0	10	08
It to Abbigell parker ffor fyering in desember and March ..	0	05	00
It to Edward Dalby for Ann Willms Indenture	0	02	06
It 10 weekes Scooleing ffor Abill Jaynes boyes	0	03	04
It to Jone Barker ffor ffyring in December and March ..	0	05	00
It to John Shott and wife at severall times	0	17	07
It ffor John Shotts ffunerall ye Minister 2s. 6d. and ye Clarke 3s. 6d.	1	10	10
It to Mary Eynion befor monthly pay at severall times ..	0	14	06
It Mary Eynion 6 months at 2s. 6d. p month ·	0	15	00
It ffor ye relife of Mary Eynion and child by ye complaynt of Her neighbours Her could not subsist wth out more pay month	0	07	06
It payd the golier ffor Mary Eynion	0	02	06
It desember the 3rd to a soldier yt was wounded and boud ffor Gloster	0	01	00
It ffor yses at severall times	0	05	06
It Layd out when distributed ye Addit money	0	03	06
It 2 seamen wch was tacken	0	01	00
It gave 3 Seamen wch was tacken in January	0	03	00
It to Hopkins ffor makeing the rate	0	01	00
It to Willm Wither when Leame and payd ye Surgin ..	0	15	00
It ffor Cloathers for Mary James and children	0	10	00
It ffor Sara Shott for House rent	0	10	00
It ffor Clothing of Abill Jaynes and children	0	10	06
It ffor William Withers children He being lame	0	12	00
It ffor Mary Eynion and child and House rent	0	15	00
It ffor Willm Peacocks being tacken	0	07	00
It Jone Barker being in want..	0	05	00
It gave ye widdow Eiles	0	02	06
It ffor My Expence of gooing to ye Justis	0	02	06
It Richard Jones being in want	0	05	00
	31	06	05
It I crave alowance ffor Ann Jones	00	02	00
	31	08	05

	£	s.	d.
Wm Stainer Charges Him Selfe wth ..	31	11	4
one rate at 8d. p £ cometh	31	08	5
	00	02	11
It ffor a warrant to bring in ye new Clector and for Caring and Sineing ye booke	00	02	11
	00	00	00

llowed by us
amuell Price
o Lambe
ho Smith
os Jackson
Villiam Martin
ames Dymer
William White

allowed by us

Page 250.

The Account of William Selfe Colector for ye Tithing of The Tithing of Westbury-uppon-Trim for ye yeare 1693.

	£	s.	d.
payd Robert Wade 12 months pay at 6s. the month ..	3	12	0
payd margaret Haskins 12 months pay at 4s. ye month ..	2	8	0
payd Ann Legge 12 months pay at 4s. ye month	2	8	0
payd William Bower 12 months pay at 2s. ye month ..	1	4	0
payd Jone Wilde 8 months pay at 8s. ye month and 4 months pay at 10s. ye month	5	4	0
Imp Gave To Robert Wade and his wiffe	0	7	0
Gave To Margret Haskins at severall Times	0	1	0
Imp payd John Clavill for goeing to Lauford gate	0	1	6
payd for 2 shirts for Thomas Wilee	0	5	0
payd for 2 warrants	0	2	0
payd for my expences 4 times goeing to Laufords gate ..	—	4	0
payd for Sineing of The rate..	0	1	0
payd for 2 payre of shoes and 2 payre of stockings and ffower yards of fflaning for Jane Wilde children ..	0	6	2
Imps gave To Jane Wilde To buy he children Close	0	10	0
ffor washing Jane Willdes bedding when she went from her children	—	1	6
payd for Buring Jane Willds Childe	0	2	6
payd ffor a warrant To Bring in ye new Colector	0	1	0
payd ffor draughing up my Accounts	0	1	0
payd ffor carring ye Booke To The Jusstis	0	0	6
The whole given	17	0	2
payd ffor Bringing Edward pullen To his Master 3 Times..	0	1	6
pd to William White for ye Keeping goody Wilds Children 3 weeks more	0	7	6
pd to Mr. Lane for ye rent of goody Pamers house.. ..	1	14	2
	19	03	4

	£	s.	d.	
Recd by a rate att 5d. p £ wch comes to ..	16	19	2	
	02	04	02	
Allowed by us Wm Martin		4	0	A bale I
Edm Hunt				crave dew to
Richard Grumwell	2	0	2	selfe
John Smyth				

Page 251.

Memorandum ye above £2 — 2d. on ye other side and £1 dew for ye rent of a house where Mrs. Cuffe dwell is .. .. 3 — —

	£	s.				
recd Mr. Martin	1	6	—			
recd popt church rate Jo Jackson	0	9	—			
recd popt poer rate Rich Selman	0	14	—			
recd popt poer rate Tho Washorow ..	0	14	—	3	3	—

Page 252.

STOAKE BISHOP.

The account of John Barwick one of the overseeres of ye Poore of ye Paresh of Westbury-upon-Trym for ye yeare 1693.

	£	s.	d.
Imp paid goody Pullin 12 mo pay att 9s. p monnth	5	08	00
to Goody Calender 12 mo pay att 2s. p mo	1	04	00
to Goody Greffin 12 mo pay att 2s. p mo	1	04	00
to Mrs. Cuff 12 mo pay att 3s. p mo	1	16	00
to John White 5 mo pay att 6s. p mo	1	10	00
to Alice Dowle 3 mo pay att 9s. p mo and 9 mo pay att 6s. p mo	3	06	00
to Goody Vaughan 10 mo pay 3 mo att 4s. p mo and 7 mo att 6s. p mo	2	14	00
to Eliz Hughes 6 mo att 6s. p mo and 6 mo att 8s. p mo ..	4	04	00
to Goody Hughes a fortnights pay more	0	04	00
to Goody Hughes att severall times	0	02	06
for Goody Hughes is rent	0	15	6
to John White att severall times	0	03	00
It for Shooes for John White..	0	03	6
It to Goody Dowle att several times..	0	04	0
It to Goody Vaughan att several times	0	02	6
It Buring of goody Vaughan	1	00	00
to Goody Chandler att times..	0	01	00
for 2 shefts and a paere of Shooes for ye child at Goody Pullens and Stocking	0	04	11
to Goody Griffin	0	02	06
It for going to the Justices several times according to these warrants	00	05	00
Gave to ye woman which was sent from St. Austins parish wth a warrant of removeall	00	03	8
It going to Charleton about John Whites business.. ..	00	01	00
for a warrant of removeall	00	02	00
It att a parish meating	00	02	06
It att a meating Conserning ye man wch fell over the rocks	00	01	06
It for a warant to bring in ye over seers of ye high waies ..	00	01	06
spent warning out of ye intruders in ye pish	00	01	06
pd the tything man to goe to warne ye intruders in ye prish before ye Justices	00	00	06
more paid to Alice Dowle two weekes pay	00	05	00
for the warant to bring in ye next oversere	00	01	00
for carring ye book in	00	00	06
for entering my account in the booke	00	1 02	00
	25	16	1

Page 253.

				£	s.	d.
Recd by a rate att 5s. p £ which comes to				19	4	4½
Recd of Mr. Wm Martin				05	0	0
	£	s.	d.			
Disburst	25	16	1	24	4	4½
due to Jo: Barwick	01	11	8½			

Allowed by us Wm Martin				
Edm: Hunt	Dew	1	06	08
John Smyth Richard Grumnell	more the month to the poore ..	1	09	00
		2	15	8½

Page 254.

The Acct of Mr. George Petre one of the overseers for ye poore of ye tything of Sheere-hampton in ye parish of Westbury-upon-Trim for ye yeare 1693. And haveing a rate at five pence p pound which comes to £19 07s. 06d. for ye tything aforesaid.

The Disburstments are as followeth	£	s.	
Impr Payd to John Barker 13 moneths pay at 2s. p moneth comes	01	06	00
It Payd to Mary Atkins 13 moneths pay at 5s. p moneth comes to..	03	05	00
It Payd to Mary Onion 7 moneths pay at 5s. p m.. ..	01	15	00
It Payd for keeping of Mary Onions Child 6 months pay at 6s. p moneth comes to	01	16	00
It Payd to Elianor Jayne 13 moneths pay at 5s. p month comes to..	03	05	00
It Payd to Sarah Shott 13 moneths pay at 3s. p moneth comes to..	01	19	00
It Payd to William Bowry 13 moneths pay at 2s. p moneth comes to	01	06	00
It Payd for Bread, Cheese, Coale for fireing for Mary Onion and Shoes for her child..	00	09	00
It Payd to Abigaile Parker for tending of Mary Onion in her sickness	00	05	00
It Payd for Shoes for Anne Williams	00	01	08
It Payd for a Warrant for John Parker	00	01	00
It Gave to Joane Baker at severall times	00	10	00
It Gave to Richard Jones in his Lameness..	00	05	00
It Gave to ye Whore yt was at Jones being sent by an order from St. Augustines pish in Bristoll to us ..	00	07	00
It Gave to Dinah Hughes to buy Cloaths for her children	00	10	00
It Payd for Burying of Mary Onion	01	02	09

Page 255.

	£	s.	d.
It Gave to Sarah Shott in her sickness	00	05	00
It Payd to Chirugion for Cureing of Richard Jones Legg..	00	10	00
It Payd for Signing ye Poore Rate..	00	01	00
It Gave to Abigaile Parker	00	01	00
It payd for makeing ye Poore Rate..	00	02	00
It Gave to a poore passinger going for Ire-Land by ye Justices order	00	01	00
It Allowed Capt Davis for a rate being Surveyor of ye High ways	00	01	06
It I crave to be allowed for Anne Jones	00	00	10
It Payd for entering of this acct in ye Books	00	02	00
	01	04	04
Sum over ye other Side ..	18	03	05
Disbursed in all	19	07	09

Allowed by us Wm Martin
Edm Hunt
John Smyth
Richard Grumnell

Ap: ye 10th 1694
Wee doe nominate and appoint
for ye yeare insuing officers

John Smith
Nicholas Cox } Overseers of ye Poore
Jeremy Gush

Allowed by us as far as true
J S Lenton
Tho Chester

Page 256. March 26 1695

Officers chosen ffor ye pish of Westbury-upon-Trim ffor ye yeare ensuing
Jno. Collins ffor Mrs. Knight Estate Southmead Westbury Tithing
Tho. Evered Churchwarden ffor Sherehampton

ffor Westbury	}	overseers
Sr. Tho. Cann ffor Stokebishop	}	
Edward ffishpool for Sherehampton	}	

The pticalers of ye poores rate at 7d. p £ gathered by Nicolas Cox overseer ffor Mr. Richard Crump 1694 ffor ye tithing of Stokbishop.

	Assesm				
Sr. Tho. Cann	130		3	15	10
Sr. Ro. Southwell	77		2	00	10
Sr. Sam. Astry	11		–	6	5
Sr. Richard Crump	37		1	1	7
Sr. Simon Lewis	6		–	3	6
Lady Yeamans	44		1	5	8
Lady ffane tithe	9		–	5	3
Mr. Jos. Jackson	84		2	9	–
Mr. Wm. Martin	84		2	9	–
Mrs. Dymer	64	10	1	17	7½
Mr. tho. Edwards	33	10	–	19	6½
Mr. David Phillips	6	—	–	3	–
Mrs. Joice Bevan	38		1	2	2
Capt. Price	18	10		10	9½
Mr. Jon. Blackwell	5			2	11
Mrs. Knight	22			12	10
Mr. Grenetts Aldworth	37	10	1	1	10½
Mr. Bill Adams	20		–	11	8
Mr. Biss for Mr. Hurtnell	8		–	4	8
Mrs. Mitchell	12	10	–	7	3½
Mr. Dawson	10	10	–	6	1½
Mr. Homes	31		–	18	1
Alde Creswick[1]	9			5	3
Mr. Hort	8			4	8
Widow Holbrook	9			5	3
Mr. Page	8			4	8
Mr. Gallop	3			1	9
Mrs. Peters	8			4	8
Wm. Self	3			1	9
Mr. Hurn	10			5	10
Arthur Sawer	4	10		2	7½
Mr. Sam. Sandford	2			1	2
Mr. Barwick	2			1	2
Mr. Loyd	4			2	4
Mr. Tompkins	18	10		10	9½
Mr. Kirk	18	10		10	9½
Mr. Robert Kirk	33			19	3
			26	17	7½

[1] The Creswick family had a great mansion in Small Street, the site of which is now

Page 257.

STOKBISHOP TITHING.

The Accot of Nicolas Cox Overseer of ye poor ffor Sr. Richard Crump Disburst as ffolloweth vizt

Sarah pulling 13 mth pay at 9s. p mth ..				5	17	–
Jno White 7 mth pay at 6s. p mth £2 2s. 4 at 7s. p mth £1 8s. 2 at 8s. p mth £0 16s. all				4	2	–
Jane Griffin 4 month pay at 2s. p mth 8s. 9 mth at 4s. p mon 1s. 16d.				2	4	–
Mrs. Cuffe 5 monthes pay at 4s. p mth ..				1	–	–
pd Wm White Keeping Wild Children 5 mth at 10s.				2	10	–
pd Sarah Pulling Keeping Wild children 8 mth at 11				4	8	–
pd Wm White ffor 4 months keeping Rob Cuffe				4	–	–
gave to Wm White	0	1	–			
pd Goody Sudamore ffor Tom Evans ..	0	5	–			
gave James Taynt	0	3	–			
pd for 2 pr shooes ffor Wild children ..	0	3	–			
pd for shifts and stocking for Wild children..	0	6	–			
gave Joane Griffin at 3 times..	0	5	–			
pd Sarah Sudamore abt Tom Evans.. ..	0	5	–			
pd for attendance on Mrs. Cuffe at sevl times	1	2	6			
pd buriall of Mrs. Cuffe	1	3	–			
paid Sarah Scudamore about Tom Evans at twice	0	10	–			
pd for Shooes Stockigs and bookes	0	2	6			
pd for Clothes	0	18	–			
pd for a Coat for Tom Evans	0	06	–			
pd for Shooes book and neckclothes.. ..	0	02	6			
pd for Clothes for Mary Candler	0	15	2			
gave Robt Cuffe 1s. more 1s 4d.	0	1	9			
gave at my Door	0	2	4			
a pair shooes and stockigs for Tom Evans ..	0	2	6			
a shirt for Robt Cuffe	0	2	6			
a pair Stocking ffor Tho Evans	0	0	9			
2 shirts for tom Evans 3s. 3d. britches and wascoat 6s.	0	9	3			
pd at Severall times	0	4	–			
making ye rate and entring in ye Book ..	0	4	–			
				7	14	9
I crave allowance ffor Will Self	0	1	9			
				31	15	9
ffor wh recd Short on Wido Kirk			9½			
ffor wh recd Short of Mrs. Tompkins ..			9½		3	4
				31	19	1
recd by ye rate on ye other side				26	17	7½

Page 258.

	£	s.	d.
perused and allowed this rate and there is due	5	01	05

to Nicolas Cox five pounds one
shilling five pence

Jos Jackson
Abraham Badman
Samuell price
Tho Wasborowe
John Hortt
Will Davis

Memorandum N Cox recd Jer. Gush ye overseer of ye poor for Sheerhampton after making up the accts	1	00	1
	4	01	4

Page 259. Aprill ye 3th in 1695 The account of Richard Sellman overseear of The poore of the parrish of Wesbury-uppon-Trimn and haveing a rate made at 7d. ye pound which comes to £24 7s. 1d. and my disbursment is as ffolloweth.

	£		
Imp payd Robert Wade and Wiffe at 10s. ye month 13 month pay	06	10	0
payd Margreet haskins 13th months pay at 4s. ye month ..	02	12	0
payd Thomas Teege 13th months pay at 4s. ye month ..	02	12	0
payd William Bower 13 months pay at 4s. ye month ..	02	12	0
payd Widdow Chandler 5 months at 2s. ye month	00	10	0
payd Widdow chandler 6 months pay at 4s. ye month ..	01	04	0
payd Alice Dowle 13 months pay at 6s. ye month	03	18	0
payd Mary ffenell for keeping of Thomas pruett	00	07	0
payd Thomas pruett 4 months and ½ at 4 sh ye month ..	00	18	0
payd to Thomas pruett at severall Times in his sicknes ..	—	04	0
pay for a warrant for removeall of Thomas White	00	01	0
payd for a warrant for Sarah prueett and a coppy	00	03	0
payd for carrying of Sarah pruett to ffillton	00	05	6
payd for goeing to Bartly to agree with ye keepper	00	06	0
payd for a payre of stockings and shoos for Tho willd ..	00	03	6
payd for a warrant and ye coppy	00	02	0
payd for keeping Sarah pruett 12th week in prison at 3s. ye week	01	16	0
payd for Clothing Sarah pruett and caring her to Torthworth	01	18	6
payd for keeping Tho Willd 5 weeks at 1s. 6d. ye week ..	00	07	6
payd for Burying Thomas pruett	00	10	0
payd to mary ffenell for Sarah pruetts Diatt	00	18	0
payd for a warrant for ye ffidlers wife	00	01	0
payd for carrying Sarah pruett to allmensbury	00	04	0
payd for Draughing a coppy of ye order	00	01	0
payd the wittnes for goeing to glossester	00	15	0
payd in exspences to glossester for 4 days	02	01	0
payd for hors hiar for my selfe and my and my self to Glossester 4 days	00	10	0
payd in Expensses Adiautt Day	00	06	6
payd for a payre of shoes for margrett haskins	—	02	6

Page 260.

	£	s.	d.
payd for shoes and stockings for mary Willd	00	00	0
payd for one shiffte	00	00	0
payd for bead stoffe	00	0	0
payd for approns	0	00	0
payd for a sarge gound	0	00	0
spent in goeing to sessions at severall times..	00	02	0
gaue to passes at severall Times	00	03	0
for keeping Mary Willd 4 month at 4s. ye month.. ..	00	00	0
for entring of in the Booke	00	02	0
The som	0	07	0
	£	s.	d.
In all as i have disbursted The whole sums..	33	5	6
	33	12	6
I crave Allowance i could not receve			
Mr. Richard Lane stopt for rent palmer house	2	0	00
William Selfe	0	14	0
gills nuosse	0	0	3½
	39	12	9½

	£	s.	d.		£	s.	d.
recd by a rate	24	07	1				
recd of Mr. Jo Jackson ..	3	00	–	disburst as above	33	12	6
	27	7	1	gave him with Ma Wild as apprenticed	4	0	0
Due to Richard Selman having allowed him £4 ffor	12	19	8				
taking Mary Wild as An Apprentce remaine due twelve					37	12	6
pounds nineteen shillings eight pence	40	6	9	ffor wh not recd	2	14	3½
					40	6	9½

Apr 11th 1695
allowed by us
Jos Lenton
Tho Chester

Jos Jackson
Abraham Badman
Samuell price
Will Davis
Tho Wasborowe
John Hortt

Page 261.

WESBURY 1694

A rate made by ye parrish of Wesbury-uppon-Trimn Towards The releffe of ye poore for ye yeare 1694 att 7d. p £.

		£				
Imp	the Lady Fane	18		00	10	6
	Mrs. Knight	94	10	03	2	4½
	Mr. Wasbrow	30		02	6	80
	Mr. Jackson	43		01	3	1
	Mr. Geering	42		01	4	6
	Mr. Tunbridge	21		00	12	3
	Mr. Walter	16		00	09	4
	Mr. Edward Sampson	75		02	03	9
	Mr. Ralph Sampson	08		00	04	8
	Mr. Richard Lane	82		02	07	10
	Captin Samuell prisse	48		01	08	0
	Sur. Richard Crump	03		00	01	9
	Mrs. Walter	12		00	07	0
	Thomas Wasbrow	15		00	08	9
	Captin Web	14		00	08	2
	Widdow Douttin	27		00	15	9
	Widdow Clavill	13		00	07	7
	Thomas Adlam	24		00	14	0
	Captin Ardnall	20		00	11	8
	Mr. Gallop	07		00	4	1
	Mrs. Sarah Wasbrow	03		00	1	9
	Mr. William Whitte	27		00	15	9
	Mr. John Burgiss	28	10	00	16	7½
	Mrs. hoart	26		00	15	2
	Jonathan new	08		00	04	8
	Mrs. Web	12		00	07	0
	Mr. Samuell Sandford	09	10	00	05	6½
	Mr. Thomas hoart	08		00	04	8
	Mr. Tisson	12		00	07	0
	Mr. Chesser	03		00	01	9
	John Adlam	02		00	01	2
	Richard horwood	05		00	02	11

Turne over for ye rest.

Page 262.

Mrs. Nickolls	07		00	04	I
Mrs. Clark	06		00	03	6
Robert hodges	01		00	00	7
John Wasbrow	03		00	01	9
Mr. Jackson for Wall	01		00	00	7
Gills Nuss	00	10	00	00	3½
Edward Jocham	01		00	00	07
The ratte comes to			24	7	I

Page 263—Blank.

Page 264—Blank.

Page 265—Blank.

Page 266.

An account of Jeremiah Gush overseer of the poore of Sheerehampton of ye parish of Westbury-upon-trim for the yeare 1694 and haveing a rate at seaven pence the pound wch comes to £27 09s. 06d. his disbursMents are as followeth:

	£	s.	d.
Impr Payd to John Baker 13 moneths pay at 2s. p moneth comes to..	01	06	00
It Payd to Mary Atkins 13 moneths pay at 2s. p moneth comes to..	01	06,	00
It Payd to Sarah Shott 13 moneths pay at 3s. p moneth comes to..	01	19	00
It Payd for keeping of Mary Onions child 13 moneths pay at 6s. p mo comes to	03	18	00
It Payd for keeping of Abel Jaynes Children 13 moneths pay at 5s. p moneth comes to	03	05	00
It Payd for keeping of James Whittiers Child 13 moneths pay at 6s. p mò comes to	03	18	00
It Payd to Elizabeth Hughs 5 moneths and 3 weeks pay at 8s. p moneth comes to	02	06	00
Elizabeth Hughs was Struk of ye book on ye 14th day of September 1694			
It Gave to ye Widdow Iles	00	01	00
It Gave to Abigail Parker in time of her sickness.. ..	00	03	00
It Gave to Tom Playford in time of his sickness in ye Small Pox at severall times	00	08	00
It Gave to Abigail Parker for tending of Tom Playford in ye Small Pox..	00	05	00
It Gave to Abigail Parker in time of her Childs sickness in ye Small Pox..	00	06	06
It Payd for one Payre of Shoes, one paire of stockings and one shift for Mary Onions Child	00	05	00
It Payd for makeing the rate	00	02	00
It Spent at the distributeing ye Audit money	00	01	06
It spent at ye Receiving of ye Audit money	00	05	00
	19	15	00

Page 267.

It Payd for a warrant for the removeing of Magdalen Harvey	00	02	06
It Payd for a warrant to Richard Jayne for bringing in the Surveyor of the highways	00	01	00
It Payd for a warrant to bring in the next overseer ..	00	01	00
It Payd for makeing Anne Williams's Indentures.. ..	00	04	00
It Payd for makeing the rate anew..	00	01	00
It Payd for entering this account	00	02	00
It Payd to Charity Jones 5 moneths pay for keeping of Anne Williams at 5s. p m comes to	01	05	00
It Payd to Charity Jones 6 moneths pay for keeping of Anne Williams 5s. p m comes to	01	10	00
It Payd to Thomas Hopkins for tending the book ..	00	00	06
Received of Mr. Geoge Petre on the 3d of October 1694 the sum of £2 03s. wch money was payd to him by John Parker for Anne Williams			
It Spent at the Parish meetings	00	02	06
It Spent at three several sessions	00	01	06
	03	11	00
Sum over ye other side ..	19	15	00
	23	06	00
Gave wth Anne Williams to bind her Apprentice.. ..	05	00	00
My whole disburstments for ye yeare is..	28	06	00

	£	s.	d.
I received the Sum of	29	12	06
	28	06	00
Comeing to ye Parish	01	06	06

I do crave allowance for William walcomes Estate being moneys wch I cannot Receive wch comes to 4s. 8d. and for Anne Jones 1s. 9d. soe there is	–	4	8
		1	9
coming to the parish 20s. 01d. pd to Nicholas Cox	1	0	1
	29	12	6

Tho Wasborowe
John Hortt

Jos Jackson
Abraham Badman
Samuell price

Page 268.

Aprill ye 11th 1695.

Seen and allowed by us

? J. S. Lenton

Tho Chester

Att a meeting of ye parish ye 3d June 1695 It was Agreed that a rate of 7d. p £ should be made ffor ye maintenance of ye poor for ye ensuing year wch comes to 78 14 2

	£	s.	d.						
Sherehampton tithing to pay p.mo.	1	18							
Itt . . . Whithers child	0	6	0						
Jno Baker	0	2	–						
Mary Atkins ..	–	2	–						
Sarah Hatt	0	3	–						
Mary Onion Children	0	6	–						
Abel Jaen children	0	5	–						
	1	4	0	13 mo pay ..	15	12			
Eliza Hughes children		6	–	14s. for 12 mo	8	8			
Tho Tagg		4	–				24	—	–
Wm Bowry		4		Remained to paye the charges			3	9	6
	1	18		Sherehampton rate ..			27	9	6
besides casually ..		7d.							

	£	s.					
Westbury Tithing to pay	1	14	–	p month Viz			
Robt Wade and wife	0	10	–				
Sarah Pullen for her self and child ..	0	9	–				
Margaret Haskins ..	0	4	–				
	1	3	–	13 moneths pay	14	19	–
Sarah Pullen for Wild children	0	11	–	12 monthes pay	6	12	–
pd Alice Dowle 1 mo pay						5	–
pd Tho Jagy 1 month pay						4	–
pd Wm Bowry 1 month pay						4	–
					22	4	–
remains to pay other charges					2	3	1

7d. pd rate comes to 24 7 1

Page 269.

Sto Bishop Tithing comes to £1 17s. p month

	£									
Robt Cuffe ..	1	—	—							
Jno White ..		8								
Joane Griffin ..		4								
	1	12		for 13 mo R	20	16	—			
Alice Dowle ..		5		for 12 m R	3					
					23	16	—			
pd Sarah Pullen for keeping Wild children ..						11	—			
					24	7	—	£	s.	d.
remaines over to pay charges					2	10	7	26	17	7
Sherehampton ..								27	9	6
Westbury ..								24	7	1
								78	14	2

Monthly pay

	£						
Sherehampton ..	1	18	—				
Westbury.. ..	1	14	—				
Stokebishop ..	1	17	—				
	5	9		p month for ye whole parish	70	17	-
				remaines to pay other Charges	7	17	2

Jos Jackson
Tho Cann

Page 270.

WESTBURY-SUPER-TRIM IN COM GLOUCR.

A rate made by ye Inhabitants of Westbury aforesd for collecting mony towards ye Releife of ye poore there for ye yeare 1695 at 7d. p £

		£		£	s.	d.
Imp	The Lady ffane	18 p annu		00	10	06
	Mrs. Knight	94	10s.	03	02	4½
	Tho. Wasborow	80		02	06	08
	Mr. Jackson	43		01	05	01
	Mr. Geering	63		01	16	09
	Mr. Wm. Walter	16		00	09	04
	Mr. Edward Sampson	75		02	03	09
	Mr. Ralph Sampson	08		00	04	08
	Mr. Richard Lane	82		02	07	10
	Mr. Samuell Price	48		01	08	00
	Sr. Richd. Crump	03		00	01	09
	Mr. Walters	12		00	07	00
	Tho. Wasborow	15		00	08	09
	Capt. Webb	14		00	08	02
	Widdow Dowding	27		00	15	09
	Sam. Clavell	13		00	07	07
	Tho. Adlam	24		00	14	00
	Capt. Arundell	20		00	11	08
	Mr. Gallopp	07		00	04	01
	Mrs. Katherine Wasborow	03		00	01	09
	Mr. Wm. White	27		00	15	09
	Mr. Day	28	10s.	00	16	07½
	Mr. Jo. Hort	26		00	15	02
	Jonathan New	08		00	04	08
	Mrs. Webb	12		00	07	00
	Mr. Sam. Sandford	09	10s.	00	05	06½
	Mr. Tho. Hort	08		00	04	08
	Mr. Tyson	12		00	07	00
	Mr. Chesier	03		00	01	09
	Jo. Adlam	02		00	01	02
	Richd. Horwood	05		00	02	11
	Mr. Nicholas	07		00	04	1
	Mrs. Clarke	06		00	03	06
	Robt. Hodges..	01		00	00	07
	Jo. Wasborow	03		00	01	09
	Mr. Jackson p Wallis	01		00	00	07
	Giles Nurse	00	10s.	00	00	03½
	Edward Jotcham	01		00	00	07
	p annum	826	10	24	07	01

Page 271.

The Acct of Thomas Wasborow overseer of the poor of ye Tything of Westbury-upon-Trim for ye yeare 1695 his disburstmts (as followeth)

		£	s.	d.
Impr	pd Wm Bowry 1 months pay att 4s. p month	00	04	00
Itm	pd Thomas Tagg 1 months pay att 4s. p month	00	04	00
Itm	pd alice Dowell 1 months pay att 6s. p month	00	06	00
Itm	pd Robt Wade 13 months pay att 10s. p month	06	10	00
Itm	pd Sarah Pullen 12 months pay for her selfe 2 chiloren att 14s. ye month	08	08	00
Itm	pd Martha Smyth 12 months pay for a bastard child att 6s. p month	03	12	00
Itm	pd Margarett Haskings 8 months pay and ½ att 4s. ye month	01	14	00
Itm	pd Martha Smyth for 2 payre of shoes and stockings and shifts for ye parish child she keepes	00	08	06
Itm	pd her likewise 14 shillings 4d. for making Wilds childrens cloths and ye childs cloths she keeps	00	014	04
Itm	pd Mr. Sam Bayley for severall yards of stuff for wades children to make cloth then as appears p. note ..	01	14	10
Itm	pd Mr. Bowdler for 8 yds ¼ of cloth for Wilds boy.. ..	00	08	01
Itm	pd Mr. Caviell fore payer of shooes for Wilds children ..	00	03	06
Itm	pd ffrances Wasborow for ale for Margarett Haskins in her tyme of sickness	00	01	07
Itm	pd Sarah Pullen for looking after Margarett Haskins ..	00	02	00
Itm	pd for a warrt to remove betty	00	02	06
Itm	pd Mr. Lane Goody Palmers house rent	02	00	00
Itm	paid Mr. White for a warrt	00	01	00
Itm	pd Richd Horwood for warrt	00	01	00
Itm	pd Tho Hopkins for carrying ye booke to ye Justices ..	00	00	06
Itm	pd for a warrt to bring in ye next overseer..	00	01	00
	The whole disburstmts ..	26	16	10
	The rate comes to for ye yeare ..	24	07	01
	There is due upon ye ballance of the Acct	02	09	09

Page 272.

I doe crave Allowance for mony yt I cannot receive of Mr. Tho Hort	00	04	08
I doe crave allowance for mony yt I cannot receive of Wm Selfe	00	14	00
due to me on the ballance ..	03	08	05

This acct allowed by us on the
21th day of April 1696

Samuell price
William Martin
John Collins Churchwarden
Thomas Everet Churchwarden
Westbury

Wee doe nominate and appointe
William ward two serve the offic
of oversere for the yeare insuing
ffor the Tything of Stoake Bisshop
We doe nominate and appointe
Capt Coockman or the Lady yeamans two serve
the offic of over seare for the yeare
in suing for Stoake Bisshop

Wee doe nominat and appoint Edward Long
two serve the offic of over seare of the
poore for the year in sueing for the
Tything of Sherhampton

Page 273.

COM. GLOUC.

A Rate made by ye Inhabitants of ye Tything of Stoake Bishop for collecting mony for the Releife of ye poore for ye yeare 1695 att 7d. p £

		£ p ann				
Impr	Sr. Thomas Cann	130		03	15	10
	Sr. Robt. Southwell	70		02	00	10
	Sr. Samuell Astry	11		00	06	05
	Sr. Richd. Crump	37		01	01	07
	Sr. Symon Lewis	06		00	03	06
	The Lady yeamen	44		01	05	08
	The Lady ffane	09		00	05	03
	Mr. Jackson	84		02	09	00
	Mr. Martin	84		02	09	00
	Mr. Edwards	33	10s.	00	19	06½
	Mr. Phillipps	06		00	03	06
	Mrs. Joyce Beavan	38		01	02	02
	Mr. Price	18	10s.	00	10	9½
	Mr. Blackwell	05		00	02	11
	Mr. Knight	22		00	12	10
	Mr. Aldworth	37	10s.	01	01	10½
	Mrs. Tyladams	20		00	11	08
	Mr. Bysse	08	–	00	04	08
	Mr. Mitchell	12	10s.	00	07	3½
	Mr. Dawson	10	10s.	00	06	1½
	Mr. Holmes	31		00	18	01
	Mr. Creswick	09		00	05	03
	Mr. Tho. Hort	08		00	04	08
	Widow Holbrocke	09		00	05	03
	Mr. Poope	08		00	04	08
	Mr. Gallop	03		00	01	09
	Mr. Dymer	64	10s.	01	17	7½
	Mr. Robert Kirk	33		00	19	03
	Mr. Tomkins	18	10s.	00	10	09½
	Mr. Kirk	18		00	10	—
	Mr. Petre	08		00	04	8
	Mrs. Selfe	03		00	01	09
	Jo. Hurne	10		00	05	10
	Arthur Sawer	04	10s.	00	02	08
	Sam. Sandford	02		00	01	02
	Jo. Barwicke	02		00	01	02
	Joseph Lloyd	04		00	02	04
		922	00	26	18	02

Page 274.

The Acct of Jo Clavell for Sr. Tho Cann overseer of ye poore of ye Tything of Stoakebishopp for ye years 1695—his disburstmts (as followeth)

		£	s.	d.
Impr	pd Jo White 13 months pay 10 months att 10s. p month and 3 months att 8s. p month..	06	04	00
Itm	pd Joane Griffin 13 months pay att 4s. p month	02	12	00
Itm	pd Alice Dowle 12 months pay att 6s. p month	03	12	00
Itm	pd Robt Cuffe 3 months pay att 20s. p month and 6 months att 15s. p month..	07	10	00
Itm	pd ye Widdow Skydmore for Hughes children 10 months pay att 6s. p month and 1 month att 5s.	03	05	00
Itm	pd Sarah Pullen 1 month pay	01	00	00
Itm	pd for buryeing Ratchell Rowland..	00	15	00
Itm	pd for removeing Anne Bennett	00	02	00
Itm	pd for making Rates and signeing of them..	00	03	00
Itm	Gave to Elizabeth Hughs	00	01	00
Itm	pd for a passe and keeping George Rowland	00	12	06
Itm	pd for cloths for Hughs's children	01	16	06
Itm	pd for a shirt for Robt Cuffe..	00	05	00
Itm	pd for keeping Luce Mulling and burying her child ..	01	05	00
Itm	pd for removeing Henry Longford his wife and child ..	00	15	09
Itm	pd Mr. Martin for a warrt to bringing overseers of ye highways	00	01	06
Itm	payd for removeing Elizabeth Wade to Horfield.. ..	00	04	00
Itm	pd for ye buriall of Robt Cuffe	01	07	02
Itm	pd for removing Jo Price his wife and child	00	02	06
Itm	pd Jo Organ for Jo Stuckey..	00	05	00
It	payd for entering ye accts	00	02	00
It	Payd for a warrant for ye bringing in the new overseer ..	00	01	00
It	gave to Thomas Haskins for Carrying ye book	00	00	06
	This acct comes to ..	32	02	05

Page 275.

		£	s.	d.
Impr	I doe crave allowance for monies wch I have not received of Thomas Hort wh he stops for keeping of Tom Wild ..	00	04	08
It	I doe crave allowance for ye Lady ffane	00	01	03
		00	05	11
	My Disbursments for the whole yeare is ..	32	02	05
	My rate comes to £26 18s. 02d. whereof I have received	26	12	03
	There is comeing to me from the parish the sum	05	10	02

Allowed this Acct this 20th Aprill 1696

John Collins Churchwarden

Thomas Everet Churchwarden

Jos Jackson

William Martin

Samuell price

Page 277.

SHEEREHAMPTON.

A rate made by ye inhabitants of ye Parish of Westbury for and towards the relief of the poore at 7d. p £ for ye yeare 1695 as followeth.

	£	s.	£	s.	d.
Impr Lady ffane for ye tythe	55	00	01	12	01
Sr. Samuel Astry for ffishpools	54	00	01	11	06
Sr. Samuel Astry for Harrices	28	00	00	16	04
Sr. Samuel Astry for ye ship	02	00	00	01	02
Mrs. Rogers	76	00	02	04	04
Phillip Reed or tent	31	00	00	18	01
Mrs. Sarah Wasborrow	05	00	00	02	11
Mrs. Holloway	35	00	01	00	05
Richard Grumwell	40	00	01	03	04
Mr. Hellier	19	00	00	11	01
William Stainer	26	00	00	15	02
William Stainer for Catherine	04	00	00	02	04
John Willis	05	00	00	02	11
John Smyth Pilot	12	00	00	07	00
Charity Matthews	20	00	00	11	08
Mary Smith and Edw: Tippet	12	00	00	07	00
William White	13	00	00	07	07
Mr. Dorney or tent	15	00	00	08	09
Wirkhouse	15	00	00	08	09
Widow Edwards	16	00	00	09	04
George Petre	17	00	00	09	11
Widow Stoakes	09	00	00	05	03
Widow Thomas	20	00	00	11	08
Thomas Everett	08	00	00	04	08
Richard Pritchard	07	00	00	04	01
Richard Smyth	14	00	00	08	02
Mr. Christmas or tent	28	00	00	16	04
Avenhouse	16	00	00	09	04
Thomas Joyner for Dightons	50	00	01	09	02
Richard Pritchard for Dees	24	10	00	14	03½
Robert Cornish for Dees	02	10	00	01	05½
Richard Jayne for Dees	02	00	00	01	02
Jonathan Perkins for Dees	03	00	00	01	09
Anne Cox	01	00	00	00	07
Richard Pritchard for Dees	01	00	00	00	07
John Smith	25	00	00	14	07
Widow Berry	07	00	00	04	01
Charity Berry	05	00	00	02	11
Thomas Herring or tent	11	00	00	06	05
Widdow Smyth	15	co	00	08	09
Thomas Smyth	16	00	00	09	4
Thomas Smyth for Berries	07	00	00	04	1
Thomas Smyth for Peacock	04	00	00	02	4
John Jackson	07	00	00	04	1
John Willis for Greens	24	00	00	14	0
Widdow Green	06	10	00	03	9½
Widdow Gush	10	00	00	05	10
Samuel Robins	08	00	00	04	08
William Davis	12	10	00	07	3½
Gregory Bush	10	00	00	05	10
	854	00	24	18	02

Widdow

Page 278.

	£	s.	£	s.	d.
Widdow Haynes	04	00	00	02	04
Edmund Hunt	15	00	00	08	09
William Walcome	08	00	00	04	08
James Smyth	06	00	00	03	06
Mr. Sampson for ye Inne	10	00	00	05	10
Esqre Lewis	16	00	00	09	04
William James	06	00	00	03	06
Mrs. Sedgwick for Cox	16	00	00	09	04
Widdow Green for fully grove	02	00	00	01	02
Mrs. Everett	02	00	00	01	02
Anne Jones	03	00	00	01	09
	088	00	02	11	04
	854				
	942	00			
The sum from over ye other side			24	18	02
The rate comes to for ye yeare 1695			27	09	06

Page 279.

An account of Edward ffishpoole overseer of the poore of Sheerehampton of ye Parish of Westbury-upon-Trim for ye yeare 1695 and haveing a rate at Seaven pence ye Pound which comes to £29 09s. 06d. his Disbursments are as followeth—

	£	s.	d.
Impr Payd to Thomas Tagg and to his wife one moneths Pay at 4s. p moneth and more ten moneths Pay at 6s. p moneth comes to in all	03	04	00
It Payd to William Bowry eleven months Pay at 4s. p moneth comes to	02	04	00
It Payd to Keeping of John Hughs Children a 11 moneths pay at 6s. p month comes to	03	06	00
It Payd to John Baker 13 moneths pay at 2s. p moneth comes to..	01	06	00
It Payd to Mary Atkins 13 moneths pay at 2s. p moneth comes to..	01	06	00
It Payd for ye Keeping of Mary Onions child 13 moneths pay at 6s. p mo comes to	03	18	00
It Payd for ye keeping of Abel Jaynes children 13 moneths pay at 5s. p moneth comes to	03	05	00
It Payd to Sarah Shott 13 moneths pay at 3s. p moneth ..	01	19	00
It Payd for ye Keeping of James Whittiers child 13 moneths pay at 6s. p mo comes to	03	18	00
It Gave to Henry ffishpoole in time of Sickness	00	06	00
It Gave to Abigaile Parker for tending a Boy	00	05	00
It Payd for a Paire of Shoes for Mary onions Child	00	01	06
It Payd for makeing a Gown for Mary onions child	00	00	06
It Payd for a paire of Shoes for James Whittier	00	01	06
It Paid for a garment and —— ? for Mary onions Child ..	00	02	00
It Payd for makeing rates and spent at ye makeing of it in all	00	03	00
It Spent at ye distributeing of ye Audit money	00	03	00
It Payd for mending of one pair of shoes for Mary Onions Child	00	00	03
It Paid to William Downs for quartering the Whore and her Bastard	00	06	00
It Payd at another time for quartering ye whore and her Bastard to Willm Downs	01	02	00
	26	16	09

Page 280.

	£	s.	d.
It gave to Elianor Reed at severall times	00	06	00
It Spent ye day wee brought Benjamin Albright and others to ye overseers of the parish of Henbury	00	01	00
It Payd to Willm Downs more for ye whore and Bastards quartering	00	13	00
It Payd to abigail Paker for ye whore and Bastard	00	02	00
It Payd for a Warrant for ye bringing in of the surveyors of ye Highways	00	01	00
It gave for ye entering of this account and rate in ye book ..	00	02	00
It Payd for a warrant for ye bringing in a new overseer ..	00	01	00
It Gave for the makeing of two Certificates for ye Dischargeing of the parish of St. Augustins of ye whore and Bastard	00	01	06
	1	07	06
The sum from over ye other side.. ..	26	16	09
The whole disbursments	28	04	03
The rate comes to for ye yeare	27	09	06
There is Due upon ye Ballance of this acct to Edw ffishpoole ye sum of	00	14	09
It I doe crave allowance for money wh I cannot Receive of Anne Jones	00	01	09
It gave to Thomas Hopkins for carrying the booke to ye Justices	00	00	06
There is due upon ye Ballance pd him by William Martin	£00	17	00

Jos Jackson

Samuell price

William Martin

John Collins Churchwarden

Thomas Everet Churchwarden

Page 281.

Aprill the 27th 1696

Allowed by us

J. S. Lenton

John Meredith

Page 282—Blank.

Page 283.

The accompt of William Ward overseer of the poore of ye tything of Westbury-upon-Trim for the yeare 1696 are as followeth.

	£	s.	d.
Imprs Paid to John Smith 13 months pay at 6s. p moneth comes to	03	18	00
It Paid to Robert Wade 13 months pay at 10s. p month comes to	06	10	00
It Paid to Sarah Pulling 13 months pay at 14s. p month comes to	09	02	00
It Paid to Thomas Wade 2 months pay at 6s. p month and 2 months pay at 4s. p month comes to in all ..	01	00	00
It Gave to a poore woman and Six Children yt had a Pass	00	00	06
It Paid for Signing ye Rate	00	01	00
It Paid to Captaine Price	00	04	00
It Paid for two Shifts and a neck-cloth for Gooddy Wade	00	07	06
It Paid for two yards and ¾ of Sarge for John Smith Girle	00	06	10
It Paid to John Smith for makeing ye Girles Coate ..	00	02	00
It Paid for Stockings and Shoes for John Smiths Girle ..	00	02	06
It Gave to two Seamen wch had a Pass to travaile ..	00	01	00
It Gave to an Irish woman wch had a Pass to travaile ..	00	00	06
It Gave to Thomas Wade in his Sickness at several times	00	14	08
It Paid for a Warrant for William Thomas	00	01	00
It Paid to Mr. Lane for Gooddy Palmers house rent ..	02	00	00
It Paid to Mr Wasborrow wch he was out ye Last yeare ..	03	00	00
It Paid for 11 Ells of cloth for Parish Children	00	11	00
It Paid for makeing ye childrens shifts	00	02	00
It Paid for Shoes and Stockings for Wilds Children ..	00	05	00
It Paid for a Paire of Shoes for Sarah Pulling	00	02	08
It Paid for a Paire of shoes for John Smiths Girle.. ..	00	01	06
It Paid for Cloth and makeing of Clothes for Wilds Children	01	01	09
It I crave allowance for money wch I could not Collect ..	00	10	01½
It Paid for a Warrant to bring in ye new Collector ..	00	01	00
It Paid for a Warrant to Streine upon Richard Symmons	00	01	00
It Spent at Severall times in makeing ye Rate ..	00	03	06
It Gave to Thomas Hopkins for carrying ye booke to have it signed by ye Justices	00	00	06
It Gave for ye entering of this acct..	00	01	00
The whole Disbursmts ..	30	12	06½
This acct chargeth with a rate ..	31	01	09
Due to ye Parish upon ye ballance here of	00	09	02½
It Payd for makeing ye rate and for a warrant	00	01	06
Paid Mr. Still ye said Ball ..		7	8½

April 14th 1697

Allowed by us	John Hort	John Smyth
Samuell price	William Martin	Tho Wasborowe

Page 284.

Wee doe nominate and appoint to
serve Collectors for ye poore for parish of
Westbury-upon-Trim for ye yeare 1697
Capt Price for ye tything of Westbury
Edward Jayne for Stoke Bishop
John Seagar for Sheerehampton.

Page 285.

An Acct of William Steele one of the overseers of the poore for ye tything of Stoke Bishop of ye pish of Westbury-upon-Trim for ye yeare 1696 are as followeth—

	£	s.	d.
Imprs Paid to Sarah Scudamore two months pay ending ye 12th of June at 12s. p moneth comes to	01	04	00
It More Paid to Sarah Scudamore eleventh months pay at 16s. p month	08	16	00
It Paid to John White 13 months pay at 10s. p month	06	10	00
It Paid to Joane Griffin 13 months pay at 4s. p month..	02	12	00
It Paid to Alice Dowle 13 months pay at 6s. p month..	03	18	00
It Paid for keeping a Bastard to Sarah Scudamore 2 months pay at 10s. p month comes to	01	00	00
It more Payd to Sarah Scudamore 4 months pay for keeping ye same child at 8s. p month comes to ..	01	12	00
It Gave to Joane Jones in Sickness	00	12	06
It Paid for drink and Biskett for those yt carried her to ye Grave	00	06	00
It Paid ye Clerk and Sex Stone	00	03	08
It Paid for a Shroud for her	00	02	06
It Paid to them yt Laid her out..	00	01	00
It Paid for a Coffin for her..	00	07	00
It Paid to ye Minister	00	02	06
It Paid for Coales	00	02	00
It Paid to two women yt made oath	00	01	00
It Paid to woman to looke to her in her sickness ..	00	02	00
It Paid to Thomas White for George Benetts child ..	00	03	00
It Paid for 3 paire of shoes for Hughes Children.. ..	00	04	06
It more laid out for 3 paire of Stockings..	00	01	10
It Paid ye Tailor for makeing ye boy a Coate and breeches and ye wench a Gowne	00	02	00
It Paid to poore travellors at severall times	00	02	06
It Disbursd for Alice Dowle for Coale	00	05	00
It Paid to her in money ye time Shee lay in at sever times	00	05	00
It Paid to John White in her sickness by ye Justices order	00	03	00
It Paid for makeing ye rate	00	02	00
It Paid going to ye Justice wth Prudence Parker and a warrant to send her away and money gave her ..	00	03	06
It Paid for an order to remove Prudence Parker and to warn old Wheeler and a man yt lived at Clackmill out of ye Parish comes to in all	00	06	00
It Paid for a Shift for Joane Griffin and in money ..	00	05	00

Page 286.

	£	s.	d.
nprs for serving ye order and Carrying Prudence Parker to Broom-yard in Herefordshire hosehire and other charges came to	03	00	00
It I crave allowance for wh Sr. Thomas Cann stoped which was	04	17	06
It Likewise I crave allowance for wh Mr. Jackson stoped on my rate	03	00	00
and I crave allowance for wh Mr. Pope stoped ..	00	06	00
It I charge for myselfe for 4 days yt I was out when I carried Prudence Parker to Broom-yard.. ..	00	08	00
It Gave for carrying ye booke to be signed	00	00	06
It Gave for a warrant to bring in ye new Collectr ..	00	01	06
It Gave for ye entering this acct in ye booke	00	01	00
	11	14	06
The sum from over ye other side ..	29	15	06
The whole disburstmts..	41	10	00
This acct chargeth wth a rate comes to..	39	02	00
Parish indebted to ye Collector	07	08	00

	£	s.	d.	£	s.	d.
Paid to Mr. Steel by Edward Long ..	1	10	05			
Paid to Mr. Steel by Willm Ward ..	0	07	8			
	1	18	01			
Paid by Mr Hort	0	11	00	3	08	7
	2	09	01			
To recd of Sr Thomas Cann	0	19	06			
	3	08	07	3	19	5
Due to Mr. Steel on ye Ballance				3	19	5

Aprill 14th 1697 this accounte
allowed by us

Samuell Price Tho Smith
Will Davis John Willis
John Hort William Martin
Tho Wasborowe

Aprill 29—1697

By money to Mr. Steele the Ballance paid Mr. John Hort 3 19 05

Page 287.

An Acct of Edward Long one of the overseers of the poore for ye Tything of Sheerehampton of ye parish of Westbury-upon-Trim for ye yeare 1696 are as followeth—

	£	s.	d.
Impis Paid to John Baker 13 moneths pay at 2s. p month ..	01	06	00
It Paid to Mary Atkins 13 months pay at 2s. p month ..	01	06	00
It Paid for keeping of Mary Onions child 13 moneths pay at 6s. p month comes to..	03	18	00
It Paid for keeping Abel Jaynes children 13 months pay at 5s. p month comes to..	03	05	00
It Paid to Sarah Shott 13 months pay at 3s. p month..	01	19	00
It Paid for keeping of James Whittier 13 months pay at 6s. p moneth comes to..	03	18	00
It Paid to ye Widd Tagg 13 months pay at 6s. p month	03	18	00
It Paid to William Bowry 13 months pay at 6s. p month	03	18	00
It Paid for wollen cloaths, shirts, shoes and tockings for Old Bowry Mary Onions child and James Whittier the sum of	02	03	06
It Gave to Elianor Reed at Several times..	00	08	06
It Gave to Joane Baker at Severall times	00	02	06
It Gave to William Withers at Severall times	00	05	00
It Gave to Elizabeth Smith at severall times	00	03	00
It Gave to Mary James	00	03	00
It Gave to William Peacock	00	02	06
It Gave to Abigaile Parker..	00	05	00
It Gave to Anne Jones	00	02	06
It Gave to John Baker	00	02	06
It Gave to Sarah Shott	00	02	06
It Gave to Joane Rosser	00	02	06
It Gave to Richard Jones	00	01	06
It Gave to Widdow Iles	00	01	00
It Gave for a warrant to bring in ye New Collector ..	00	01	06
It Gave for Carrying ye booke to be signed by ye Justices	00	00	06
It Gave for tending old Bowry when he was sick.. ..	00	07	00
It Gave for ye entering of this acct..	00	01	00
The whole Disbursmts	28	03	06
I crave allowance for money yt I could not Collet..	01	08	03
Wee doe take Mrs. Mary Roger Deptor to ye parrish (£ 00, s. 16, d. 6)	29	11	09
The rate comes to	35	03	06
Due upon ye ballance to ye Parish ..	05	11	09

Page 288.

		£	s.	d.
Impr	Paid Nicholas Cox	04	01	04
	It Paid William Steel	01	10	05
	towards ye ballance of their accts..	05	11	09

Aprill 14 1697 This Account
allowed by us
Samuell price
John Hort
William Martin
Tho Wasborowe
Will Davis
Thomas Smith
John Willis
John Smyth

Page 289.

1697. A rate made by the inhabitants Churchwardens and Overseers of the poore or the Parish of Westbury for and towards the reliefe of the poore at the rate of 8d. a pound to be paide monthly.

		the yearely value of Westbury		rate		
		£		£	s.	d.
Impr	The Lady Fane for her Tythe	18		00	12	00
	Mr: Thomas Wasborow	80		02	13	04
	Mrs. Knight	94	10	03	03	00
	Mr. Joseph Jackson	43		01	08	08
	Mr. Geering	63		02	02	00
	Mr. William Walters	16		00	10	08
	Mrs. Sampson	75		02	10	00
	Mr. Ralph Sampson	08		00	05	04
	Mr. Richard Lane	82		02	14	08
	Capt. Price	48		01	12	00
	Sr. Richard Crumpe	03		00	02	00
	Mrs. Walters	12		00	08	00
	Tho. Wasborow Senior	15		00	10	00
	Capt. Webb	14		00	09	04
	Mrs. Dowding	27		00	18	00
	Samuell Clavill	18		00	08	08
	Thomas Adlam	24		00	16	00
	Capt. Arendall	20		00	13	04
	Mrs. Knight for Gallops	07		00	04	08
	Mrs. Katherine Wasborow	03		00	02	00
	Mr. William White	27		00	18	00
	Mr. Thomas Daye	24		00	16	00
	Mr. John Hortt	26		00	17	04
	Mr. Jonathan New	08		00	05	04
	Mrs. Webb	12		00	08	00
	Mr. Samuell Sandfoord	09	10s.	00	06	04
	Mr. Thomas Hortt	08		00	05	04
	Mrs. Tyson	12		00	08	00
	Mr. Cheshire	03		00	02	00
	John Adlam	02		00	01	04
	Richard Horwood	05		00	03	04
	Mrs. Nickolls	07		00	04	08
	Mrs. Clarke	06		00	04	00
	Goodman Hedges	01		00	00	08
	John Wasborow	03		00	02	00
	Mr. Jackson for Wallises	01		00	00	08
	Edward Jotcham	01		00	00	08
	Giles Nurse	00	10s.	00	00	04
	Thomas Symons	04		00	02	08
		825		£	s.	d.
	The rate comes to			27	10	04

Page 290.

1697. A rate made by the Churchwardens and overseers of the poore and other the inhabitants of the Prish of Westbury for and towards the releife of the Poore at the rate of 8d. p £ to be paide monthley.

			The yearely value of Stoak Bishops rate				
			£		£	s.	d.
	Impr	Sr. Thomas Cann	130		04	06	08
		Sr. Robert Southwell ..	70		02	06	08
		Sr. Samuell Astry	11		00	07	04
		Sr. Richard Crumpe	37		01	04	08
		Sr. Simon Lewis	06		00	04	00
		The Lady Yeamans	44		01	09	04
		The Lady Fane	09		00	06	00
		Mr. Joseph Jackson	84		02	16	00
		Mr. Martin	84		02	16	00
		Mr. Edwards	33½		01	02	04
		Mr. Phillips	06		00	04	00
		Mrs. Joice Bevan	38		01	05	04
		Capt. Price	18½		00	12	04
		Mr. Blackwell..	05		00	03	04
£3 to add for		Mrs. Knight	22		00	14	08
agro: fel by		Mr. Aldworth.. .. £40	37½		01	05	00
Brookes Death		Mr. Tilladams..	20		00	13	04
on Alders		Mr. Byss	08		00	05	04
on Alder £2		Mrs. Mitchell	12½		00	08	04
on Watts £2		Mr. Dawson	10½		00	07	00
		Mr. Holmes	15		00	10	00
		the heires of Mr. Brookes £15	16		00	10	08
		Alderman Cresswick ..	09		00	06	00
		Mr. Thomas Hortt	08		00	05	04
		The Widow Holebroake ..	09		00	06	00
		Mr. Pope	08		00	05	04
		Mrs. Knight	03		00	02	00
		Mrs. Dymer	64½		02	03	00
		Mr. Robert Kirk	33		01	02	00
		Mr. Peters	08		00	05	04
		Mr. Tomkins	18½		00	12	04
		Mrs. Kirke	18		00	12	00
		Willm. Self	03		00	02	00
		John Hurne	10		00	02	08
		Arthur Sawyer	04½		00	03	00
		Mr. Samuell Sandfoord ..	02		00	01	04
		John Barrett	02		00	01	04
		Joseph Loyde..	04		00	02	08
			—	the rate			
			918	comes to	30	14	08

Page 291.

1697. A rate made by the Churchwardens and overseers of the poore and other the inhabitants of the Prish of Westbury for and towards the reliefe of the poore at the rate of 8d. p £ to be paide monthly.

		The yearely value of Sheerehamton rate				
		£		£	s.	d.
Impr	The Lady Fane for the Tythes	55		01	16	04
	Sr. Samuell Astry for Fishpools	54		01	16	00
	Sr. Samuell Astry for Harrises	28		00	18	08
	Sr. Samuell Astry for the Ship	02		00	01	04
	Madam Rogers	76		02	08	00
	Phillip Read or tenant	31		01	00	08
	Mrs. Sarah Wasborow	05		00	03	04
	Mrs. Holloway	35		01	03	04
	Richard Grumwell	40		01	06	08
	Mr. Hollier	19		00	12	08
	Mrs. Stainer	26		00	17	04
	Mrs. Stainer for Katherines	04		00	02	08
	John Willis	05		00	03	04
	John Smith Pilatt	12		00	08	00
	Charity Mathews	20		00	13	04
	Mary Smith and Edward Tippett	12		00	08	00
	William White	13		00	09	04
	Mr. Dorney or tenant	15		00	10	00
	Wirkhouse	15		00	10	00
	Widow Edwards	16		00	10	08
	Mr. George Petre	17		00	11	04
	Widow Stoakes	09		00	06	00
	Widow Thomas	02		00	01	04
	Thomas Everatt	08		00	05	04
	Richard Prichard	07		00	04	08
	Richard Smith	14		00	09	04
	Mrs. Christmas or tenant	28		00	18	08
	Aven house	16		00	10	08
	Dightons	50		01	13	04
	Richard Pritchard for dees	18		00	12	00
	Robert Cornish for dees	02	10s.	00	01	08
	Richard Jayne for dees	02		00	01	04
	Jonathan Perkins for dees	03		00	02	00
	Anne Cox	01		00	00	08
	Richard Pritchard for dees	01		00	00	08
	John Smith of the Ivyhouse	20		00	13	04
	Widow Berry	07		00	04	08
	Charity Berry	05		00	03	04
	Thomas Herring or tenant	11		00	07	04
	Widow Smith	15		00	10	00
	Thomas Smyth	16		00	10	08
	Thomas Smyth for Berries	07		00	04	08

Page 292.

	£ p annum		£	s.	d.
Thomas Smith for Peacocks..	04		00	02	08
John Jackson	07		00	04	08
John Willis for greens	24		00	16	00
Widow Green	06½		00	04	04
Jeremiah Gush	15		00	10	00
Samuell Robins	08		00	05	04
Capt. Davis	12½		00	08	04
Gregory Bush..	10		00	06	08
Widow Haines	04		00	02	08
Edmond Hunt	15		00	10	00
William Wallrond	06		00	04	00
James Smyth	06		00	04	00
Mr. Sampson for the Inne	10		00	06	08
Sqr. Lewis	16		00	10	08
William James	06		00	04	00
Mrs. Sedgwick for Coxes	16		00	10	08
Widow Green for fully Grove	02		00	01	04
Mrs. Everatt	02		00	01	04
Anne Jones	03		00	02	00
Giles Garret	16		00	10	08
Henry Gooding	04		00	02	08
	193		06	8	08
935 10	742	10			
Brought from the other side			23	15	00
			30	04	8

'ee do nominate and appoynt
› serve Collectors for ye poore
r ye pish of Westbury-upon-Trim
r ye yeare 1698
r. Wm White for ye Tything of Westbury
›hn Smyth Pilate for ye Tything of
ıerhampton
r. Henry Little for ye Stoak Bishopp

›35	10
›25	10
›12	00
›73	00

Page 293—Blank.

Page 294.

		£	s.	d.
1697.	The account of Mr. Samuell Price overseer of the Poore for the Tything of Westbury for the yeare 1697 and haveing a rate of eight pence in the pound which comes to £27 07s. 08s.	27	07	08
	the disbursstments as followeth	£	s.	d.
Impr	To Robert Wade and his wife 9 months at 10s... ..	04	10	00
	To old goody wade 4 months at 6s. p month	01	04	00
	To Sarah Pulling 13 months at 14s. p month	09	02	00
	To John Smith in part for the prentice maid	03	00	00
	allowed him for Clothers	01	00	00
	To John Smith makeing Clothers for Wild Goose Children and what he laide out	00	08	02
	It Paide for setting Holdbrookes sons Knee	00	05	00
	To John Hopkins making the rates and entring them in the booke and going to Sheerehampton ..	00	03	06
	Itt To Palmers Girl goeing to fetch Robert Wades son to bury him	00	00	06
	Itt for a warrant to bring Ralph to the Justice ..	00	01	00
	Itt for a warrant to remove him and spent	00	03	00
	Itt to John Palmer the kings tax for burying Robert Wade	00	04	00
	To Dorithy Wade in both her Sickness..	00	13	00
	for a Coffin and ale for the men carying her	00	06	00
	To Mary Fennell for 19 weeks diett for Holdbrookes son at 2s. 6d. a week	02	07	06
	Itt Paide for dressing his leg	00	10	00
	Itt Paide for the burying of Dorithy Wade to Mr. Goldenham and the Clark	00	05	02
	Itt Paide for Clothers for Wildgoose children	00	17	10
	To Mr. Lane for rent for widow Palmer	02	00	00
	Itt Paide for Shoes and Stockings Apron and Buckram and Canvas for Wildgoose children..	00	14	01½
	Itt To Joane Pearce at severall times	00	08	06
	Itt Gave to Robert Wade in his sickness	00	04	00
	To severall men and others with Passes..	00	03	04
		28	10	7

Page 295.

	£	s.	d.
To Mr. Chocke for endentures for ye maid	00	03	00
To money spent when the rates was made and Cost when they was signed..	00	03	00
Itt Paide for 3 shirts for Holdbrookes boy two sacks of Cole and when he was sick and spent when we meett about him	00	08	02
To Hobes wife attending him when he was sick and men for carrying him to Robert ffennells.. ..	00	02	06
	£		
for a Warrant for to bring in the new Collector ..	00	01	00
for Carrying the book to be signed	00	00	06
for entring the account in the Booke	00	01	00
	00	19	02
brought from the other side ..	28	10	07½
	29	09	9½

28th Aprill 1698
Samuell price

	£	s.	d.
To a rate for the poore for the yeare 1697	27	07	08
Red of John Seyar overseer of the poore	02	02	01
Sheerehamton the ballance			
	29	09	09

pp Contra Cr			
By money disboshd	29	09	09

Allowed by us
John Seager
William White
John Willis
Thomas Smith

29th Aprill 1698
Allowed by us
J. S. Lenton
Tho Chester

Page 296—Blank.

Page 297—Blank.

Page 298.

1697. The acount of John Seagar overseer of the poore for the Tything of Sheerehamton for the yeare 1697 and haveing a rate of eight pence in the pound which comes to

	£	s.	d.
The acount of John Seagar overseer of the poore for the Tything of Sheerehamton for the yeare 1697 and haveing a rate of eight pence in the pound which comes to	31	01	04

The disbursments are as followeth

	£	s.	d.
Impr Paide the Widow Tag 13 months pay at 6s. a month which comes to..	03	18	00
Itt Paide Charity Jones 13 months pay at 6s. a month for Whit Churches boy	03	18	00
Itt Paide to Charity Hartford 13 months pay at 6s. a month for Mary Onions bastard	03	18	00
Itt Paid to old Griffin 13 months pay at 5s. a month for Abell Jaynes boy	03	05	00
Itt Paide to Ellinor Reed 13 months pay at 3s. p month	01	19	00
Itt Paide to Sarah Shott 13 months pay at 3s. p month	01	19	00
Itt Paide to John Baker 10 months pay at 2s. p month	01	00	00
Itt Paide to old Bowry one months pay..	00	06	00
Itt Paide to Edith Bowry for attending him	00	04	00
Itt Paide to the Widow Iles one months pay	00	07	00
Itt Paide to Thomas Hopkins for the buriall of old Bowry	00	03	04
Itt Paide for a paire of Shoes and Stockins for onions bastard	00	02	08
Itt Paide for bringing the rate to me	00	00	06
Itt Spent a makeing the rates	00	01	06
Itt Paide for the Cloth and makeing the letters for the poore people	00	02	06
Itt Paide to Thomas Everat for taping James Whitchurches shoes	00	00	10
Itt Gave to the Widow Iles towards reliefe..	00	06	04
Itt Paide for cloth for two garments for onions bastard and makeing them	00	05	02
Itt Paide to Joane Baker when her goods was attacht towards reliefe	00	04	00
Itt Paide to Thomas Reed for Cheese for the Widow Iles	00	01	04
	22	02	02

Page 299.

	£	s.	d.
Itt Paide for Edward Cawlys Coffin and shroud.. ..	00	09	00
Itt Gave to him in his time of sickness	00	10	06
Itt Paid for ale at his buriall	00	07	06
Itt Paide to Mr. Stump for burying him..	00	02	06
Itt Paide for makeing the grave	00	01	06
Itt Paide for bread and cheese	00	09	06
Itt Paide for attending him in his sickness..	00	03	06
Itt spent when sale was made of his goods	00	00	06
Itt Paide Joane Joyner and Abigall Parker for goeing with the Certificate	00	01	00
Itt Paide to Richard Jayne the Kings tax for the buriall of Edward Cawly	00	04	00
Itt Paide to Dorcas Parker for washing Edward Cawlys Cloaths	00	03	10
Itt Gave to Ellinor Reed towards reliefe..	00	02	06
Itt Gave to Goody Iles towards reliefe	00	01	06
Itt for a warrant to bring the Collector in..	00	01	00
Itt Gave for Carrying the book to be signed	00	00	06
Paide for entering the acount	00	01	00
	02	19	10
brought from the other side	22	02	02
	25	02	00
I crave allowance of Anne Jones..	00	02	00
Paide to Capt. Davis for warrants which hee laide out ..	00	05	03
Mrs. Stainer stopt of Sarah Shott	00	01	00
I crave allowance of Mary James	00	03	04
Spent at Mr. Selmans	00	04	00
	00	15	7
For money to buy two children Cloaths..	01	10	00
paid to Capt, Price the ballance of his acompt	02	02	01
Paide to John Smith the Tailor for the prentice maide in part being the full ballance of my acount.. ..	01	11	08
	31	16	11

allowed by us
Samuell price
William White
John willis
Thomas Smith

29 Aprill 1698
J. S. Lenton
Tho Chester

Page 300.

1697. The acompt of Edward Jayne one of the overseers of the poore for the Parish of Westbury for the Tything of Stoak Bishop for the yeare 1697 and haveing a rate of eight pence in the pound which comes to

	£	s.	d.
The acompt ... a rate of eight pence in the pound which comes to	30	14	08
The Disburstments as followeth			
Impr Paide 13 months pay for John Hueses two children at ten shillings p month..	06	18	08
Itt Paide Joane Griffin 13 moneths pay at foure shillings a month	02	12	00
Itt Paide Alce Dowle 13 months pay at 6s. p month ..	03	18	00
Itt Paide Seaven months pay for the bastard child to the Widow Skudimore at 8s. a month	02	16	00
Itt Paide to John White	01	00	00
Itt Laide out for one of Hueses boy	00	12	06
Itt for Clothing the children at one time..	02	04	07
Itt Paide for a truss for the child..	00	00	06
Itt Paide for the charge of John Adys	01	06	06
Itt Paide for the burying of the bastard child	00	15	00
Itt Paide to Capt. Price for John Smith[1]	02	00	00
Itt Paide the Kings Tax for three burialls	00	12	00
Itt Gave Alce Dowle at severall times	00	09	06
Itt Paide for one paire of shoes for hues child	00	01	08
Itt Paide for the burying of Joane Griffin..	01	00	00
Itt Paide for makeing the letters and cloth for the Poore people	00	01	06
Itt for a shift for the poore child	00	01	08
Itt for expenses at severall times at Parish meetings ..	00	04	00
Itt Paide for a warrant for to bring the new Collector in	00	01	00
Itt Paide for Carrying the book to be signed	00	00	06
Itt Paide for entring the Acompt in the book	00	01	00
I crave allowance for money which I cannot gather of Mr. Jackson	02	16	00
	29	12	07
dew to the parish the ballance of this acc..	01	02	01
	30	14	08

Allowed by us	29th Aprill 1698
Samuell price	Allowed by us
John Willis	J. S. Lenton
Thomas Smith	Tho Chester

Page 302.

1698. The Acount of William White one of the Overseers of the poore of the Parish of Westbury-super-Trim for the Tything of Westbury for the yeare 1698 and haveing a rate at 8d. p £ to.. .. .. .. 37 10 04

	£	s.	d.
haveing a rate at 8d. p £ to..	37	10	04

The disburstments are as followeth

	£	s.	d.
Impr Paide to Jane Wade 13 months at 6s. a month.. ..	03	18	00
Itt Paide to Sarah Pulling 2 months at 14 a month ..	01	08	00
Itt paide eleaven months more to her at 9s. p month ..	04	19	00
Itt paide to John Hunt 9 months at 10s. a month ..	04	10	00
Itt paide two months more to Hunt at 8s. a month ..	00	16	00
Itt paide to George Wade and Sarah Seaven months pay at 12s. a month..	04	04	00
Itt Gave to Tho: Wade when he was sick..	00	07	06
Itt pd to Joane Dyer for tending of Wade..	00	03	00
Itt pd for mending of Wades childrens Cloathes.. ..	00	01	06
Itt Gave to David Humphrys in his sickness	00	01	00
Itt paide for a Coate for George Wade	00	05	03
Itt for mending George Wades shoes	00	01	00
Itt for makeing the rate	00	01	06
Itt Gave to Willm Jones in his Sickness..	00	05	00
Itt paide for two Shifts and stockins and shoes for Wilds wench	00	07	00
Itt paide for keeping of Richard Holdbroakes boy 19 weeks at two shillings sixpence a week	02	07	06
Itt paide for Sarah Wades Indentures	00	06	08
Itt for entring the Acount in the Booke..	00	01	00
Itt for Carrying the booke to be signed	00	00	06
Itt for a warrant to bring the new Collector in	00	01	00
Itt pd to John Hunt's wife when he was at Bath.. ..	00	03	06
I crave Allowance of Alderman Lane for the rent of Pitt	02	00	00
I crave Allowance of Capt. Price	00	04	10
I crave Allowance of Mr. Wasborow	00	10	07
I crave Allowance of Richard Horwood..	00	04	00
I crave Allowance of Giles Nurse..	00	00	04
	29	07	08
There remaines due to the Collector to Ballance this acount	01	17	04
Reced of Mr. Wasborow for Mr. Fanes money ..	00	12	00
and there is due to me ..	01	05	04

Page 303.

Allowed by us

Wm Martin
Jeremiah Gush
Tho Wasborowe
Will Davis
John Hort
John Willis
Edm: Hunt

We doe nominate and apoint to be Overseer for the yeare ensuing

Joseph Jackson for the Tything of Westbury
Robert Symons for the Tything of Stoak Bishop
John Willis for the Tything of Sheerehampton
Examined by us and allowed

B Bromwich

Wee doe nominate and appoynt to be overseers for ye yeare ensuing

John Hollyman for ye Tything of Westbury
David Barwick for ye Tything of Stoak Bishop
William England for ye Tything of Sherehampton.

Page 304.

		£	s.	d.
1698.	The Acount of Mr. Henry Little one of the Overseers of the poore of the Parish of Westbury-super-Trim for the Tything of Stoak Bishop for the yeare 1698 and having a rate of 8d. pence p £ comes to	30	14	08
	more reced of Mr. Holmes ..	00	08	08
		31	03	04

	The disburstments are as followeth	£	s.	d.
Impr	Paide Alce Dowle 4 months pay at 7s. p month	01	08	00
Itt	Paide Alce Dowle 9 months pay at 8 p month ..	03	12	00
Itt	Paide Goody Scudimoore for Keeping Hueses children 12 months at 10s. 8d. p month	06	08	00
Itt	paide for the Buriall of William Vaughon	00	03	00
Itt	paide Michaell Quintin the Clarke of St. Michaells ..	00	05	04
Itt	paide for a Coffin and Shrowde and two women makeing Oath	00	09	06
Itt	for a shift and two Aprons for one of hueeses children	00	02	06
Itt	Spent about putting out of Hueses child	00	00	08
Itt	for Clothers for Hueses Children	00	05	02
Itt	paide Joane Dyer for Keeping Wades two Children a month	00	12	00
Itt	for a paire of Stockins for one of Hueses children ..	00	00	07
Itt	paide Joane Dyer another months pay	00	12	00
Itt	paide for a paire of shoes and a shift for Hueses children	00	04	00
Itt	Spent at makeing the rates for the poore	00	07	10
Itt	Spent a goeing to the Justices About Goody Brown..	00	06	00
Itt	paide Katherine Browne for her weeks pay	00	03	00
Itt	paide for makeing the rate	00	01	06
Itt	paide Mary Hardin for Katherine Browne a week ..	00	03	00
Itt	paide Margarett Nicholls a week for Goody Brown ..	00	03	00
Itt	paide Margarett Nickolls another week	00	03	00
Itt	for a paire of Bodices for Hueses child..	00	02	00
Itt	paide Margarett Nickolls another week	00	03	00
Itt	paide for a man to goe with Katherine Brown to Bristoll and back againe	00	01	00
Itt	paide Margarett Nickolls for goody Browne	00	06	00
Itt	paide Margarett Nickolls for goody Browne	00	03	00
Itt	paide Margarett Nickolls for goody Browne	00	03	00
Itt	Lent Mr. Martin to fee Mr. Knight about the removeall of Goody Brown	00	06	00

Page 305.	£	s.	d.
Itt paide for Signeing the poores rate	00	01	00
Itt paide Tobias Doales man for a paire of Shoes.. ..	00	03	08
Itt paide Margaret Nickolls for the Widow Brown ..	00	06	00
Itt Spent at Signening Robert Fennells Indentures ..	00	01	06
Itt Spent at a parish meeting	00	10	00
Itt paide Margarett Nickolls for goody Browne	00	06	00
Itt Gave to a woman that Came with a pass	00	00	06
Itt paide Margarett Nickolls for goody Browne	00	03	00
Itt paide Mr. Chock for a warrant..	00	00	06
Itt paide Margarett Nickolls for goody Browne	00	03	00
Itt paide for a rugg for John Hues..	00	06	06
Itt Laide out a looking after the mother of the Child which was left neare pitch and pay	01	02	09
Itt paide Margarett Nickolls for Goody Browne	00	03	00
Itt paide Samuell Jotcham a Salesman	07	09	02
Itt paide Margarett Nickolls for Goody Browne	00	03	00
Itt paide for carrying the Child to Westbury, Coffin and the Clarke	00	04	00
Itt paide Tho White for keeping George Bennets boy a month	00	06	00
Itt paide Harry Pages wife..	00	00	06
Itt paide John Skudimoore for keeping John Hueses children a fortnight and three nights..	00	06	06
Itt Paide for entering the acount in the Booke	00	01	00
Itt for Carrying the booke to be Signed	00	00	06
	11	18	01
brought from the other side ..	16	14	01
	28	12	02
I crave Allowance for money which I cannot gather of Lewis the malt man	00	01	08
	28	13	10

The Collector is debtor to the parish £2 9s. 6.

John Willis

Allowed by us

pd the ballance of this acount to Mr. Martin

Wm Martin
Jere: Gush
Tho Wasborowe
John Hort
Edm Hunt

Examined and allowed by us
Jo: Bromwich

Page 306.

1698. The Acount of John Smith one of the Overseers of the Poore of the Parish of Westbury for the Tything of Sheerehampton for the yeare 1698 and haveing a rate of 8d. pence a pound Comes to .. .. ..

	£	s.	d.
1698. The Acount of John Smith one of the Overseers of the Poore of the Parish of Westbury for the Tything of Sheerehampton for the yeare 1698 and haveing a rate of 8d. pence a pound Comes to	31	05	08

The disburstments are as followeth

	£	s.	d.
Impr Paidē James Whitchurch 3 months pay at 6s. p month ..	03	18	00
to Sarah Onion 13 months pay at 6s. p month	03	18	00
to Harry Jayne 13 months pay at 5s. p month	03	05	00
to Sarah Shott 13 months pay at 3s. p month	01	19	00
to Ellinor Reede 13 months pay at 3s. p month.. ..	01	19	00
to Widow Iles 13 months pay at 7s. p month	04	10	00
to Widow Tagg 13 months pay at 7s. p month	04	10	00
to Mary Preston 3 months pay at 6s. p month	00	18	00
to Mary Prestons child 8 months pay at 6s. p month ..	02	08	00
Itt Gave to Mary Preston at severall times before she had monthly pay	00	06	00
Itt Paide for a new hatt for Harry Jaynes..	00	02	00
Itt for two new paire of stockings for harry Jayne ..	00	02	00
Itt for a new paire of shoes for harry Jayne	00	03	04
Itt for mending harry Jaynes shoes twice..	00	01	04
Itt for two paire of stockings for James Whitchurch and Sarah Onion	00	01	08
Itt for mending James Whitchurch and Sarah Onions shoes twice	00	01	09
Itt for cloth to make each of them a shift and makeing	00	03	06
Itt for 2 aprons and neck cloths and cloth to make Sarah Onion bead clothers	00	05	00
Itt Spent at makeing the rate and makeing him.. ..	00	03	00
Itt for 10 months scoolling for James Whitchurch ..	00	05	00
Itt for 10 months scoolling for Sarah Onion	00	03	00
Itt Gave to three poore passengers that was bound for Ireland which had orders from the Mayor	00	03	00
Itt Gave to a poore man that Came out of Turkey ..	00	01	00
Itt Gave to severall poore people that was goeing to Ireland that was in great distress	00	04	00
Itt Gave to Jane Barker before she died..	00	03	00
Itt paide for rent for Sarah Shott..	00	08	00
Itt paide to Abigall Parker for Pauls wench	00	08	00
	30	09	07

Page 307.

	£	s.	d.
Itt Paide to Abigall Parker for keeping Tauls wench ..	00	01	06
Itt for a new paire of Shoes for James Whitchurch ..	00	02	02
Itt for mending WhitChurches shoes and Sarah Onions..	00	01	00
Itt for two new paire of Stockings for them	00	01	06
Itt for a new Waskott for James Whitchurch	00	03	00
Itt for makeing the rate and signeing him	00	02	00
Itt Spent at severall times about parish business ..	00	05	00
Itt Gave to John Baker at severall times	00	10	00
Itt paide for entring the acount in the booke	00	01	00
Itt paide for Carrying the booke to be signed	00	00	06
	01	7	8
brought from the other side ..	30	09	07
	31	17	03
There is due to ballance this acount to the Collector from the parish	00	11	07
I crave Allowance for money which I cannot gather ..	00	06	00
Soe there remaines due to the Collector	00	17	7

Allowed by us
Wm Martin — Edm: Hunt .
Jere Gush
Tho Wasborowe
John Hort
Will: Davis

12 Aprill 1699
Examined and allowed by us
B Bromwich
Thomas Walter

Page 308.

		£	s.	d.
1699.	The Acount of Robert Symons one of the overseers of the poore of the Parish of Westbury for the Tything of Westbury for the yeare 1699 And haveing two rates one at 6d. in the pound and the other at 3d. in the pound comes to ..	30	18	01½

The disburstments are as followeth

		£	s.	d.
Impr	pd Ann Tagg one months pay at 7s. p month and 12 months pay at 8s. p month	05	03	00
	pd John Hunt 13 months pay at 8s. p month	05	04	00
	pd Jane Wade 13 months pay at 6s. p month	03	18	00
	pd William Browne 5 months pay at 6s. p month ..	01	10	00
	pd for Clothers for John Hunt and his boy and Wildgooses wench	03	17	00
	pd for a warrant and order and Carrying John Hunts boy to St. Georges in Somersetshire	00	15	06
	pd Mr. Lane for Ellinor Palmer's rent ½ a yeare	01	00	00
	pd Joane Dyer for Keeping George Wade one month at 2s. p week	00	08	00
	pd to Margarett Humphreys at severall times	01	04	08
	pd Mr. Jackson for what he disburst dureing his time of overseer for the Tything of Westbury	00	19	00
	pd Mr: William White towards what was due to him on the ballance of his account	00	07	03
	pd Robert Fennell towards the apprentice of Tho Wades wench	00	05	03
	I crave allowance for money which I cannot of Richard Horwood stopd for his Tything rate..	00	04	03
	I crave allowance of Giles Nurse	00	00	04½
	I crave allowance for what I cannot gather of Mr. Fane..	00	13	06
	pd for makeing the rate	00	01	00
	pd for signeing the rate	00	01	06
	Gave to a poore woman and a child at a Vestry meeting	00	00	06
	pd for a warrant of Disturbance for Walter Star ..	00	01	00
	pd to Mr. White to ballance his acount	00	06	11
	I crave allowance for what I cannot gather of Mr. Jackson	00	10	09
	Itt paide for a warrant to bring the new Collector in ..	00	01	00
	Itt paide for carrying the booke to be signed	00	00	06
	for entering the acount in the book	00	01	00
	This acount comes to ..	26	13	11½

Page 309.

	£		d.
And there remaines due to the Prish to ballance this acount	04	04	02

Page 310.

1699. The acount of Robert Symons one of the Overseers of the poore of the Parish of Westbury for the Tything of Stoak Bishop for the yeare 1699.

		£	s.	d.
	And haveing two rates one at 6d. in the pound and the other at 3d. pence Comes to	34	11	06
	The Disburstments are as followeth			
Impr	Paide Alce Dowle 13 months pay at 10s. p mon:	06	10	00
	pd Sarah Pulling for her self and Wilds wench 13 months pay at 9s. p month	05	07	00
	pd Hannah Tant 6 months pay and a halfe at six shillings p month	01	19	00
	Paide for charges of severall things in James Taints Sickness as appears by bill	01	10	03
	Paide for a warrant and Mittemas for carrying James Taint and his dayghter to Bridwell and other charges about them	00	18	02
	Paide for goeing to Glosester on a tryall with Whitchurch Prish concerning Yeamans Family	02	15	00
	Paid for Warrants and Orders for Carrying Richard Yeamans and his two sons to Whitchurch and copying of them and expences about them	04	01	08
	Paide for orders for carrying Betty Crowder to St. Peters Prish and charge about finding out witnesses ..	00	13	06
	Paide for goeing to Glosestr on the Tryall of Elizabeth Crowder and two witnesses and 4 horses and all charges about that Business against the Prish of St. Peters	06	17	06
	Paide for Clothers for 4 of Alce Dowles children and Hannah Taint	06	00	09
	pd for a warrant and order for removeing of Joseph Holstock his wife and child out of the Prish and getting security for them	00	09	10
	Paide Elizabeth Giles for cureing Tants child	00	04	06
	Paide to Mary Bartlett	00	03	00
	Paide to Elizabeth Hughes at Severall times	01	06	00
	Paide for makeing the rates..	00	02	06
	Paide for signeing them	00	02	00
	Paide Robert Fennell towards the apprentice maide ..	00	18	08
		39	19	4

Page 311.

	£	s.	d.
I crave allowance for what I cannot gather of Mr. Jackson	01	01	00
I crave Allowance for money which I cannot gather of Mr. Fane	00	06	09
Paide for a warrant to bring in the new Collector and carrying the book to be signed..	00	01	06
for entring the acount in the Book..	00	01	00
Brought from the other side	39	19	4
	41	09	07

	£	s.	d.
Due to the overseer of this acount..	6	18	1
Due to the Parish of Westburys acount from the Collector	4	4	2
due to the overseer from the Prish to ballance this acount	2	13	11

Samuell price
William Martin
John Hort
Richard Grumwell

We doe nominate and appoint to be Collectors
for the poore for the yeare ensuing 1700
Edward Rogers for the Tything of Westbury
Thomas Hortt for the Tything of Stoak Bishop
Richard Cromwell for the Tything of Sheerehampton

Page 312.

		£	s.	d.
1699.	The Account of John Willis one of the Overseers of the poore of the Prish of Westbury for the Tything of Sheerehampton for the yeare 1699 and haveing two rates one at 6d. in the pound and the other at three pence comes to	35	03	10½
	The Disburstments are as followeth			
Impr	Paide to the keeping of James Whitchurch 13 moneths pay at 6s. p month	03	18	00
	Itt Paide Sarah Onion 13 months at 6s. month.. ..	03	18	00
	Itt Paide for keeping Prestons child 13 months pay at 6s. p month	03	18	00
	Itt Paide for the keeping of Tants Child 7 months and a halfe at 6s. p month..	02	05	00
	Itt Paide the Widow Reed 13 months at 3s. p month..	01	19	00
	Itt Paide Sarah Shott 13 months pay at 3 p month ..	01	19	00
	Itt Paide John Baker 13 months at 2 p month ..	01	06	00
	Itt Paide Henry Jayne on months pay	00	05	00
	Itt Paide the Widow Iles 8 months at 7s. p month ..	02	16	00
	Paide her five months more at 6s. p month	01	10	00
	Itt Paide for the Binding of Henry Jayne apprentice to Mr. Martin	04	00	00
	Itt Gave to John Baker	00	01	00
	Itt Paide to cloth to make shifts for the Prish children and makeing of them	00	13	00
	Itt Paide for Shoes for the Prish children	00	09	06
	Itt Paide for 4 paire of stockins for the children ..	00	03	01
	Paide for woollen cloth to make them Cloaths.. ..	01	01	01
	Itt for (?) lining and Buttons	00	01	02
	Itt for a paire of lather Breekhes for James Whitchurch	00	02	06
	Itt for makeing the childens woollen Cloaths ..	00	04	06
	Itt for 3 yards and a half Carsey to make Prestons Child an upper Coat and under Coat	00	05	06
	Itt for whalebone and Canvas	00	00	10½
	Itt for makeing Prestons Childs Cloaths..	00	02	00
	Itt for two Aprons for prestons Child	00	01	03
	Itt for mending James Whitchurchs Shoes twice ..	00	01	04
	Itt for grafting a paire of stockins for Henry Jayne ..	00	00	06
	Itt for lengthing Sarah Onions Coat	00	00	04
	Itt for makeing the rates and signeing them	00	04	06
	Itt Paide Richard Jayne the Kings Tax for the buriall of Joane Baker..	00	04	00
		31	10	01½

Page 313.

		£	s.	d.
Itt	For my expences in Prish Business..	00	03	06
	I crave allowance for mony which I cannot gather of Charity Berry	00	03	09
	I crave allowance for money which I cannot gather of Anne Jones	00	02	03
	Paide to John Smith the last Collector which was due to him on the ballance of his acount	01	06	03
	Paide to Mr. White to ballance his acount..	00	09	09
Itt	paide for a warrant to bring the new Collector in.. ..	00	01	00
	Itt for entring the acount in the book	00	01	00
	Itt for Carrying the book to be signed	00	00	06
		02	08	00
	brought from the other side ..	31	10	01½
	my disburstments is	33	18	01½
	There is due upon this acount to the prish	01	05	09

Paide the ballance of this acount to Robert Fennell

Tho Wasborowe
Samuell price
William White
John Hort
Richard Grumwell
Thomas Smith

3 April 1700
allowed of this Account
if true Richard Haynes
Nath Wade
Tho Walter

Page 314—Blank.

Page 315.
geaven by Elizabeth Helling
unto the poore of the parrish of Westbury £5

Page 316.
Joseph faye of St. Nicholas Parish Bristyll having 4 children
now Living at ye hope and Anchor
Wee Have In Westbury man and woman came out of Bristoll
Charles Newth and his wife on ye Gallows hill
have notice given them to goe out of the prish
Augt. 27 90 by Christmas or to give Security
Walter Rudge and his wife late of Clifton to bring
a Certificate by ye 8th September.
ffrances Osborne and his wife of Blagden In
Sommersettshire now living at ye Gallows Hill
ye prsons at ye house say they are going away at
Michellmas.

NOTE.—This "Poor Book" is bound in parchment, and once had a clasp and fastening attached, but they have disappeared. It is written on coarse paper, 11 by 7½ inches.

CPSIA information can be obtained at www.ICGtesting.com
Printed in the USA
LVOW132001151211
259596LV00015B/217/P